When the Levees Break

When the Levees Break

Re-Visioning Regulation of the Securities Markets

KAREN KUNZ AND JENA MARTIN

LEXINGTON BOOKS
Lanham • Boulder • New York • London

Published by Lexington Books
An imprint of The Rowman & Littlefield Publishing Group, Inc.
4501 Forbes Boulevard, Suite 200, Lanham, Maryland 20706
www.rowman.com

Unit A, Whitacre Mews, 26-34 Stannary Street, London SE11 4AB, United Kingdom

British Library Cataloguing in Publication Information Available

Library of Congress Cataloging-in-Publication Data Available

978-0-7391-9604-5 (cloth)

978-0-7391-9606-9 (pbk.)

978-0-7391-9605-2 (electronic)

Contents

APPENDICES

Figures and Tables

Acknowledgments

A friend and colleague of ours, Charles DiSalvo, famously (or infamously) said "writing a book is like giving birth"—even though neither of us has had that experience, we are now certain we would agree. And, just like no one wants to go into delivery alone, we believe that this book would not be what it is today without the incredible help and support of the following people: Chris Bauer, Lorrie Farrington, Pam Fritz, Joshua Fershee, Bertha Romine, Stephen Selby, Craig Slaughter, Melanie Stimeling, and our editors, Emily Roderick and Joseph Parry. Special thanks to Kevin Kunz and Jaison Simms for their extraordinary support. And finally, we are grateful for the support received from a Hodges Grant at the College of Law and a faculty development/ book subvention grant from the Eberly College of Arts & Sciences at West Virginia University. We know that there are others whom we have failed to thank, but know that our gratitude goes well beyond these pages and deep into our hearts.

Introduction

Have you ever stood in front of a twenty-foot dam and watched as a tidal wave crashed over it?

No?

Neither have we. However, if we *were* to imagine such a scene we believe that it would be replete with chaos, destruction and confusion, with almost nothing left in its wake.

Now imagine that, instead of a twenty-foot dam, we have the Hoover Dam. At 726 feet tall, it can make you feel protected. But now, instead of a tidal wave, it's a tsunami[1] that comes with such a quick and ferocious force that it destroys *everything* in its path.

Think back to 2005—do you know where you were when hurricane Katrina struck New Orleans? Most of us watched on TV as floodwaters surged through the city, destroying buildings and lives, leaving some residents stranded on their rooftops, waiting for help. The culprit was not the hurricane itself but the levees. Most thought the government had prepared for such emergencies. The dikes and dams were there to contain local bodies of water and enable them to absorb everyday rains and the occasional downpour or severe thunderstorm; the levees were for the major events, such as deadly floods resulting from tropical storms and hurricanes or even a tsunami. But they were all old and faulty and not remotely in shape to withstand Katrina.

In the United States, that describes our current securities framework. The regulatory dikes, levees and dams—the regulatory agencies and regulations that have been enacted since the stock market crash of 1929—surround us and make us feel protected. Holes in the dike appear every once in a while, but if the leaks become too serious, we know the US government will activate the levees and patch things up when the waters calm down. But what happens when the dikes crumble and the levees break?

In this book we explore those concerns. From our combined forty-five years of experience in industry, regulation and academia, we have examined the world of securities regulation and are preparing the lifeboats as we write. This book is for those who work in the securities industry, whether for a Wall Street or boutique firm, an exchange or self-regulatory agency or a federal or state regulator, as well as those policymakers, consultants, lobbyists and academics who study it. It is for investors who want to better understand the structure of the securities markets and those fearful of another, pending flood or curious about how regulation might prevent future failures. The purpose is to start a national, or better yet a global, conversation about how to shore up the securities markets before the next floodwaters wreak even more havoc.

The truth of the matter is that the evolution of the markets, advancements in technology and development of quantitative trading and the consolidation of firms and exchanges have punched a multitude of new holes in the regulatory dikes. Enforcement as we know it and the Dodd-Frank reforms are ineffective at plugging any one leak, let alone containing the flood of changes that have occurred in the industry in the last decade. This is primarily because the regulatory structure envisioned when federal securities laws were enacted in the 1930s is not applicable to financial markets that no longer remotely resemble those it was designed to control.

Here we identify these leaks—the changes that have taken place in the industry, particularly over the last few decades—and the ways they have caused the dams to crumble. And instead of devising one more way to patch the holes in the hope that the barriers will hold a little longer, we offer plans to build a whole new levee system that will ensure that we are prepared to weather any storm.

To this end, we develop a regulatory framework that incorporates the paradigm shift necessary to embrace alternative interpretations of investment products and markets and the role of regulation. We begin with a discussion of the increasing sophistication of new products and the impact of technological progress on trading and execution processes. We then examine how the regulatory environment has attempted but failed to keep up with these advancements and the ways in which pending rulemaking is ill-equipped to keep pace, let alone become equipped to move ahead and engage in proactive measures.

On that foundation, we begin to develop a transformational framework that incorporates an entirely new market orientation, one that goes beyond the current regulatory shortfalls. Our model is initially applied to US markets; however, we conclude the book with ideas about how the implementation of our model implicates an international framework.

Our model is predicated on two key arguments. Our central premise is that there is a disconnect, or more precisely a disaggregation, in the markets between the companies within our regulatory framework and the stocks that purport to represent them. No longer do participants in the stock market purchase a particular stock because they would like to invest in the company. Now investors—or more accurately, purchasers—buy stock because of its value, separate and apart from the company. Specifically, we document how modern traders no longer typically look at the fundamentals of a particular company in deciding whether or not to buy its stock. Instead, they examine the stock as a product in and of itself (like a toaster or a car), with a value that is separate and apart from the value of the underlying corporation.[2] This disaggregation marks a fundamental shift from an investor paradigm to a consumer paradigm. This perception is evidenced at all levels of investing activity, from mom-and-pop investors and day traders to institutional investors and Wall Street traders.

An example of this disaggregation at the micro level is the recent LinkedIn acquisition by Microsoft, a publicly traded company that was purchased for $26.2 billion without ever having shown a profit.[3] More pernicious still is its manifestation on a macro level where computerized trading—the use of algorithms that barely take into account the fundamentals of a company—represents the majority of trading volume on US and international exchanges. We argue that, since the markets have become dominated by this new consumer paradigm, we should completely divorce the theory of the firm and corporate governance from the regulatory market structure, treating the securities of the firm as a "widget" that consumers buy, and regulate them as such.

Our second premise follows from the first: we assert that the regulatory structure currently in place is woefully inadequate to regulate the products and markets as they have evolved to their present form. Specifically, the fundamental regulatory DNA of all federal securities agencies (spearheaded by the Securities and Exchange Commission) is one of disclosure. As regulation continues to focus on disclosure, it ignores the use of increasingly complex electronic systems and equipment that can be sabotaged by sophisticated hackers, the ascent of social media, and the reliance on self-regulatory organizations to police their own—all while corruption extends to even those setting market standards.[4]

There are numerous books written about the financial markets, investing, quantitative trading, and technical analysis, as well as regulatory structures, crisis management, and reform efforts. This book is unique in that it proposes a radical new way of looking at investment products and markets and encompasses that paradigm shift within our regulatory model. For example, while the 2008 financial crisis was inexorably intertwined with the derivatives markets, we consider it to be merely the most extreme manifestation of the growing disconnect between the perception of securities as investments and their actual use as something far different.[5] Our method of plugging the leaks, which we envision as a total reengineering of the system, deals with this disconnect head on and addresses all products in the securities markets system. Nonetheless, our primary focus is on the equity markets and their role in the overall stability of the system.

For ease and clarity, this book is divided into three primary parts. Loosely, they describe what is, what should be, and how we plan to get there from here. Part 1 provides a thorough description of regulatory life as we now know it. Since the dawn of regulation, the greatest single change in the securities markets is the way in which securities are bought and sold. Increasingly complex investment products and the introduction and adaption of increasingly sophisticated technologies used in trading, execution and operation have revolutionized the exchanges, making them virtually unrecognizable from those envisioned when the Securities Act of 1933 and the Securities Exchange Act of 1934 were enacted. Here, we identify the ways in which the financial markets have changed, the failure of regulations to keep up and the resultant risks and vulnerabilities.

We begin in chapter 1 with a discussion of the technological advancements that have revolutionized individual and institutional trading, execution and broker/dealer operations over the last few decades. As a result of these innovations, a seismic shift has taken place in the securities markets. The fault lines have been present for quite some time; however, it is only now, in the last few years, that the ramifications of these displacements have been felt. The typical approach for traders has gone from examining companies to determine whether they will be a good long-term investment to examining the markets as a whole. Nowhere is this shift more apparent than in the rise and increasing prevalence of quantitative trading models. As a result, there is now a disconnect between the markets themselves and the companies that are traded on the markets. Algorithmic trading embodies this theoretical model on a ubiquitous level. What a company does or does not do matters very little to whether the company's stock should be bought or sold. Instead, algorithms are used to determine whether the company's stock is a good "buy" based on how the *stock* is doing and how the *market* is behaving. This shift has had a broad impact on retail and institutional investor behavior and the global economy at large, but relatively little impact on regulatory structures and the role of government in oversight.

The regulatory framework that historically and currently dominates our markets has failed to keep pace with technological advancements. In chapter 2 we address the shortcomings of the regulatory structure currently in place, with emphasis on the evolution of the responsibilities of the Securities and Exchange Commission. Here we show that the SEC's focus on disclosure is inadequate and dangerous. Subsequently, in chapter 3 we offer a detailed critique of the overall regulatory model, identifying the numerous agencies, self-regulatory organizations and exchanges that are charged with oversight of various aspects of the securities markets, their development and their relationship to each other and state regulators.

In Part II we present our view of a new regulatory and structural paradigm. To start with, in chapter 4 we talk about alternative options for reforming our current investor protection system that take into consideration the advancements in technology and recent changes to trading patterns. Our discussion of these alternatives provides the basis for our argument regarding the shift to *whole market regulation* based on a *consumer protection* orientation.

As we elaborate on our consumer protection model, we offer a detailed analysis of how securities would be traded and regulated. In chapter 5 we set forth our thesis on treating securities as products that can be regulated, with a modified *caveat emptor* orientation, in much the same way that we buy, sell and regulate toasters or cars. Among the proposals set forth is an incredibly comprehensive IPO process that acts as gatekeeper to ensure that only legitimate companies' stock trade on the securities exchanges. This extensive review eliminates the need for subsequent disclosures and the market fluctuations that often accompany them. This provides the basis for a much more consumer-oriented approach for an issuer's "products" (i.e., its stocks). This approach, we argue, generates cost savings for companies while enabling them to supply information that investors want. We also discuss the advantages present in our current disclosure-based system—for example, the baseline of confidence that is provided for investors—and discuss how our product-based model, with its labeling analogy, provides that same stability albeit without the same degree of onerous regulation on companies.

In chapter 6 we explore the complementary, whole-market regulatory structure necessary to support our model. The shift in focus from disclosure to fraud prevention includes proactive measures built into the oversight structure to catch glitches and intrusions and anticipate the advantages and effects of innovative new technologies. Our structure encourages regulation to correct or adapt as needed—in much the same way the SEC has begun to dabble—but on a larger and more comprehensive scale. One of the greatest advantages of this model is that it embraces the integrated electronic basis of contemporary financial markets and sets forth an accompanying regulatory framework.

In Part III, we turn to the details. Specifically, we discuss the mechanics of implementation, including the regulatory hurdles that we will need to overcome in order to make the transition to a consumer-product orientation. We also tackle the very real issue of how the political will necessary to accomplish such a seismic shift might be achieved. In this section we provide preliminary blueprints for establishing such a system both substantively, through legislation, and by overhauling our current agencies. In addition, we offer an honest and critical assessment of the effect the new regime will have on the market. We consider how the new market structure could affect everything from business and human rights issues to stabilizing global markets to assisting in capital formations.

This section begins with a point-by-point discussion of the impact of our new holistic market regulation system on the current regulatory system. In chapter 7 we propose a new agency structure that is much more nimble and streamlined. With less to regulate on a micro level, it can devote its attention to prognosticating on the strengths and weaknesses in the markets. This will enable it to take quick and decisive actions when necessary (e.g. implementing trigger mechanisms or re-routing order flow) and to develop proactive alternatives that can be employed to stop leaks and floods before they happen.

From there we illustrate in chapter 8 how this innovative perspective offers companies less regulation and more freedom in the markets and is beneficial to corporate America and to society. Here we describe, step by step, how companies navigate the IPO process to bring their products to market. In addition, we discuss how our more aligned approach to regulation actually reflects where the market is and protects customers where they need the protection the most.

Finally, in chapter 9 we look at what it would take politically to realize the transition to this new regime. What underscores the reluctance and, in some cases, actual push back from stakeholders? What is in it for them to take the plunge? We also briefly examine how our scheme might fit within global markets' activities and regulation. We look at threats posed to global economies by current practices and structures, such as those triggered by social media and electronic order activation, and begin to look at ways that the consumer protection paradigm could minimize those risks worldwide. Making this shift gives the US an opportunity to take a leadership role—or at least a seat at the table, which is considerably more than our antiquated system currently provides—in developing a collaborative global markets paradigm and regulatory structure.

*   *   *

We realize that this is a complete paradigm shift. And, let's be honest, nobody likes change. Even when faced with a leaky Hoover Dam, many (indeed most) people would rather bail out the water (or the companies) and plug up the leaks than confront the problem at its source, *up river*, so to speak.

Recent events in the securities markets have shown us our vulnerabilities. Right now, there is no levee to hold back a hurricane-size storm. There is not even a current infrastructure to weather the small leaks that can quickly transform into catastrophic floods. The only way to fix it is to start over—to build a new levee—with the technology and equipment needed to stop both small leaks and big floods before they come.

Just so you know, there's a difference between a dike and a levee. A dike normally runs along or parallel to a body of water such as a river or a sea, a dam runs across or through a body of water. A dike has water only on one side, a dam has water on both sides. The main purpose of a dike is protecting the land behind it from flooding, whereas a dams' purpose is to retain the water. Dikes and levees are embankments constructed to prevent flooding. Levees may be formed naturally or artificially. They prevent the water from overflowing and flooding surrounding areas.[6]

Similarly, in our markets, there are many different infrastructures at play that help to keep our economy afloat. We have agencies, we have SROs, we have private plaintiffs and we have legislatures. Right now however, each of these entities seems to be working at cross purposes rather than in harmony. The results are not pretty.

Gone are the days of the Little Dutch Boy[7] who plugged leaks with his thumb. With all the technology we have at our disposal now we can use not just better equipment, but the *right* equipment for the job. That way, when the waters rise, we'll be ready.

Notes

1. According to the US Geological Survey, "although both are sea waves, a tsunami and a tidal wave are two different . . . phenomena. . . . A tidal wave is a shallow water wave caused by the gravitational interactions between the Sun, Moon, and Earth . . . Tsunamis are ocean waves triggered by large earthquakes that occur near or under the ocean, volcanic eruptions, submarine landslides, and by onshore landslides in which large volumes of debris fall into the water" (http://www.usgs.gov/faq/catego ries/9755/3141). Comparatively, the flash crash of 2010 could be considered a tidal wave, whereas the more fundamental market crash in 2008 and the resulting depression would be a tsunami.

2. Stu Woo and Lynn Cowan, "LinkedIn 4.2 Billion Valuation Raises Eyebrows," *The Wall Street Journal* (May 19, 2011).

3. "Microsoft Purchase of LinkedIn is one of the Most Expensive Tech Deals in History: It May not be One of the Smartest," *The Economist* (June 18, 2016). Equally amazing is that when the acquisition was announced, the stock price jumped approximately $60 per share, from $130 to $190.

4. Alyssa Chang, "When Lobbyists Literally Write the Bill," *NPR, Its all Politics* (Nov 11, 2013). See also Jonathan Spicer and Emily Stephenson's, "Secret tapes of Fed meetings on Goldman prompt call for US hearings," in *Reuters' Business News* (Sep 26, 2014).

5. To that end, there are numerous scholars who, in the wake of the financial crisis, have discussed the perils of derivatives and their comparison to gambling (Eric A. Posner and E. Glen Weyl, "A Proposal for Limiting Speculation on Derivatives: An FDA for Financial Innovation," *University of Chicago Institute for Law & Economics*, Olin Research

Paper No. 594), speculation; (Lynn A. Stout, "Regulate OTC Derivatives by Deregulating Them," *Cornell Law Faculty Publications*, Paper 754. http://scholarship.law.cornell .edu/facpub/754), and even weapons of mass destruction (Buffett, as quoted by Tony Boyd in "Warren Buffett still says derivatives are 'weapons of mass destruction," *Financial Review* [July 15 2015]). We tend to agree with these intellectuals' assessment of the derivatives market and discuss this further in Part III.

6. Agriwaterpedia. http://agriwaterpedia.info/wiki/Dikes,_dams,_levees.

7. Peter Miller, *The Little Dutch Boy* (Encyclopedia Mythica, 2016), http://www .pantheon.org/articles/l/little_dutch_boy.html. "Dutch legend has it that there was once a small boy who upon passing a dike on his way to school noticed a slight leak as the sea trickled in through a small hole. Knowing that he would be in trouble if he were to be late for school, the boy poked his finger into the hole and so stemmed the flow of water. Sometime later a passerby saw him and went to get help. This came in the form of other men who were able to effect repairs on the dike and seal up the leak. This story is told to children to teach them that if they act quickly and in time, even they with their limited strength and resources can avert disasters. The fact that the Little Dutch Boy used his finger to stop the flow of water is used as an illustration of self-sacrifice. The physical lesson is also taught: a small trickle of water soon becomes a stream and the stream a torrent and the torrent a flood sweeping all before it, dike material, roadways and cars, and even railway tracks and bridges and whole trains. This tale originates from the American writer Mary Mapes Dodge and is in fact not a real myth, although many people believe it is. She published this tale in 'Hans Brinker, or the Silver Skates' in 1865."

Part I

THE DISCLOSURE PARADIGM

Stories about the financial markets have become a staple in news reports and on the Internet. Reading them can sometimes be like watching a train wreck, especially when the reports are about market crashes or malfunctions—whether you fully understand what they're telling you or not, it's hard to turn away. The information can be confusing, particularly when the commentators are not specific about which aspect of the financial markets they are talking about. There is commercial banking, which is responsible for checking and savings accounts, investment products such as certificates of deposit, commercial paper, and other interest-bearing products. And there is investment banking, which encompasses the securities markets—stocks, bonds, options, commodities, futures, derivatives, etc.—and the efforts by bankers to produce new issues that are bought and sold on exchanges within these markets. Up until the late 1990s, commercial banks could only engage in the securities markets in two ways: they could sell investment products such as stocks, bonds and mutual funds through a partnership with a securities firm, and they could invest their cash reserves—the funds they use to make loans, for example—in securities as a way to increase profits.

That bright line between the two meant that commercial banks were not allowed to engage in investment banking activities and investment banks shied away from commercial banking activities (which is still the case). Regulation and lines of authority and responsibility—which regulatory bodies oversaw securities products and markets and which were accountable for deposit accounts, lending, commercial paper and Treasury securities—were clearer then as well. Now, absent those delineations, making the distinction between which agencies are responsible for regulating which products and markets can be confusing even to writers and regulators.

Our focus throughout this book is on the securities markets and the relevant participants involved. We do touch on the banking industry, where we focus on

Treasury securities and more specifically on the investment banking portion of the markets. While the too-big-to-fail banks have become so, in part, through their engagement in securities activities—JP Morgan Chase and Citibank come to mind here—commercial banking and regulation are not included in this conversation, except to any extent that those activities and regulations pertain directly to the securities markets. Our interest lies solely in investment products and participants, trading and regulation.

In this section we examine the current structure of the US securities markets and identify some of the fundamental flaws in the current system. We begin with a broad overview of the markets, the salient issues and the potential pitfalls. We contend that the disintegration of the wall between commercial and investment banking, proliferation of unregulated products, advancements in technology and institutionalization of electronic trading have substantially changed how we view and engage with these markets.

In the second chapter we move on to an analysis of the disclosure paradigm on which the existing regulatory structure is based. The SEC's regulatory regime, aka, the disclosure model, was designed around corporate financial disclosures, in part, to ensure investor protection. This method assumes that investors use information provided in those disclosures to make intelligent investment choices. However, there are flaws in that design. The disclosure system was based on the failings of the 1920s securities markets. Things have changed considerably since then. Moreover, companies have found a multitude of ways to skirt the requirements. The disclosure system is woefully out of date.

The history of the changing nature of the securities markets and the failure of regulation to keep up is the focus of the third chapter. Since the 1933 and 1934 Acts, the regulatory structure has been chasing advancements and has been consistently unsuccessful in its attempts to catch them. The result is a sophisticated market system overseen by a patchwork of uncoordinated, ineffectual regulatory organizations, SROs, exchanges and ancillary entities.

All of this to state the obvious: the regulators have run out of fingers and toes to use to plug the holes in the now-crumbling regulatory dike. The last tsunami in 2008 almost wiped it out. The next one is sure to.

CHAPTER 1

Watching the Waves Roll In

In previous generations, employees worked for their employers for their lifetime, retiring after 25 or 30 years of service with a gold watch and a pension. Similarly, during that time, a securities purchase represented a person's investment in the underlying company itself—a show of faith in the company's intrinsic performance and ability to succeed.[1] Our financial markets were symbolized by the retail investor.[2] These were individuals or families who would purchase a company's stock—often the company they worked for—and then hold onto it for years, if not decades, trusting in the company's long-term performance.[3] Any profit that the investor realized in the short term came, not from selling a portion of his initial investment, but from dividends that the company returned to the investor year after year.[4]

Now, however, investing and trading patterns are unlike anything that we have seen before. As noted author Michael Lewis writes: "The line between gambling and investing is artificial and thin."[5] This is evident in a number of different ways. First, retail investors have been replaced by institutional investors who dominate the market,[6] which favors them over their retail counterparts. For instance, the nature of the current disclosure system focuses on the sellers' disclosures (i.e., corporations who must disclose information so that investors can make a decision to buy or sell). However, the institutional buyers, whose influence on and share of the market is substantial, are not under the same disclosure obligation or scrutiny. It is now common for institutional holdings to constitute more than 50, or even more than 75 percent of the outstanding shares of a company's common stock. Such one-sided oversight misses at least half of the activity in the market, which arguably gives institutional players unrestrained power to call the plays.

Second, the rise of computerized technology has allowed market participants to trade in ways that would have been inconceivable a decade ago. The use of algorithmic trading formulas and the rise of college degrees in financial engineering serve to make this even more evident.

Finally, focusing on the fundamentals of a company and using that data to make decisions about whether to purchase or to not purchase shares in a company has become passé. The emphasis on buy-and-hold investing, with a focus on the intrinsic value of companies and their stock,[7] has given way to a calculated, short-term trading approach.

Now investors and traders are examining the value of the stock itself, separate and apart from the underlying company. This disconnect, or "disaggregation," between the security and the company, is at the heart of the new securities marketplace.

Keep in mind, the concepts of investing and trading are intertwined. There are practical differences, of course; some traders buy and sell for their firm's accounts while others buy and sell large blocks for customer investment allocations. Traders may even take the other side of an investment when a buyer or seller cannot be found for the offsetting transaction. Conceptually, however, trading is associated with short-term profit-seeking, in which securities are bought and sold with a quick turnover in mind. Investing, on the other hand, had long been thought to be a buy and hold strategy. Retail and institutional investors, however, have adopted this short-term trading perspective, enabled in part by individuals' access to do-it-yourself electronic brokerage firms (i.e., E-Trade, Scott Trade, Ameritrade and others) and access to algorithmic strategies (i.e., Algorithmic Trading for Dummies and The Beginners' Guide to Quantitative Trading)[8] and institutional adoption of algo methods. As a result, we use the terms investing and trading interchangeably as a reflection of this universal approach to buying and selling securities.

These three issues—institutional dominance, technological advancements and disaggregation—make up the substance of this chapter's focus.

The Investors' Advocate

"The Securities and Exchange Commission thinks of itself as the investors' advocate, by which it means retail investors—individuals and households—as opposed to institutional investors."[9]

The last three decades have witnessed a precipitous rise in the volume of trading done by institutional investors. There are a number of reasons for this. First, with the gradual (and then explicit) lessening of regulation of trading activities, banks that once were confronted with an either/or investment plan are now free to engage in both commercial and investment banking. Second, this ease of trading enabled investment companies to enter the markets in unprecedented numbers through pension funds and other institutional investor entities. Finally, the rise and proliferation of computerized trading has made it incredibly profitable for institutional investors and investment banks to enter the market and trade for their own benefit on a level that eclipses retail traders.

To reiterate, until 1993, most of the equity in the United States securities markets was situated in the hands of retail investors.[10] Since then, however, the total amount of equity held by institutional investors has skyrocketed.[11] As a result, the rise of the institution as a principal player is a significant factor in the shift in our securities markets.[12] The sheer volume of the markets that institutional participants claim bears this out: current statistics show that institutional investors account for more than half of the market participation in the US.

As a result, institutional investors dominate the market.[13] For instance, the rise of institutional players has affected overall investment strategies. While an increasing number of people invest in the securities markets, they do so indirectly, using institutional investors, such as mutual funds and pension funds, as intermediaries.[14] In 2014, for example, just 14 percent of families in the US held shares in individual stocks, such as Google or Apple. And less than half (48%) of adults have money invested in the stock market directly or indirectly, through pension plans, mutual funds, EFTs, etc. [15] Consequently, institutional investors gain even more power in the securities market because of the vast amount of wealth they control by trading with other people's money.

In a discussion of institutional investors, former SEC Commissioner Louis Aguilar notes:

> The role and influence of institutional investors has grown over time. For example, the proportion of US public equities managed by institutions has risen steadily over the past six decades, from about 7 or 8 percent of market capitalization in 1950, to about 67 percent in 2010. The shift has come as more American families participate in the capital markets through pooled-investment vehicles, such as mutual funds and exchange traded funds (ETFs). Institutional investor ownership is an even more significant factor in the largest corporations: In 2009, institutional investors owned in the aggregate 73 percent of the outstanding equity in the 1,000 largest US corporations. . . . Simply stated, institutional investors are dominant market players, but it is difficult to fit them into any particular category. This poses a challenge for regulators, who must take into account all the many different ways institutional investors operate, and interact, with the capital markets. [16]

A Glossary Refresher

Algorithmic trading: computerized trading using models based on proprietary mathematic formulas.

Alpha model: Part of the *black box trading* system, using algorithms to model and predict the behavior of a security.

Angel Investor: A wealthy person who provides funding for start-up businesses in exchange for ownership equity or debt commitments.

Black Box: The inscrutable, super-secret portion of an algorithmic investment system that contains formulas and calculations used to generate various types of data, including buy and sell signals.

Dark Pool: A private, alternative trading exchange or forum that is not accessible to the public, and where the size and price of orders are not revealed to other participants.

Derivative: A financial contract whose value is based on, or "derived" from, a traditional security (such as a stock or bond), an asset (such as a commodity) or a market index.

Exchange: a brick-and-mortar or electronic marketplace in which securities are bought and sold.

Floor Broker: Member of an exchange who is an employee of a member firm and executes orders, as an agent, on the floor of the exchange for clients.

Fundamentals: Information about a corporation's (or firm's) business model, including but not limited to earnings, dividends, interest rates and risk evaluation.

Institutional Investor: Organizations that invest, including insurance companies, depository institutions, pension funds, investment companies, mutual funds and endowment funds.

Investment Company: A firm that that invests the funds of investors in securities appropriate for their stated investment objectives in return for a management fee.

Quant: An expert in managing and analyzing quantitative data.

Securities: Paper certificates or electronic records evidencing ownership of equity (stocks) or debt obligations (bonds).

For more, see the full glossary in the back of the book.

Taken from: NASDAQ, *Financial Glossary*, http://www.NASDAQ.com/investing/glossary/a, and *Investopedia*, Investopedia.com.

Among institutions, the hedge fund is in the forefront of the trend of purchasing or selling stock as stock.[17] At their core, hedge funds are organizations that pool and manage securities for an incredibly wealthy group of investors.[18] The dominance of these hedge funds goes hand in hand with the dominance of algorithmic trading, and, because they are regulated to a lesser extent than other institutions and participants in the financial markets,[19] these funds and their investments have been allowed to grow by leaps and bounds, creating a vicious cycle where retail investors are increasingly edged out of the market.

In spite of the changing dynamic in market dominance, the SEC's mode of regulation has yet to address the fact head-on: it is still narrowly focused on a now largely marginalized class of investors, the retail investors.[20] As one scholar puts it, albeit more politely, our markets have "fundamentally changed in recent decades while financial regulation has moved far more slowly."[21]

In short, the growing influence of institutional players cannot be overstated. That influence has been key in the shifting paradigm and necessitates the demand for new technologies to keep pace.

Investing in the Digital Age

In the last few decades the amount of information and data that can be stored has increased exponentially. Concomitant with this rise in storage space is the speed with which it can be processed.[22] While the data and how it is used in the securities market have been advancing in an unprecedented fashion, the technology necessary to complete these transactions has simultaneously been shrinking.[23] The sheer space needed to perform these mighty calculations is minute compared to what was needed a generation ago. Data analyses that would have been nearly impossible a few decades ago (and even then only with a number of supercomputers) can now take place on a handheld device.[24]

The rise in innovation and technology has led to another curious consequence: the increased separation between man and machine. With the sheer speed at which many of these trades occur (where thousands of shares are moved in under a second), the "human factor"—a typical backstop against, at minimum, computer glitches, or at most, flaws in formulas—has been all but lost.[25] Hedge funds and other institutional investors have taken this even further and allowed for the rise of computer trading—buy and sell orders with huge trading volumes executed with virtually no human intervention or oversight. Nowhere is this human disconnection seen more than in the rise of algorithmic trading.

Algorithmic trading can refer to a number of electronic trading practices, all of which use computerized models to analyze data and effect large volume transactions in exchange and off-exchange markets. In this book, we use this term interchangeably with various practices that fit within this framework including black box, quantitative and high frequency trading (HFT). The growth of these forms of electronic trading and the ways in which their use has changed the development, interpretation and dissemination of research and trade execution have been well documented. The change has also occurred at every level;

computer-trading practices have been embraced by small private equity firms and hedge funds as well as established global investment banks such as Goldman Sachs, Merrill Lynch and (the former) Lehman Brothers. Even individual retail investors may now participate in algorithmic trading due to increased access to and advantages in computer software,[26] as well as books, websites and blogs that promote 'algorithmic trading for dummies.'[27]

Electronic or computer trading often refers to the broader idea of using technology to deliver market activity. Quantitative or algorithmic trading uses arithmetic calculations, or algorithms, in its creation of trading patterns. What goes into those trading patterns is often known as the "black box."[28]

Alpha Model Portfolio Construction

The components within a basic black box make up an alpha model. The alpha model contains the value added brought to the endeavor by the quant. "They are in essence designed to *time the selection and/or sizing of portfolio holdings.* They hold at a core the premise that no instrument is inherently good or bad, and therefore no instrument is worth always owning or perpetually ignoring."[29] While there are a limited number of trading strategies that can be employed, they can be implemented in a variety of ways, allowing for an enormous diversity of schemes. Further, quants tend to base development of their alpha models on either theoretical or empirical underpinnings.[30]

One writer offers a succinct commentary on the rise of computerized trading:

> As part of a high frequency trading (HFT) strategy, computer gener-ated algorithms dominate daily trading volumes. Algorithmic trading uses computer programs to enter trading orders with the computer algorithm deciding aspects of the order, such as the timing, price, and quantity of the order, or in many cases, initiating the order without human intervention. [. . .] HFT firms may hold their position for a very short horizon and try to close the trading day in a neutral position. Therefore, HFT must be a type of algorithmic trading, but algorithmic trading need not be HFT.[31]

Algorithmic trading itself has now been incorporated into the securities in-dustry at an institutional level, representing the dominant trading model at most hedge funds and a significant part of the curriculum for a financial engineering degree. The premise behind algorithmic trading and its ascent into securities markets is based on the fundamental belief of many of its adherents that the mar-ket is run by a mathematical "truth" (creatively named the "Truth"). The perfect trading formula is one that captures this inherent truth of the markets and uses that truth to yield high returns for investors. "The Truth," simply stated is "a universal secret about the way the market worked that could only be discovered through [. . .] the study of obscure [mathematical] patterns in the market."[32] As such, many traders in today's markets are on a quest to find *the* formula that encapsulates that Truth and insulates its wielders from significant market failure.[33]

The pinnacle of the shift to computerized trading came with the institutionalization of this methodology at the academic level.[34] By the turn of the century, financial engineering programs that endeavored to develop algorithmic trading patterns were proliferating across the country.[35] These graduates, in turn, either went to work for large institutional investors (usually brokerage firms or hedge funds) or set up their own shops—getting investors to fund millions upon millions of dollars into these new trading models with the potential for incredible returns.[36] In addition, the rise of this form of trading has become widespread enough to infiltrate all aspects of the exchanges themselves.

The birth in 1967 of Instinet, the first off-exchange trading platform designed to compete with the New York Stock Exchange (NYSE), marked the beginning of automated financial markets. Over a decade later, the NASDAQ, originally designed as a computer bulletin board system, was founded by the National Association of Securities Dealers (NASD)[37] and ultimately became the first electronic stock exchange. The NYSE embraced automation at a much slower pace, becoming the largest and first global exchange through its acquisition of Euronet in 2007.

More recently, the purchase of the NYSE by the Intercontinental Exchange (ICE) was designed to enable the venerated exchange to better keep pace with rapid and rapidly changing electronic trading and expand its reach into futures and derivatives, also in demand by high-frequency traders.[38] Similarly, the Chicago Mercantile Exchange (CME), the largest futures market worldwide and the strongest competitor to ICE in the futures and derivatives markets, acquired the Kansas City Board of Trade and is eyeing several other targets, including NASDAQ and Eurex, a group of European derivatives exchanges, while developing a London futures exchange from scratch.[39]

The same technological progress that spurred consolidation within the big boards also fostered the growth of additional trading platforms, providing supplemental sources of liquidity to "exchanges and non-exchange trading venues, such as alternative trading systems (ATS) in the United States and Canada, multilateral trading facilities (MTFs) in Europe, and brokers' internal crossing networks."[40] The result of this proliferation is that equity markets "for which on-exchange trading was prominent, have become more fragmented and, in some instances, less transparent. With the further development of multiple trading venues, liquidity in a particular share is often split amongst different pools of liquidity"[41]

For example, large traders once used floor brokers to hide the full sizes of their orders. The brokers displayed size only to traders that they trusted would not unfairly exploit the information. Now large traders use the hidden order facilities of electronic exchanges and dark pools to control the exposure of their orders. These facilities generally are more reliable than floor brokers and much less costly to use. The traditional NYSE floor was the forerunner of today's electronic "dark pools" that only disseminate information to trusted traders.[42]

Trading venues continue to develop new and innovative trading functionalities to attract and maintain order flow. Their "electronic systems . . . provide affordable remote access to investors by retaining unexecuted orders in a consolidated order book for possible matching with future orders. On automated electronic trading systems, profit-seeking value traders can closely monitor the market and become suppliers of liquidity even without a presence on the trading floor."[43] As a result, the use of *dark liquidity* for trading equities and the development of so-called *dark orders* and *dark pools,* again facilitate liquidity while maintaining anonymity. As a result, block trades executed away from the central exchanges have increased substantially.[44]

In this regard, technology and algorithmic trading are inexorably intertwined. First, technological advances ensure that enormous amounts of numbers can be computed in a fraction of a second. Second, increasingly sophisticated software allows for more and more complicated calculations. Third, there is greater access to and ability to process vast amounts of data from disparate sources. As a result, data analyses that would have been nearly impossible a few decades ago can now take place on your iPad with a few swipes. Finally, the rise of financial engineering as a recognized discipline and sought after degree has created a new breed of market analyst who can combine technology with innovative equations to process, employ, and distribute market data.

The Impact of Advancing Technologies

The use of quantitative trading methods has increased exponentially over the past two decades, to the point where it is commonplace in traditional brokerage firms. But to what extent does it account for market activity? By 2009, algorithmic and high frequency trading dominated trading volume. The use of electronic order flow and fulfillment systems had grown to represent over 60 percent of all trading volume in 2009.[45] Trading volume on the exchanges increased just as dramatically. Between 2003 and 2009 the US average daily trading volume rose from approximately 3 billion shares to almost 10 billion shares, respectively. Yet market share of the NYSE for its listed equities declined over the same period from 80 percent of all volume to just over 25 percent by the end of 2009, illustrating a substantive shift in trade execution to off-exchange venues. Further,

> Average trade size fell substantially as computers made slicing large blocks into small pieces a cost effective means of limiting adverse costs of trading large positions. Automated traders began providing liquidity, supplementing and displacing traditional liquidity suppliers. The number of quote updates per trade, as well as the number of orders cancelled per executed trade, increased dramatically as traders employed new electronic strategies for offering and searching for liquidity.[46]

In 2005 algorithmic trading made up between five and seventeen percent of all trading volume and, at an estimated growth rate of seven percent per year, it was seen as the largest growth area in electronic trading. By 2012, estimates of the share of trading volume varied. Some claimed that high-frequency trading firms accounted for 73 percent of all equity orders in the United States, 40 percent in Europe, and 5–10 percent in Asia.[47] Data from the NYSE indicated that the daily trading volume of "traders using complex mathematical programs to automatically execute buy and sell orders . . . skyrocketed 164 percent between 2005 and 2009. . . . These traders were competing for pennies in millions of transactions and accounted for 61 percent of the trading volume on the NYSE in 2009."[48] On the other hand, in 2012 the *New York Times* reported declines of algorithmic trading by about 75 percent from their peak of $4.9 billion in 2009, and decreases in HFT volume of approximately 10 percent, to a market volume share of just over 50 percent. These declines appear to correspond to overall volume declines for the broad financial markets over the same periods.

In short, despite varying estimates, it is undisputable that quantitative trading now makes up a significant portion of market activity. So, what exactly, have we gotten ourselves into?

Algorithmic trading enthusiasts espouse its many benefits. In the plus column, electronic trading enables economies of scale, makes for more effective transactions through efficient pricing, provides routing and pricing stability and adds efficiency to trading and markets. It can reduce the cost of capital by reducing trading and investor commissions, adding liquidity and making quotations more informative.[49]

However, there are equally as many concerns, many of which seem to come right from the pages of the latest thriller. Chief among them, from both individual and quantitative perspectives, is the degree to which algorithmic trading relies on and can be impacted by advancements in technology. The slightest hiccup in the markets can trigger large-scale buys and sells that can wreak havoc on the exchanges and investors' portfolios even before the regulatory shutdown rules kick in. For example, in 2012 alone "Knight Capital, Facebook, BATS, the Madrid Stock Exchange, the New York Stock Exchange and the Tokyo Stock Exchange all suffered at the hands of technological limitations as outages and flash crashes traversed the world's exchanges."[50] And in April 2013 phony Twitter messages reported that explosions at the White House

> sent the Dow Jones Industrial Average into a tailspin, shaving 150 points, or about 1 percent, in the blink of an eye. The fake Tweet dealt a hammer blow to other markets as well: The S&P 500, the NASDAQ and crude oil all dropped 1 percent. The S&P 500's losses alone wiped out about $136.5 billion, according to Reuters; the broader market lost nearly $200 billion in value, U.S.A. Today reported. At the same time, the yield on the 10-year U.S. Treasury note fell 4 basis points, and the CBOE Volatility Index—the so-called 'fear index'—surged 10 percent.[51]

This is of particular interest as algorithmic trading is applied increasingly to a broader range of investment products and international trading venues, which by their very nature are targets of cyber-attacks.[52] In the commercial banking sector, international banks have been the focus of particularly sophisticated hackers over the last few years. Hackers enter each bank through an integrated global system, meaning that the penetration of just one bank puts the entire system at risk. "There have been at least four known cyber-attacks against a bank involving fraudulent messages on the SWIFT (the Society for Worldwide Interbank Financial Telecommunication) payments network, one dating back to 2013. . . . Banks around the world use secure SWIFT messages for issuing payment instructions to each other."[53] While these cyber-catastrophes threatened commercial rather than investment institutions, a similar penetration of that magnitude could crash securities markets simultaneously across the globe.

Equally alarming is the markets' interconnectedness with social media such as Facebook and Twitter[54] and their vulnerability to breaking news and social commentary, particularly given the impact of the phony Twitter report.[55] The fact that social media can be used to create "shocks" in the market which then create disturbances in the economy, adding to national and global "financial fragility, is alarming"[56] The Twitter report "also raised new questions over the security of the plethora of social media sites.[57] "The ability of hackers to use Facebook, Twitter and other social media sites to affect global markets and economies presents altogether new and unforeseen needs for controls on algorithmic trading.

To be sure, concerns about technological reliance within the securities markets go deeper than that. Dependence on electronic algorithms as a replacement for comprehensive analysis creates a false sense of security and engenders a herd mentality, wherein investors are likely to follow major market movements created by algorithmic triggers. For example, retail investors are likely to sell into a declining market and buy into a strong market as preset triggers produce large block sell and buy orders.

Cyber "events" at public institutions and commercial entities are becoming commonplace, making institution and exchange systems and investor data increasingly vulnerable. A significant cyber breach at the FDIC, for example, was caused when 44,000 customers' records were "inadvertently" downloaded on to a departing employee's thumb drive just before he left the organization.[58] More significantly, the Federal Reserve reported that they experienced over 50 cyber "breaches" labeled "unauthorized access" or "information disclosure" between 2011 and 2015—with four in 2012 described as "espionage"—as well as hundreds of "incidents."[59] And those were just attacks on the Federal Reserve's Board of Governors; the bank's twelve branches are privately owned so cyber intrusions experienced by any of them would not be publically reported. In the private sector, huge amounts of personal data stolen from numerous government, financial and retail establishments—JP Morgan Chase and Target, to name just a few—could easily be used to access and liquidate investor accounts, simultaneously and globally.

The use of electronic execution, clearing and customer account systems also plays a role in security framework. Cyber security has not been a primary concern for regulators and spending by firms to keep up with the latest in system upgrades and security is often curtailed by concerns for the bottom line. While it may seem that this has little to do with electronic trading, in fact, these electronic systems make it possible for execution and recordkeeping for large share and big dollar transactions and for customer accounts impacted by these trades.

So, while the increased reliance on technology to run all aspects of the securities markets and the advancement of social media to influence behavior have set the door to cyber issues ajar, algorithmic trading and industry reliance on electronic systems have propped it wide open.

Disaggregation: The New Norm

Traditionally, financial planning and securities trading were based on analyses that were tied to the underlying security. Certainly, for many financial professionals, there were various theories that were posited regarding the numerous trading patterns to determine whether a buy, hold or sell recommendation was in order. Commentators put forth many different theories regarding how the market would behave or what the trading patterns would be, but, at their heart, all of these theories were tied directly to the fundamentals of an individual corporation (or even an industry).

A few years ago, that all began to change.

In the book *The Quants* reporter Scott Patterson discusses the source of this change: the rise of quantitative analysis as a framework for trading in the market.[60] According to Patterson, this methodology was originally developed by Ed Thorp, who first applied it to Blackjack.[61] It soon became clear, however, that this methodology could be translated into the securities arena, with dramatic results.[62]

It seems fitting that a form of Thorp's Blackjack model ended up being applied to the stock market. Initially—before the 1929 crash and subsequent creation of the SEC—for many investors, that's what the securities market was: it was speculating; it was gambling. For a few decades, we retreated from that model, focusing instead on a company's fundamentals. But now, we have come full circle, using ever more sophisticated technology to buy stocks, whether we know anything about the company that they represent or not.

We call this shift a disaggregation—where the stock is considered separately, apart from the company it represents. As such, we believe that what we are witnessing is a very important shift, from an investor paradigm to a consumer paradigm. Under an investor paradigm, you would buy the stock because you believed it to be a good investment, because you agreed with the company's potential, or at least its fundamentals and wanted to show your support for that company, all the while making money for yourself. In a consumer paradigm, you could care less about whether the company was a good investment. The question becomes: Is it a good buy; how quickly can I make money from it? There are many ways that we can track this: Two examples are, first, the increased focus on short-term financial gain of the market and our absolute fascination with quarterly results, and, second, our ability to keep buying a stock even when all indications from the company's fundamentals would indicate that we shouldn't. There is also the rise of short term trading itself—we mean *really* short-term traders. This was recognized in the early part of the century with the focus on day traders but has now become standard within the realm of quant firms (those who devote themselves to algorithmic trading) even to the point of liquidating their holdings every night.

Quantitative firms are notoriously secretive about the formulas and data needed to execute these strategies.[63] These proprietary formulas, once created, are protected with the same intensity and paranoia as some of the highest held trade secrets[64] or top-level government security information.[65] The only thing that is clear is that the amount of data being processed through these funds is enormous.[66]

Outsiders, therefore, know very little regarding what type of information is used for these formulas. However, what has become clear is that not much of the information is derived from the fundamentals of the corporation to which the security is attached.[67] What the corporation is doing, what its long term prospects are, or what its balance sheets contain matter very little, if at all, for these formulas.[68] In fact, given that many HFTs require that the position be liquefied at the end of *each day of trading*, one can see why the long-term fundamentals of a company would have very little to do with the actual trading.[69]

This disaggregation is at the heart of the shift from an investor paradigm to a consumer paradigm. Since it is clear that traders are buying stock for reasons that are fundamentally different than the investment prospects of the corporation, then the logical conclusion is that they are purchasing the particular stock solely for its gains—for its value as a product that is divorced from the company rather than as a proxy for the company itself.[70]

As such, this habit of buying and selling the thing itself is much more characteristic of a consumer rather than an investor. The trader is purchasing the stock for its value today and then selling the stock, like an informed connoisseur, before the value decreases. Admittedly, this is a fast-paced version of the consumer model but a version nonetheless.

The disconnect between an equity's position in the securities market and the underlying company's position in the overall commercial market is increasingly being recognized. For instance, one author reports that, "the markets are full of companies with powerful positions and sluggish stock prices."[71] The changed pattern of trading allows for traders to leverage bad performing assets and can ensure liquidity in the markets. However, these benefits can only be seen if the models—the formulas on which trades are based—perform as predicted. The 2008 financial crisis revealed the flaw in this thinking.

The financial crisis was deemed by many to be a black swan—a statistically unpredictable disaster that, in the words of one commentator, "occurs so infrequently that they are virtually impossible to analyze using standard statistical inference."[72] To the more cautious investor, this merely highlighted the flawed nature of the statistical prediction model of market performance and, in particular, its heavy reliance on the rational investor. Indeed, even financial engineers acknowledge the impact of behavioral economics on trading decisions. As Andrew Lo and Mark Mueller state, "the incentive structures of hedge funds, proprietary trading desks and most non-financial corporations have a non-trivial impact on the attendant risks those financial institutions face."[73] In other words, traders at these firms are often motivated not by gains to the market but by short-term greed to make decisions that affect millions. This greed may in fact be rational and even benefit the market. When self-interest rather than concerns of market performance for investors trumps decision making, however, this leads to classic agency conflict in which traders may in fact put their own interests ahead of those upon whose behalf they are investing.[74]

Moreover, the traditional use of hedging (leveraging against one security by buying another security with offsetting risks in order to diversify an investor's portfolio) has now become an end in and of itself rather than a means to maintain a stable portfolio.[75] Essentially, while hedging used to be the way to create diversification, now hedging has simply become a new way to play the markets to get at the Truth of the market—and it would seem to create money where none existed before.

All of these factors have combined to bring the US to the point where disaggregation has now been embedded, on an institutional level, within the securities markets.[76] As a result, the shift from an investor paradigm to a consumer paradigm appears to be complete. Given this, having a market that is regulated by disclosure, which seems to consider only the investor paradigm, brings us dangerously close to the crashing waves.

Notes

1. One of the ways that this was expressed was in discussions of the fundamentals of the securities and how those fundamentals added value to the security that embodied it (but in many ways that has changed). *See, e.g.*, Neil Irwin, *Washington Post*, "Twitter could end up being really profitable. But it's a super risky stock," *Wonkblog* (Nov. 4, 2013) http://www.washingtonpost.com/blogs/wonkblog/wp/2013/11/04/twitter-could -end-up-being-really-profitable-but-its-a-super-risky-stock/ (stating that at the time of its IPO, Twitter was being valued at $13.6 billion although it has never earned a profit); Daniel Gross, "Amazon Stock May Be Up, but the Company Still Doesn't Make Any Money," *The Daily Beast* (Oct. 25, 2013) http://www.thedailybeast.com/ar ticles/2013/10/25/amazon-stock-may-be-up-but-the-company-still-doesn-t-make-any -money.html; Matthew Yglesias, "The Prophet of No Profit: How Jeff Bezos won the faith of Wall Street," *Slate* (Jan. 30, 2014) http://www.slate.com/articles/business/money box/2014/01/amazon_earnings_how_jeff_bezos_gets_investors_to_believe_in_him. html; *and* Trefis Team, "Why LinkedIn's Fundamentals Don't Support Its Share Price," *Forbes* (July 15, 2011) http://www.forbes.com/sites/greatspeculations/2011/07/15/why -linkedins-fundamentals-dont-support-its-share-price/.

2. Matthais Burghardt, *Retail Investor Sentiment and Behavior: An Empirical Analysis* (Gabler Verlag, 2011) arguing that retail investor trading is important to financial institutions and the market.

3. Another aim of shareholders who held their stock over many quarters was to receive corporate dividends. *See* Philip van Doorn, "Time to sell your dividend stocks? Not so fast," *Market Watch* (Apr. 10, 2014) http://www.marketwatch.com/story/time-to-sell -your-dividend-stocks-not-so-fast-2014-04-10?link=MW_latest_news (arguing that in the long run, dividends make up the majority of returns in the market).

4. Paul Sullivan, "Assessing the Value of Owning Dividend-Paying Stocks," *NY Times* (June 3, 2011) http://www.nytimes.com/2011/06/04/your-money/stocks-and-bonds/04wealth.html?pagewanted=all&_r=0.

5. Michael Lewis, *The Big Short: Inside the Doomsday Machine* (W. W. Norton & Company, 2011), 256.

6. Deborah Fuhr, "Institutional investors dominate the market," *Financial News* (Oct. 21, 2013) http://www.efinancialnews.com/story/2013–10–21/institutional-inves tors-dominate-the-market.

7. The Graham Investor describes the process of calculating intrinsic values as "estimating the average earnings over a period of years in the *future* and then multiply-ing that estimate by an appropriate capitalization factor . . . the factors which affect the capitalization rate of a company—[are] general long-term prospects, management, finan-cial strength/capital structure, dividend record, and current dividend rate. http://www .grahaminvestor.com/articles/value-investing/intrinsic-value-an-inexact-science/.

8. See "Algorithmic Trading for Dummies" at *Wildbunny* blog (2015), http://www .wildbunny.co.uk/blog/2013/03/15/algorithmic-trading-for-dummies/. And *5 Essen-tial Beginner Books for Quantitative Trading*, https://www.quantstart.com/articles/Top -5-Essential-Beginner-Books-for-Algorithmic-Trading.

9. Donald Langevoort, "The SEC, Retail Investors and the Institionalization of the Securities Markets," *95 Va. L. Rev.* 1025. *1025* (2009).

10. Allen D. Boyer, "Activist Shareholders, Corporate Directors and Institutional Investment: Some Lessons from the Robber Barons," *50 Wash & Lee L. Rev. 977* (1993).

11. Fuhr, "Institutional investors dominate the market."

12. Langevoort, "The SEC, Retail Investors and the Institionalization of the Securi-ties Markets."

13. Ibid.

14. Ibid.

15. Compared to 30 percent of households who own at least one cat, according to Matt Egan, "More US families own cats than stocks," *CNN Money* (Sept 9, 2014). Also see Heather Long, "Over half of Americans have $0 in stocks," *CNN Money* (Apr 10, 2015).

16. SEC Commissioner Luis A. Aguilar, *Institutional Investors: Power and Responsibil-ity* (speech at Georgia State College, April 2013).

17. In the 1800s farmers used hedging strategies to protect themselves from falling crop prices. It wasn't until the late 1940s that it came into use in the equities markets, when a reporter developed a strategy using short stock sales to hedge the risk of holding long positions. He combined that with the use of leveraging within a general limited partnership of wealthy investors and—Voilà!—the hedge fund was born! See Capitol Management Partners, A Brief History of Hedge Funds. http://www.capmgt.com/ brief_history.html.

18. In fact, many of the reasons why hedge funds have been able to avoid SEC regu-lation is that they have relied on the exemption embodied in using the money of these wealthy (or sophisticated) investors.

19. "Hedge funds are restricted under Regulation D under the Securities Act of 1933 to raising capital only in non-public offerings and only from accredited investors, or indi-viduals with a minimum net worth of $1,000,000 or a minimum income of $200,000 in each of the last two years and a reasonable expectation of reaching the same income level in the current year. Under Dodd-Frank, the SEC was given explicit authority to adjust the net worth and income standards for individuals as it deems appropriate. For banks and corporate entities, they must have a minimum of $5,000,000 in total assets. Many investors in larger hedge funds must also meet heightened qualified purchaser standards

under the Investment Company Act of 1940." "Global Hedge Fund Management," *Managed Funds Association* (2015) https://www.managedfunds.org/issues-policy/issues/globalhedge-fund-regulation/.

20. *See e.g.*, Langevoort, "The SEC, Retail Investors and the Institionalization of the Securities Markets," 1026.

21. Joel Seligman, "The SEC in a Time of Discontinuity," *95 Va. L. Rev., 679* (2009). Among the changes Seligman notes are the diversification of financial holding companies, the globalization of securities trading, the expansion of instruments for securities trading and the increase in the amount of investors in the market. Ibid. at 669–70. We would add to this three other significant changes: (1) the rise of the institutional investor; (2) the increase in the use of technology in investing and; (3) the changed behavior for investors' buying patterns for stocks.

22. Michael Lewis, *Flash Boys: Cracking the Money Code* (W.W. Norton & Company, 2014).

23. Jena Martin and Karen Kunz, "Into the Breach: The Increasing Gap Between Algorithmic Trading and Securities Regulation," *Journal of Financial Services Research* (2013).

24. Ibid.

25. One example of these consequences occurred during the 2010 flash crash, in which the Dow Jones lost 1,000 points in minutes because of what was later discovered to be a computer glitch. See Ken Sweet, "Flash Crash Worries Go Global," *CNN Money* (May 6, 2011) http://money.cnn.com/2011/05/06/markets/flash_crash/.

26. The 2nd edition of *Day Trading for Dummies* (For Dummies, 2011), by Ann C. Logue, MBA, contains a section entitled, "How to use Fibonacci Numbers and the Elliot Wave when Day Trading." See www.dummies.com/how-to-Use-fibonacci-numbers-and-the-elliot-wave-.html.

27. For example, see the blog "Algorithmic trading for dummies" accessible at http://www.wildbunny.co.uk/blog/2013/03/15/algorithmic-trading-for-dummies/.

28. Scott Patterson, *The Quants: How a New Breed of Math Whizzes Conquered Wall Street and Nearly Destroyed it* (Crown Business, 2010), 17–20.

29. Rishi K. Narang, *Inside the Black Box: A Simple Way to Quantitative and High Frequency Trading* (Wiley, 2010), 21, italics in original).

30. Ibid.

31. Nathan D. Brown, "The Rise of High Frequency Trading: The Role Algorithms, and the Lack of Regulations, Play in Today's Stock Market," *11 Appalachian J.L. 209* (2011–2012), 12 (comment).

32. Scott Patterson, *The Quants: How a New Breed of Math Whizzes Conquered Wall Street and Nearly Destroyed it*, 8.

33. Ibid.

34. Ibid.

35. Ibid.

36. Ibid.

37. "The National Association of Securities Dealers, Inc. (NASD) formerly ran the NASDAQ stock exchange and NASD Regulation, Inc., which was Wall Street's self-regulating agency. The NASDAQ became a public corporation in 2005, and the NASD

sold its ownership share in 2006. In July 2007, the NASD merged its regulatory functions with the enforcement arm of the New York Stock Exchange to form the Financial Industry Regulatory Authority (FINRA)." http://law.lexisnexis.com/infopro/zimmer mans/disp.aspx?z=1728. FINRA is a non-profit organization whose membership is comprised of investment firms and which is funded by member fees. Like its predecessor, the NASD, FINRA is responsible for auditing and enforcing member compliance with SEC regulations. This quasi-regulatory "fox guarding the hen house" structure serves to enable the SEC's limited approach to trading oversight.

38. J.E. David, "Ice to Buy NYSE for $8.2 Billion, Ending Era of Independence." *CNBC US News* (2012). http://www.cnbc.com/id/100330589.

39. L. Marek, "How the sale of the New York Stock Exchange affects CME's future," *Crain's Chicago Business* (2013). http://www.chicagobusiness.com/article/20130105/IS-SUE01/301059983/how-the-sale-of-the-new-york-stock-exchange-affects-cmes-future.

40. International Organization of Securities Commissions (IOSCO). "Regulatory Issues Raised by the Impact of Technological Changes on Market Integrity and Efficiency," *Technical Committee, Consultation Report* (2011), 13. http://www.iosco.org/library/pubdocs/pdf/IOSCOPD354.pdf.

41. T. Hendershott, C.M. Jones, and A.J. Menkveld, "Does Algorithmic Trading Improve Liquidity?" *The Journal of Finance, LXVI, 1* (2011), 1–33.

42. J. Angel, J. Harris, and C.S. Spatt, "Equity Trading in the 21st Century," Working Paper No. FBE 09–10 (2010), 2. http://ssrn.com/abstract=1584026 or http://dx.doi.org/10.2139/ssrn.1584026.

43. P.K. Jain, "Financial Market Design and the Equity Premium: Electronic versus Floor Trading," *Journal of Finance, 60, 6* (2005), 2956.

44. James Angel, Lawrence Harris & Chester S. Spatt, "Equity Trading in the 21st Century."

45. L.O. Rameriz, *High Frequency Trading* (Manuscript, 2011). http://scholar.googleusercontent.com/scholar?q=cache:2YlzRRdps4oJ:scholar.google.com/+supercom puter+trading+&hl=en&as_sdt=1,49.

46. James Angel, Lawrence Harris & Chester S. Spatt, "Equity Trading in the 21st Century."

47. C. Elias, "Regulators globally seek to curb supercomputer trading glitches." *Reuters Financial Regulatory Forum* (2012). http://blogs.reuters.com/financial-regulatory-forum/2012/08/31/regulators-globally-seek-to-curb-supercomputer-trading-glitches/.

48. Holly A. Bell, "Regulator, Go Slow on Reining in High-Speed Trading," *The Wall Street Journal,* A13 (February 8, 2013), 1.

49. For details see Karen Kunz & Jena Martin, "Into the Breech: The Increasing Gap Between Algorithmic Trading and Securities Regulation" and Rishi K. Narang, *Inside the Black Box: The Simple Truth about Quantitative Trading.*

50. C. Elias, "Regulators globally seek to curb supercomputer trading glitches."

51. 21st Century Wire, "'White House Attacked, Obama Injured' AP Tweet Hoax Crashes US Stock Market" (2013), 1. http://21stcenturywire.com/2013/04/24/white-house-attacked-obama-injured-ap-tweet-hoax-crashes-us-stock-market/.

52. PBS News Hour, *International ATM Cyber Hackers Hid 'in Plain Sight' to Overcome Computer System* (May 10, 2013). http://www.pbs.org/newshour/bb/world/

jan-june13/bank2_05–10.html; and Baker Institute Blog, "Hacking the international financial system," *Chron (The Houston Chronicle)* (June 13, 2011). http://blog.chron .com/bakerblog/2011/06/hacking-the-international-financial-system/; and Dustin Voltz and Jeremy Wagstaff, "Cyber firms say Bangladesh hackers have attacked other Asian banks" *Reuters* (May 27, 2016).

53. James Angel, Lawrence Harris & Chester S. Spatt, "Equity Trading in the 21st Century."

54. Heidi Moore & Dan Roberts, "AP Twitter hack causes panic on Wall Street and sends Dow plunging," *The Guardian* (Apr 23, 2013).

55. Wallace Witkowski and Sital S. Patel, "Twitter trading influence laid bare by fake tweet," *Market Watch* (Apr 24, 2013).

56. C.W. Calomiris, "Financial fragility: issues and policy implications," *Journal of Financial Services Research, 9* (1995), 241.

57. Heidi Moore & Dan Roberts, "AP Twitter hack causes panic on Wall Street and sends Dow plunging."

58. Joe Davidson, "'Inadvertent' cyber breach hits 44,000 FDIC customers," *Washington Post* (April 11, 2011).

59. See Jason Lange & Dustin Volz, "Fed records show dozens of cybersecurity breaches," *Reuters* (Jun 1, 2016), http://www.reuters.com/article/us-usa-fed-cyber -idUSKCN0YN4AM; and Jose Pagilery & Patrick Gillespie, "Federal Reserve under attack by hacker spies," *CNN Money* (Jun 2, 2016), http://money.cnn.com/2016/06/01/ technology/federal-reserve-hack/.

60. Scott Patterson, *The Quants: How a New Breed of Math Whizzes Conquered Wall Street and Nearly Destroyed it*, 40.

61. Ibid., 15.

62. Ibid. As Patterson notes, this transition wasn't always smooth. For instance, many of the most serious market glitches were, at least in some way, tied to the use of quantitative analysis.

63. Rishi K. Narang, *Inside the Black Box: The Simple Truth about Quantitative Trading*.

64. Scott Patterson, *The Quants: How a New Breed of Math Whizzes Conquered Wall Street and Nearly Destroyed it*.

65. Ibid.

66. Ibid.

67. Ibid.

68. Ibid.

69. Ibid.

70. Google's recent decision regarding the class of stock that they offer is a prime example of this. Traditionally, corporations have offered stock that allows stockholders to exercise voting rights. Google, in 2014, decided to issue a new class of stock, one that has no voting rights attached to it.

71. Todd Zenger, "What is the Theory of Your Firm?," *Harvard Business Review* (2013), http://hbr.org/2013/06/what-is-the-theory-of-your-firm/ar/pr.

72. Andrew W. Lo & Mark T. Mueller. "WARNING: Physics Envy May Be Hazardous to your Wealth!" *Cornell University Library, v3* (Mar 20, 2010), 37.

73. Ibid., 47.

74. Ibid.

75. Used in the way it was during the financial crisis, leveraging becomes another form of speculative trading. For further discussion on the role of hedging and its contribution to the crisis, see James Crott, "Structural Causes of the Global Financial Crisis: A Critical Assessment of the 'New Financial Architecture,'" *Working Paper, University of Massachusetts, Department of Economics* No. 2008–14 (2014).

76. Henry G. Manne, "In Defense of Insider Trading," *44 Harvard Business Review 113* (1966).

CHAPTER 2

Trying to Evaporate Water with Sunshine

MOVING BEYOND DISCLOSURE[1]

In 2014, the SEC entered into its eighth decade. Founded in 1934, the agency was created in the wake of the worst financial disaster in America's history—one that came about largely as the result of speculative and manipulative trading in its securities markets.[2] Since its founding, one of the SEC's central missions is to "protect investors."[3] Nevertheless, the model that the Commission uses to serve that mandate can by and large be framed as a *laissez faire* approach to regulation.[4] Rather than directly intervene in the corporate governance of a company, the SEC primarily uses a disclosure paradigm to protect American investors.[5]

In discussing the disclosure model, many who have worked for the SEC have evoked the words attributed to Justice Louis Brandeis that "sunlight is the best disinfectant." For instance, the former Director of Corporation Finance, John White, explicitly linked the notion of sunlight with the "bedrock principles of good disclosure."[6] It is an interesting idea—to view sunlight as the means by which we can see the challenges that we face and use that light to clear any ambiguities—to clear the water as it were. Specifically, the disclosure model rests on the premise that "an educated investor is a protected investor."[7] By intention, the SEC's regulatory model requires companies to provide investors with a sub-stantial amount of information regarding their financial operations and financial well-being in the hope that investors will use that information to make sound choices for their investments. Presumably, if we shine enough light on the prob-lem then it would clear enough water to allow investors to see to the bottom.

The problem with the disclosure system is that it doesn't work.

Given the rise of the level of the water—the sheer deluge of information that the SEC is trying to regulate—trying to use sunshine to clear the water is quixotic at best. The reasons are both theoretical and practical. On a practical level, the current model is overrun with too much regulation and not enough oversight. Many of the SEC's biggest corporate scandals in the last twenty years—ones that precipitated hundreds of millions of dollars in losses to the markets and investors—would have been perfectly legal if the companies involved had disclosed what they were doing.[8] To be clear, the companies could have still engaged in the underlying practices, they just needed to tell the general public about it.

Enron,[9] the analyst conflict scandals,[10] and Goldman Sachs[11] are notable examples of scandals that were illegal, not because of the practice itself, but because the corporations in question failed to disclose them. While the causes of actions for these scandals often sound like fraud, the underlying factual claims frequently rested on non-disclosure. Indeed, the whole legal theory at the heart of a fraud cause of action—the SEC's biggest stick in getting companies to behave—arguably rests on non-disclosure because, in the end, fraud is a deception. The deception only works if the actual truth is concealed. Whether it is done through a material misrepresentation or simply an omission is almost ancillary to the underlying fact—that the real facts have not been disclosed.

Perhaps this disconnect can best be shown through a look at the now defunct Enron Corporation. Enron may be a parable for the problems of securities regulation. The company, long known for its energy operations, ran into significant trouble (and eventually, civil liability, criminal liability and bankruptcy) when regulators began to delve into the company's financials. It was only then that they discovered a web of creative accounting and financial reporting that disguised the company's true financial health.

In their efforts to escape liability, many executives of Enron contended that most of the questionable transactions that led to the company's collapse were in fact disclosed in various SEC filings. It is undisputed that Enron's collapse had significant ramifications, not just for the employees and suppliers but also for the marketplace as a whole. In the end, if the executives' arguments are to be believed, the collapse of Enron still would have occurred, leaving the SEC with no recourse with which to seek redress for investors.

More recently, the financial crisis of 2008 shows how out of step the regulators' efforts are with the ability to create market stability. While many of the symptoms of the practices that led to the financial meltdown can be traced to deception and fraudulent behavior, the root causes of the market meltdown were completely divorced from the issues that the SEC generally regulate under a disclosure model.

Moreover, on a conceptual level, a disclosure paradigm is completely out of step with the way the markets trade today. For instance, the rise of computerized trading has made the disconnect between the US securities markets and the leading regulatory body that oversees them all the more alarming.[12] By some accounts, high frequency trading accounts for up to 70 percent of all trading volume on the US markets.[13] And, as mentioned earlier, while the current status of this market regulation is by and large primarily open to large institutional investors, the continuing advancement in technology is making algorithmic trading something that is within anyone's grasp.

Scott Patterson brings the disconnect between disclosure and trading into sharp relief when he discusses quant shops: "The quants are also haunted by another fear: systemic risk. The August 2007 meltdown showed that the quants' presence in the market wasn't nearly as benign as they had believed."[14] One of Patterson's central points is the interconnectedness of all segments of the markets—those regulated by the disclosure framework (i.e., securities) and those completely outside of its structures (e.g., commodities, hedge funds). "We are seeing things that were 25-standard deviation events, several days in a row."[15] In short, disclosure doesn't work.

We recognize, that in taking this position, we are going against numerous scholars who believe that the disclosure system is in fact adequate, or at least, here to stay. Troy Paredes acknowledges the perils of disclosure.[16] Before he became an SEC Commissioner, he discussed the implication of information overload within a securities paradigm. He notes that mandatory disclosure is broken, in large part because it fails to acknowledge how investors use the information that companies' disclose.[17] Paredes correctly diagnoses part of the problem—that if "investors, securities analysts, brokers and other securities market professionals do not internalize all of the information they gather and analyze, they will invest too few resources in research and analysis."[18] In fact, according to Parades, leaving the analysis to the professionals might make matters worse rather than better;[19] however, he goes on to discuss solutions that, while taking a step in the right direction (in that they are based on less disclosure, not more) still operate within a largely faulty framework (the disclosure system itself).[20] Moreover, events that unfolded in the years after the article was written in 2003—most obviously, the financial crash of 2008—have made the disconnect between the problem of the markets and the solution of disclosure even more apparent.

Despite this disconnect between the disclosure paradigm and the underlying harm to investors, the SEC still offers disclosure as the ultimate panacea to the country's financial ailments. While the concept that knowledge is power usually rings true, in the case of securities regulation, well-informed shareholders in the US are still, by and large, powerless—they are simply aware of their powerlessness. Equally true is that many shareholders may be apathetic to the reality because they are solely interested in the returns. The dual harms of apathy and ignorance put into question the disclosure-based regime's ability to fix the underlying issues.

Another former SEC Commissioner has come to the point of understanding that disclosure is an inadequate system. Daniel Gallagher, SEC Commissioner from 2011–2015, has also acknowledged the limitations of disclosure.[21] However,

Gallagher, like Paredes, has been unwilling to take the plunge and advocate for a complete dismantling of the disclosure system.[22] Therein, lies the error.

In chapter 1 we noted that one of the main things that have changed in the market is that the participants are different: right now the securities markets are largely dominated by institutional investors. Yet despite this changing dynamic, the SEC's mode of regulation is still too narrowly focused on a now largely marginalized class of investors: the retail investors. It appears our markets have "fundamentally changed in recent decades while financial regulation has moved far more slowly."[23]

As a result, after all the changes that have taken place in the market, the SEC has been left without a significant role. There are many issues that disclosure can no longer catch. In addition, it appears that disclosure no longer functions to help the SEC with its primary mandate to protect investors by ensuring equal access to information, which is then intended to be used by investors to make informed decisions.

We should note, however, that this may be changing. Typically, the SEC's investigative focus is on corporations or individuals who either falsely disseminate or omit material information. Recently, however, the SEC has expanded its focus by bringing fraud charges against a quant manager. According to the SEC, the manager failed to disclose an erroneous calculation that affected the fund's formulas and calculations.[24] While this may be a step in the right direction in that it focuses on key players that have until now been left out of many of the SEC's investigative focuses, namely those in quantitative analysis, the regulatory tool is still the same—one of disclosure.

Investor protection is, in fact, not the SEC's only stated mission. The SEC's mission, stated in full, is to "protect investors, maintain fair, orderly and efficient markets, and facilitate capital formation." This mission statement "identifies several strategic goals that include enforcing federal securities laws, establishing effective regulation of trading markets and their participants, and facilitating investors' access to information."[25] Having a number of distinct priorities in its mission statement has often led to tension at the SEC when one priority seemingly comes into conflict with another.[26] Nevertheless, the SEC's mission is not fundamentally the problem. Or, more specifically, a new pattern of regulation could be instituted that could do a better job of fulfilling the SEC's mission. Or the mission itself could change.

Even the SEC seems to be finally coming to the understanding that a strict disclosure model may not be enough. In 2010, the SEC proposed rules that set the stage for a potential shift (albeit an incredibly gradual one) from a primarily disclosure-based model to one that is more attuned to the market as a whole. The SEC issued a Concept Release[27] that requested feedback on high frequency trading in the wake of the financial crisis.

On March 8, 2013, the SEC took additional steps to address a more holistic market solution. The proposed rule, Regulation Systems Compliance and Integrity (Regulation SCI), provides a set of enforceable rules for other market participants that require them to "carefully design, develop, test, maintain, and surveil systems that are integral to their operations. The proposed rules require them to ensure their core technology meets certain standards, conduct business continuity testing, and provide certain notifications in the event of systems disruptions and other events."[28] The primary goal of the rule is to provide some stability to the use of market participants' relationship with technology and the impact of this technology on the market as a whole.[29]

The regulation is a step forward in that it specifically acknowledges and attempts to address the new participants (high-frequency traders), their new methods (the use of computerized trading), and the impacts they have on the securities market as a whole.

However, for every step forward, there are two steps back.

First, the proposed regulation does not go nearly far enough to address the systemic way in which these changes have fundamentally altered our trading patterns. Allowing for these fixes will, at most, provide a superficial and temporary solution that amounts to little more than treating the symptoms rather than finding a cure. Second, more recently, the SEC has once again expressed a commitment to the disclosure based foundation on which it's based. On April 13, 2016, the SEC held an open meeting to discuss a Concept Release for Regulation S-K. In her opening remarks, SEC Chair Mary Jo White stated

> the SEC's disclosure mission is central to our mission to protect investors and the integrity of our capital markets. . . . Because of its critical importance to investors and issuers, optimizing Regulation S-K, and our disclosure regime more broadly, is a crucial, ongoing responsibility of the Commission and its staff.[30]

Further, on a micro level, the SEC tends not to focus on long-range patterns and practices. For example, former SEC Secretary Jonathan Katz acknowledges that until 2009, "the SEC ha[d] never recruited, hired, and retained skilled people capable of performing quantitative analysis."[31] Katz also observes that two of the biggest scandals of the previous decades were uncovered, not by staff at the Division of Enforcement, but by academics, going through publicly available information (in one instance, SEC filings).[32] He further notes, "[t]he SEC does not itself routinely analyze [those] or other filings in this way," and concludes that "[a] regulator and the investing public must accept the fact that all frauds cannot be prevented, and that it is not always possible to detect them before they explode."[33]

Yet, as central as the Securities and Exchange Commission is to the issue of national securities regulation, the failures of the disclosure paradigm are not the only issue. One of the primary problems with the current market structure is that, with all of the leaks in the dikes, the SEC is not the only agency trying to plug the holes. Instead, there are many other agencies, working at cross purposes, who all have a hand in regulating the securities markets. It is that issue—via a stop in the 1920s and 30s—that we discuss in chapter 3.

Notes

1. Portions of this chapter were adapted from an earlier article written by Jena Martin, "Changing the Rules of the Game: Beyond a Disclosure Framework for Securities Regulations," *118 W.V. L. Rev. 59* (2015).

2. Jerry W. Markham, *A Financial History of the United States* (Routledge, 2001), 149–153. Although later, Prof. Markham states that "it is difficult to isolate a single event that caused the stock market crash of 1929," certainly the speculative behavior by some of the country's top traders was a contributing factor. Of course, many of the issues that were at the heart of the Great Depression have mutated into contributing factors of the financial crisis that hit between 2007 and 2009.

3. *The Investor's Advocate: How the SEC Protects Investors, Maintains Market Integrity, and Facilitates Capital Formation* (US Securities & Exchange Commission, 2013), http://www.sec.gov/about/whatwedo.shtml#.UytLM37D_mI.

4. There are many who would disagree with this characterization of the SEC as being laissez faire. In fact, many legal scholars today have faulted Congress and the SEC for what they describe as the federalization of corporate governance. *See, e.g.,* Stephen M. Bainbridge, "Dodd-Frank: Quack Federal Corporate Governance Round II," *95 Minn. L. Rev. 1779* (2011). While it is true that some of the provisions of Dodd-Frank, Sarbanes-Oxley and the SEC's more recent rulemaking (in the realm of shareholder proposals and proxy access) does show a keener interest in corporate governance issues, as I have argued elsewhere, the underlying methodology that the SEC used to advance those issues is still, by and large, one that is disclosure based. See Jena Martin Amerson, "The SEC and Shareholder Empowerment—Examining the New Proxy Regime and its Impact on Corporate Governance," *30 No. 2 Banking & Financial Services Policy Report 2* (2011). In addition, the SEC's most recent endeavors in examining markets as a whole (for instance through their creation of the Economic and Risk Analysis Division), are precisely so notable because they are the exception.

5. Jennifer B. Lawrence & Jackson W. Prentice, "The SEC Form 8-K: Full Disclosure or Fully Diluted? The Quest for Improved Market Transparency," *41 Wake Forest L. Rev. 913* (2006). "[O]ur results reflect the [SEC's] fundamental shift in the regulatory model to one premised upon more disclosure, greater SEC involvement, heightened corporate accountability, and an increased investor demand for market transparency."

6. John W. White, *The Promise of Transparency—Corporation Finance in 2007* (The Securities & Exchange Commission, 2007), https://www.sec.gov/news/speech/2007/spch022307jww.htm#1.

7. *See, e.g.*, the Securities and Exchange Commission's investor website which states "information is the investor's best tool when it comes to investing wisely." *Microcap Stock: A Guide for Investors,* US Securities & Exchange Commission (2013), https://www.sec.gov/investor/pubs/microcapstock.htm. See also the West Virginia Securities Commission's website, which states: "Investor education is a key component of our efforts and we sincerely believe that an educated investor is a protected investor." *The Basics of Saving and Investing: Investor Education 2020* (West Virginia State Auditor's Office, 2016), http://www.wvsao.gov/securitiescommission/education/investored2020.aspx. This mantra is repeated in other markets across the globe: *see, e.g., Investor Education: Overview,* Capital Markets Authority of Kenya, 2014), http://www.cma.or.ke/index.php?option=com_content&view=article&id=5&Itemid=118 which states "we hold the view that an educated investor is a protected investor and that a protected investor is always a more willing player in the capital market place. To us, investor education is one of the most effective regulatory tools."

8. Of course, going down the "what if" path is always dangerous. For instance, it is quite possible that the disclosure framework could lead other companies from engaging in the bad behavior in the first place—knowing that they would have to disclose it. In fact, that seems to be the rationale behind the SEC's move to require companies to disclose whether or not they have a Code of Ethics (rather than substantively require companies to adopt a Code of Ethics). The act of disclosing that one does **not** have one, should, in theory, lead to companies adopting one (see, 15 U.S.C. § 7264 [2014], Code of Ethics 17 C.F.R. § 229.406 [2014]). In passing the rule in 2003, the SEC stated "the strength of U.S. financial markets depends on investor confidence. Recent events involving allegations of misdeeds . . . have undermined that confidence . . . it seems reasonable to expect that a company would hold its chief executive officer . . . to at least the same standards of ethical conduct to which it holds its senior financial officers."

9. See, for example, Michael Duffy, "By the Sign of the Crooked E," *Time* (Jan. 19, 2002), http://www.time.com/time/business/article/0,8599,195268,00.html#ixzz12FilwwCg. He writes: "Enron and Andersen officials hardly deny the dubious deals, the 881 offshore tax havens or the stupid accounting tricks. That's partly because nobody can be sure that those dodges were inherently illegal." In an even more prescient article, William Henderson discusses the Enron collapse and notes its similarity to a largely forgotten scandal of another energy titan—Samuel Insull—that occurred over seventy years ago. See, Hon. Richard D. Cudahy & William D. Henderson, "From Insull to Enron: Corporate (Re)Regulation After the Rise and Fall of Two Energy Icons," *26 Energy L.J.* 35 (2005). According to Henderson, the main lesson to be learned from this is "in recognizing that during a financial bubble driven by rapid changes in network industries . . . regulatory officials will inevitably buckle under political pressure . . . [T]he laws adopted in response to Enron are destined to be watered down and ignored during the next boom" (Ibid., 37–38). Unfortunately, we did not have to wait for the next boom to see the full impact of the lack of political pressure.

See also Steven L. Schwarz, "Enron and the Use and Abuse of Special Purpose Entities in Corporate Structures," *70 Univ. Cinn. L. Rev. 1309* (2002) noting the complex, yet arguably technically compliant disclosures made by the company.

10. Jill E. Fisch, "Fiduciary Duties and the Analyst Scandals," *58 Al. L. Rev.1083, 1084* (2007). The analyst conflict scandals emerged when it was shown that analysts were touting stocks of a company without disclosing their conflict of interest: that their investment firm had many of the touted companies as clients.

11. According to the SEC's release on the matter, "Goldman Sachs structured and marketed a synthetic collateralized debt obligation (CDO) that hinged on the performance of subprime residential mortgage-backed securities (RMBS). Goldman Sachs failed to disclose to investors vital information about the CDO, in particular the role that a major hedge fund played in the portfolio selection process and the fact that the hedge fund had taken a short position against the CDO." "SEC Charges Goldman Sachs With Fraud in Structuring and Marketing of CDO Tied to Subprime Mortgages," *SEC Release 2010–59* (Apr 16, 2010), http://www.sec.gov/news/press/2010/2010–59.htm.

12. David M. Serritella, "High Speed Trading Begets High Speed Regulation: SEC Response to Flash Crash, Rash," *2010 Univ. Ill. J.L. Tech & Pol'y 433* (2010).

13. Jena Martin & Karen Kunz, "Into the Breach: The Increasing Gap Between Algorithmic Trading and Securities Regulation."

14. Scott Patterson, *The Quants: How a New Breed of Math Whizzes Conquered Wall Street and Nearly Destroyed It*, 40.

15. Ibid.

16. Troy Paredes, "Blinded by the Light: Information Overload and its Consequences for Securities Regulation," *81 Wash. U. L. Q. 417, 422* (2003).

17. Ibid., 420.

18. Ibid., 421.

19. Ibid., 457.

20. Ibid., 459.

21. Troy Paredes, "Blinded by the Light: Information Overload and its Consequences for Securities Regulation," 420, discussing potential solutions to the "specter of information overload"; also, Daniel Gallagher's speech, *Remarks to the Forum for Corporate Directors*, Orange County, California (Jan 24, 2014), https://www.sec.gov/News/Speech/Detail/Speech/1370540680363).

22. Troy Paredes, "Blinded by the Light: Information Overload and its Consequences for Securities Regulation," 422 (stating, "As a regulatory matter, the mandatory disclosure debate has been settled for seventy years."); Gallagher, *Remarks to the Forum for Corporate Director* asks "So what should we do? Should we jump in with both feet to begin a comprehensive review and overhaul of SEC-imposed disclosure requirements under the securities laws? Or should we take a more targeted approach, favoring smaller steps towards our ultimate reforming goals? Ordinarily, I would argue for a comprehensive approach to solving almost any problem in securities regulation, since actions in one area frequently have unforeseen and unintended effects in others. Where disclosure reform is concerned, though, I would prefer to address discrete issues now rather than risk spending years preparing an offensive so massive that it may never be launched."

23. Joel Seligman, "The SEC in a Time of Discontinuity." Among the changes Seligman notes are the diversification of financial holding companies, the globalization of securities trading, the expansion of instruments for securities trading and the increase in the amount of investors in the market. *Id.* at 669–70. We would add to this three other significant changes: (1) the rise of the institutional investor; (2) the increase in the use of technology in investing and; (3) the changed behavior for investors' buying patterns for stocks.

24. US Securities & Exchange Commission, "SEC Charges Quant Manager with Fraud," *SEC Release 2011–189* (Sept 22, 2011).

25. Barbara Black, "Introduction: the SEC at 75," *78 Univ. Cin. L. Rev. 445, 449* (2009).

26. Ibid., 448.

27. The SEC publishes Concept Releases to solicit comments from the public on a given subject to ascertain the need for future rules. See, *SEC Concept Releases,* US Securities & Exchange Commission (2015), http://www.sec.gov/rules/concept.shtml.

28. Press Release, US Securities & Exchange Commission, *SEC Proposes Rules to Improve Systems Compliance and Integrity* (Mar. 7, 2013, http://www.sec.gov/News/PressRelease/Detail/PressRelease/1365171513148.

29. Zachary J. Ziliak, "Regulation Ahead: Advice and Options for Automated and High-Frequency Traders," *Bloomberg* (Apr 22, 2013), http://www.bna.com/regulation-ahead-advice-and-options-for-automated-and-high-frequency-traders/.

30. Mary Jo White, *Statement at an Open Meeting on Regulation S-K Concept Release* (Securities & Exchange Commission, Apr 13, 2016), https://www.sec.gov/news/statement/white-statement-1–041316.html.

31. Jonathan G. Katz, "Reviewing the SEC, Reinvigorating the SEC," *71 Univ. Pitt. L. Rev. 489, 501* (2010). In 2009, the SEC created the Division of Economic and Risk Analysis (DERA) to integrate financial economics and rigorous data analytics into the core mission of the SEC. The Division is involved across the entire range of SEC activities, including policy-making, rule-making, enforcement and examination. As the agency's "think tank," DERA relies on a variety of academic disciplines, quantitative and non-quantitative approaches and knowledge of market institutions and practices to help the Commission approach complex matters in a fresh light. DERA also assists in the Commission's efforts to identify, analyze and respond to risks and trends, including those associated with new financial products and strategies. Through the range and nature of its activities, DERA serves the crucial function of promoting collaborative efforts throughout the agency and breaking through silos that might otherwise limit the impact of the agency's institutional expertise. *About the Division of Economic and Risk Analysis,* US Securities & Exchange Commission (2015), http://www.sec.gov/divisions/riskfin.shtml. While DERA seems to be a step in the right direction, the SEC is still using these tools and goals within the current regulatory framework. In the end, if the SEC is still looking at regulating through issuing disclosures rather than on a more quantitative, proactive basis, all of the data in the world will not get at the heart of the problem.

32. Ibid., 496.

33. Ibid.

CHAPTER 3

Plugging the Leaks

The structure of the current investments markets system has deep historical roots. Prior to 1929, securities commerce was a relative free-for all. The investment markets were not regulated at all on the federal level. Congress preferred to delegate that activity to state authorities. The result was inconsistent and uncoordinated regulatory oversight that did little to protect investors or ensure ethical commerce.

Then came the stock market crash of 1929.

The New York Stock Exchange, then the only US securities exchange,[1] ceased trading and shuttered its ticker tapes, unsure when it would reopen. Markets dropped precipitously on several occasions in the year leading up to the crash, like dress rehearsals for the main event, as speculators, reassured by bankers, bought into every stock and foreign investment scheme that came their way. Still the crash came as a surprise to President Hoover and most lawmakers and businessmen of the day. Until then, it was believed that the markets would automatically right themselves as needed and that supply and demand would always prevail.[2]

After committee hearings and investigations and a variety of proposed bills, Congress settled on three pieces of legislation designed to prevent future market instabilities: The Glass-Steagall Act, a portion of the US. Banking Act of 1933, the Securities Act of 1933, and the Securities and Exchange Act of 1934, which established the Securities and Exchange Commission (SEC) and its responsibilities for oversight of the securities markets.

Since then Congress has endeavored to keep pace with progress, enacting a laundry list of legislation to regulate changing and expanding markets. In addition to the SEC, a wide array of self-regulatory bodies, federal agencies, Congressional committees, Congressional councils, other federal boards and working groups—as well as agencies in each state—now oversee an ever-expanding array of investment products, including stocks, options, bonds, commodities, futures, currencies, mutual funds, variable annuities and some securities derivatives, as well as those who provide investment advice. Over-the-counter (OTC) and other securities derivatives, rating agencies and other financial products and practices remain out of regulatory reach for the moment, while a myriad of federal agents wrangle over definitions and turf wars regarding enforcement of fiduciary responsibilities. Purchases and sales are transacted electronically, and in the US alone there are eighteen stock exchanges on which to trade securities and six that conduct futures transactions, all of which are also registered with the SEC.[3]

After an almost sixty-year period of relative stability, the seas started churning again. Since 1987 there have been a number of market failures—none quite as calamitous as the crash of '29—but each with generally increasing ferocity: Black Monday in 1987;[4] the United Airlines-related mini-crash in 1989; the collapse of the dot-com bubble in 2000; the catastrophic declines in 2008; and the (mini) flash crash in 2010. As in 1929, the declines were global in scope; international markets and economic activities impact US markets just as conditions here affect international stability. And, while the epic 2008 crash illustrated the effectiveness of regulatory stopgap measures to avert an even greater catastrophe, these measures simply reduced the speed of the downward slide. Like putting fingers in holes in the dike as leaks emerged, these triggers did little to prevent the eventual cascade.

In the previous chapters we discussed two reasons for the increased fragility of the markets: (1) the rapidly changing nature of the markets and (2) the inability of the disclosure-based system to keep pace. Here, we take on a third: the fragmented oversight and overlapping jurisdictions that have resulted in a lack of coordination and/or information sharing among all securities regulators. Regulation as a reactionary process is, by its very nature, not up to the task of keeping up with rapidly changing technologies and product innovation in what has become a global marketplace.

Plugging the Holes, Storm after Storm

Prior to the crash in 1929, the nation's securities markets ran on an honor system of sorts, with expectations that a laissez-faire approach, supplemented by bankers' borrowings from the Federal Reserve and contributions of their own funds would right the ship when it tilted.[5] The US experienced bear markets as the result of foreign market activity before 1929, but because bull markets[6] ultimately replaced any downturn, there was always the expectation of recovery. As President Hoover (who was inaugurated seven months before the crash) writes in his memoirs, to be sure, we were due for some economic readjustment as a result of the orgy of stock speculation in 1928–1929. . . . But even this slump started in foreign countries before it occurred in the United States, and their difficulties were themselves a contributing factor to the stock market crash. Our domestic difficulties standing alone would have produced no more than the usual type of economic readjustment, which had re-occurred at intervals in our history.[7]

Leading up to the crash, speculators seemed to buy everything that came their way and bankers borrowed more and more to extend credit. "The fact seems to be that the [Federal Reserve] Board, in January 1928, intended to curb the speculation, but was overridden by President Coolidge, who famously declared from the White House that the speculation was not dangerous and merely reflected the growing wealth and power of the United States."[8]

Yet the markets were not entirely left to their own devices. States set their own regulations for the sale of securities and the activities of those who sold them within their borders through what was known then, and now, as *blue sky laws*. For more than a generation—between 1911 and 1933—securities sales in the United States were regulated nearly exclusively by these specialized state statutes. Only with the Securities Act of 1933, adopted by Congress at a time of national economic collapse, did federal regulation begin to any significant extent. And even then federal law was little more than a pastiche of prior experiments in blue sky regulation. Because the Securities Act of 1933 expressly preserved the jurisdiction of state securities commissions, blue-sky regulation was then—and remains today—a significant part of securities law practice.[9]

After the crash, lawmakers held numerous very public and probing hearings to determine what went wrong, culminating in the famous Pecora Committee[10] investigation, so named after Ferdinand Pecora, a former rising star in the New York District Attorney's office who became Chief Counsel to the US Senate Committee on Banking and Currency. Fueled by public outcry over bankers' testimony of greed, fraud and manipulation—earning them the nickname, "banksters,"[11] lawmakers demanded broader federal regulation of the securities markets. Pecora identified the primary cause of the crash as fraudulent sales transacted through the mail and across state boundaries. These sales were exacerbated by the lack of sufficient information provided to investors.[12]

In response Congress passed the US Banking Act of 1933, containing the Glass-Steagall provisions, the Securities Act of 1933 and the Securities Exchange Act of 1934. Glass-Steagall placed severe restrictions on affiliations between commercial banks and securities firms and prohibited commercial banks from engaging in the investment business. It also created the Federal Deposit Insurance Corp (FDIC) to insure customers' bank deposits.

The Securities Act of 1933,[13] a.k.a. the "truth in securities act" sets standards for disclosure and interstate sales. As initially proposed, the Act placed regulatory oversight within the US Postal Service to ensure its constitutionality; however, in its enacted form, supervision was entrusted to the Federal Trade Commission because of its impact on interstate commerce. Shortly thereafter, the Securities Exchange Act of 1934 established the Securities and Exchange Commission as the regulatory body responsible for oversight of the securities industry. The primary themes of these two bills were to give "investors access to information about the securities they buy and the companies that issue securities"[14] and to hold issuers and sellers liable for providing fraudulent information about themselves and the securities they make available to public and private investors.[15] This last bill ensures that investors receive all relevant information prior to buying or selling shares, regardless of where the transaction takes place (and particularly for those conducted across state lines despite any state law to the contrary). These disclosure standards, coupled with the Glass-Steagall Act, formed the bedrock of the nation's securities regulation.

Since then dozens of supplemental bills, decisions and rules have been implemented in continuing efforts to prevent the recurrence of the problems identified in the Pecora Committee's report. Most often, these actions were precipitated by heightened demands that could no longer be ignored or a problem that brought the lack of oversight to the attention of the regulators. The table in Appendix B provides a comprehensive timeline of the most significant of these actions.

The various initiatives have not only created new laws and additional requirements; they also, in many instances, created new organizations that were responsible for additional oversight. Below, we provide a brief history:

1938: The Maloney Act creates a self-regulatory organization (SRO) comprised of industry firms and led by industry leaders, to police member firms. The National Association of Securities Dealers (NASD) was envisioned as the rudder that was missing when the ship was sinking in 1929. The NASD (now known as Financial Industry Regulatory Authority [FINRA]), is entrusted to "create and enforce disciplinary rules and promote just and equitable principles of trade."[16]

THE 1940s

The 1940s marked a steady addition to the legislative body, although admittedly with less of the fevered crescendo that happened in the wake of the crash and begin-

A brief "history within the history." . . .

Traditionally, being an owner of a security meant that you would have actually received a certificate that had your name, the name of the issuer—the company or municipality (in the case of municipal or treasury bonds) on it, and the amount of the company—number of shares—you owned. However, with the advent of electronic recordkeeping, things changed.

For those of you who are not well versed in securities terms—"clearing responsibilities" include any and all activities related to your ownership of a security. Because of the electronic advancements in the administration of financial markets operations, it has become rare for owners of securities to take physical possession of their purchases. Clearing houses developed to help owners and brokerage firms (aka broker-dealers) deal with all the issues that go along with being an owner of something you don't physically possess.

ning of the Great Depression. The focus in these early years was on creating and expanding the reach of federal agencies while solidifying their enforcement abilities.

1940: Congress passes the Investment Company Act and the Investment Advisors Act, both designed to prohibit fraudulent and deceptive practices by the new kids on the block—mutual fund companies and investment advisors, respectively.

1942: The SEC adopts Rule 10b-5, arguably the most important rule in securities regulation today. The rule explicitly extends prohibited practices outlawed in the Securities Act of 1933 to the sale of securities, allowing the whole marketplace (and its participants) to be under the purview of antifraud regulation.[17]

1946: The NASD takes on the responsibility for registering all securities brokers in addition to broker-dealer firms. This action significantly broadens the NASD's authority over the industry.

THE 1950s–THE 1970s

In the following decades the scope of the financial markets continued to expand and corresponding rules and oversight organizations were developed, although the pace was considerably slower than during the 1930s and '40s.

1951: Arizona becomes one of the first states to coordinate investigation and enforcement efforts with the SEC. Several years later, three-quarters of the states adopted the Uniform Securities Act, in whole or in part, which coordinated some state regulations with federal statutes.

1970: Congress passes the Securities Investor Protection Act (SIPC), an industry-financed fund to insure customers of failed broker-dealers. Similar to the FDIC for banks, it is created in response to Wall Street's inability to keep up with the ever-increasing volume of transactions.

1971: The NASDAQ opens for business. It is the nation's first electronic over-the-counter (OTC) trading system. Developed by the NASD, it is initially designed as a telephonic information portal for OTC customers.

1973: The Chicago Board Option Exchange (CBOE) begins trading listed stock options.

1975: The CBOE introduces computerized price reporting and expands to become the Options Clearing Corporation (OCC), taking on clearing responsibilities for all US options transactions. In this year Congress also creates the Municipal Securities Rulemaking Board (MSRB). The MSRB is established to ensure fair practices for underwriting and trading of municipal securities.

1976: Congress authorizes another major regulatory body, the Commodities Futures Trading Commission (CFTC). Grain commodities and futures had been traded since the mid-19th century through the Chicago Board of Trade (CBOT). The purpose of the CFTC is to regulate and transact all commodity-based securities transactions, including options and futures.

THE 1980s AND 1990s

The 1980s and 1990s marked a shift in the overarching regulatory philosophy from one of increasing regulation to one of routine limitation of federal power. This culminated in the 1990s with an explicit Congressional move towards deregulation.[18] To the extent that regulatory power increased during this time, it was almost always in reaction to a scandal or crisis.

1982: The Futures Trading Act is passed. The Act clarifies the CFTC's jurisdiction over futures and options on futures contracts and eliminates bearer securities.

1988: Congressional legislation is passed to prosecute insider trading via the Insider Trading and Securities Fraud Enforcement Act (ITSFEA). The Act is no doubt informed by federal agents' investigation and prosecution of Michael Milken, which was at the time, the biggest inside trader the SEC had investigated.

1989: In response to another crisis (this time in the savings and loan industry), Congress moves to regulate savings and loan institutions by enacting the Financial Institutions Reform, Recovery and Enforcement Act.

1990: After the market crash of 1989, the SEC's powers and responsibilities are again expanded. Congress passes the Market Reform Act, giving the SEC authorization to take action in emergency situations to maintain or restore fair and orderly markets and trade clearance. That same year Congress passes the Securities Enforcement Remedies and Penny Stock Reform Act giving the SEC the power to "issue cease and desist orders related to insider trading activity."[19]

At the same time, Congress takes a huge step toward giving the markets even more power:

1991: The New York Stock Exchange initiates after hours trading.

1996: The NASD divides itself into two separate entities, NASD Regulation Inc. and the NASDAQ stock exchange.

1999: Congress passes the Financial Services Modernization Act, more commonly known as the Gramm-Leach-Bliley Act (GLBA), which gives the SEC responsibility for securities transactions conducted by commercial banks—also the jurisdiction of the US Treasury's Office of the Comptroller of the Currency (OCC) and the Federal Reserve Board. On the surface this Act is a great expansion of SEC authority. However, most remember the Act as repealing the raison d'etre of Glass-Steagall by allowing banks to engage in both investment banking and commercial banking products. Unfortunately, the Act also paves the way for the development of institutions that become too big to fail.[20]

THE FIRST DECADE OF THE NEW CENTURY—2000–2009

The new millennium offered the markets even broader authority while continuing its pattern of inconsistent regulatory oversight. During this time, when the markets were doing well, Congress removed or limited various agencies' authority (both state and federal). However, when the next crisis or scandal happened (which was with much more alarming frequency), Congress responded with expanded regulation. This time period was also marked by Congress' limiting private plaintiffs' ability to bring securities related litigation (long viewed as a needed supplement to SEC jurisdiction).

2000: The Commodity and Futures Modernization Act prohibits federal regulation of OTC derivatives.

2002: Congress passes the Public Company Accounting Reform and Investor Protection Act (commonly known as the Sarbanes-Oxley Act, or SOX) in response to corporate scandals involving (among others) Enron, World-Com and Tyco. To preempt similar corporate failures in the future, SOX also created the Public Company Accounting Oversight Board (PCAOB) to audit the auditors of public companies. One of the primary purposes of the Act is to hold corporate officers responsible for accurate and timely financial disclosures to ensure that the public had access to reliable information.[21] The law includes substantive penalties for fraudulent activity, making it possible (albeit not probable)[22] for punishment—including fines and jail time—for corporate officers.

2005: Congress enacts the Class Action Fairness Act (CAFA), which builds on earlier legislation—the 1996 National Securities Market Improvement Act (NSMIA) and the 1998 Securities Litigation Standards Act (SLUSA), which preempt state authority and limit class actions—to further restrict state courts from adjudicating anything other than insignificant investment-related class actions. These laws direct investors' claims to federal court. "There is evidence . . . the collective effect of these statutes has been to drive smaller plaintiffs' firms out of the traditional securities litigation market, and perhaps strengthen larger firms."[23]

2009: Congress passes the Fraud Enforcement and Recovery Act. Among the authorizations given under the Act is the creation of the Financial Crisis Inquiry Commission (FCIC) to determine the causes of the 2008 financial crisis. The scope of their inquiry focuses primarily on the oversight practices of the SEC; however, it also includes other regulatory agencies.

AND THEN CAME THE BIG ONE . . .

The Dodd-Frank Wall Street Reform and Consumer Protection Act of 2010 (Dodd-Frank) was considered the most sweeping reform of financial markets regulation since the '33 and '34 Acts. The Act created additional regulatory bodies and review and reporting requirements and is purposed to give shareholders more power. Its laundry list of reforms targets banking institutions and practices as well as securities markets and participants in efforts to restrict the activities of firms that became too big to fail as a result of the Modernization Act of 1999. The sheer breadth of the Act has created significant implementation challenges. Six years later only 276 rules, or 68 percent of all those required, have been finalized, another 40 rules (or 10 percent) are pending review or approval, leaving over 21 percent of the 390 rules yet to even be considered. Dodd-Frank was remarkable for a number of reasons. One of the more controversial aspects of the Act, the Volcker Rule, prohibits commercial banks from proprietary trading, sets curbs on risky trading and establishes new, rigorous capital requirements. Aside from the impacts on the banking industry, the Act reversed earlier prohibitions on regulation of hedge fund advisors, who use a large variety of investing techniques (think "hedging your bets") to manage pools of investor dollars, and established regulatory oversight of derivatives,[24] which were also specifically exempt from regulation in earlier legislation. Oversight of securities-based derivatives became the responsibility of the SEC. OTC derivatives, which are less liquid and more volatile, now fall under CFTC supervision.

Other adopted reforms include uniform definitions of terms, rules for clearing and reporting transactions (agreements); and requirements for increase in capital requirements for non-clearing swap dealers.[25] According to the Financial Stability Board's (FSB) Ninth Progress Report on Implementation of OTC Derivatives Markets Reforms,[26] the market reforms proposed so far have been agreed to by all the countries whose markets engage in these types of transactions; however, while some progress has been made, there is substantially more to go.

Not surprisingly, Dodd-Frank also produced several new supervisory organizations. In doing so, the legislation contributed to the confusion surrounding the roles of different agencies and their oversight functions. The Consumer Financial Protection Bureau (CFPB) was the first regulatory body to come from the Act, and it represents the first federal efforts at real consumer protection and advocacy. It is designed to protect customers from deceptive and abusive practices in all aspects of the financial services markets. However, the organization's focus to date has been limited to commercial banking, and actions taken have centered primarily on consumer and payday lending. If and when it shifts focus to the securities markets, its efforts at investor protection will challenge long-standing regulation-mandated arbitration rules, under which customers are prohibited from suing investment firms and their agents for deceptive practices.

The Financial Stability Oversight Council [FSOC], a quasi-oversight group, was created to identify and monitor excessive risks to the US financial system, ideally through increased engagement between regulatory agency directors. "Chaired by the Secretary of the Treasury, voting members included the Federal Reserve Chairman, Comptroller of the Currency, Consumer Financial Protection Bureau Director, and chairs of the SEC, FDIC and CFTC."[27] Also, Section 967 of the Act required "the SEC to engage an independent consultant to conduct a broad and independent assessment of the SEC's internal operations, structure, funding, and the agency's relationship with [self-regulatory organizations] SROs."[28]

Confused by a patchwork of legislation and regulation?

A table illustrating the current regulatory oversight structure—which organizations are responsible for which aspects of the securities markets regulation—is provided in **Appendix A**.

A chronological list of the significant regulations is contained in **Appendix B**.

The Dodd-Frank Act also proposed that the SEC define and establish uniform federal fiduciary standards for the financial industry—something already codified (part of the "know your customer" concept) and included in broker-dealer examinations. In an uncoordinated effort, the Department of Labor (DOL) "proposed a wholesale revision to its regulation that redefines what it means to be a fiduciary under the Employee Retirement Income Security Act (ERISA) and the Internal Revenue Code."[29] The Act's requirements for something already in practice and the DOL's efforts to recreate the wheel have resulted in backlash and confusion.

The DOL's 1,000-page fiduciary rule, "which requires financial advisers to put their clients' interests ahead of their own when giving retirement advice"[30] adds a substantial new layer of compliance requirements on the small, boutique firms while favoring the big Wall Street firms, which have the ability to hire legions of attorneys. In contrast, smaller firms do not have the same resources to bear the cost of compliance.[31] In addition, the law allows the Wall Street firms "to sell their proprietary products more easily than they would have under the proposed rule."[32] This gives them a way to put commissions ahead of the investor interests (particularly if the proprietary product's performance is substantially below that of a competing product).[33] Since the passage of Dodd-Frank, two more laws have been passed that impact regulatory oversight. The Jumpstart Our Business Startups (JOBS) Act of 2012 exempts emerging growth companies from capital and disclosure requirements and, in a nod to the growing popularity of social media in all aspects of our lives, allows for variations of crowdfunding under certain conditions (more on the JOBS Act in Chapter 6). The Stop Trading on Congressional Knowledge (STOCK) Act, also of 2012, prohibits Congressional insider trading for personal gain.

Clearly, regulation of the financial markets has become far and away more complex than what could have possibly been envisioned in the 1930s. The Securities Act and the Securities Exchange Act have been supplemented by a host of legislative actions that have expanded the SEC's responsibilities while simultaneously creating new oversight organizations whose roles directly conflict with those of the SEC. The number of self-regulatory organizations that have roles in securities markets oversight have also expanded over the decades, as has the number and structure of securities exchanges. But through all this expansion the question remains: why hasn't all this regulation made the markets more stable and sustainable?

Charting the Waters

THE SEC

Congress always intended for the SEC to function as the leading navigator for the securities markets, guiding them through regulation to ensure smooth sailing. In practice, however, that has not been the case at all. Generally speaking, the SEC's reach is limited to general securities—stocks, options, bonds, mutual funds, and to the degree that they contain mutual funds, variable annuities. Meanwhile, the US Treasury and the CFTC have established their own regulatory jurisdictions within the securities markets, overseeing commercial bank and interest-bearing investments and commodities, futures, and derivative products, respectively. Yet the vast majority of investment brokerage firms trade in all of these products, meaning that they are audited by each of these agencies for regulatory compliance and the scope of those audits often overlap. For example, the SEC examines trades in US Treasury securities as part of its jurisdictional purview. Moreover, there is additional regulatory overlap between federal agencies, self-regulatory organizations, exchanges and state securities and insurance agencies. This section illustrates the systemic confusion created by having so many guides with oars in the waters.

The SEC began life with limited responsibilities—primarily for detecting and preventing fraud and ensuring that pertinent information, particularly financial statements, were disclosed in a timely manner by corporations listed on the New York Stock Exchange. Almost immediately the organization began to have run-ins with market participants and Congress, who continuously questioned the agency's ability to do its prescribed job.

Early on, the Hoover Commission determined that the "SEC had a backlog of un-reviewed corporate reports and was unable to examine brokers on an annual basis, in part due to the shrinkage of SEC staff and budget following the war."[34] The Hoover Commission's report in 1947 was the first of dozens to come that faulted the SEC for its inability to carry out its responsibilities despite being significantly underfunded. In the mid-1950s the SEC continued to endure budget and personnel cuts, to the point where it finally warned Congress that it could not fully perform its duties. The response from Congress: rely on state regulators for help.[35] *Time Magazine* chastised the SEC as well for being (1) "unequal to the job . . .; (2) dominated by the financial industry that it was charged with regulating . . .; and (3) choosing to prosecute small brokerage firms, rather than the indomitable Wall Street firms."[36]

Adding to the Commission's failures, Congress developed a knack for simultaneously adding to the SEC's responsibilities while restricting its ability to carry them out. For instance, in 1975, Congress passed amendments to the Securities Act. This bill required the agency to create a national clearing, settlement and composite quotation system resulting in two more SROs. The bill also required the SEC to amend any rule that imposed an unnecessary burden on competition in the securities markets.[37] While aimed at the NYSE and its members, this also gave another advantage to the Wall Street securities firms that already dominated the industry through everything from control of resources (traders, staff and technology) to control of legislation. (See Chapter 6 for details.)

Congressional and Presidential commissions continued to examine and admonish the SEC every time there was a glitch in the system. "The Presidential Task Force on Market Mechanisms (the Brady Commission Report) found that in the October 1987 crash, during which the market dropped 22 percent, "numerous mechanical and structural issues contributed to the break, including the lack of inter-market communication and regulation."[38] While not expressly stated, the report implies that the 1975 amendments likely exacerbated the structural shortcomings. More importantly, this report contains the first—and only—recommendation of single agency oversight and whole market regulation.[39] Interestingly, the Task Force found that the Federal Reserve would be best suited to fill that role.

While the SEC was struggling to do more with less, the turn of the century brought a new level of dominance to the markets—this time from the nation's largest securities firms. Coupled with Congressional actions towards de-regulation (as discussed earlier), the SEC continued to become less and less effective.

THE CFTC

The SEC shares the regulatory stage with the Commodities and Futures Trading Commission (the CFTC), a regulatory body whose scope of responsibility encompasses commodities, futures and specific swaps and derivatives. The CFTC's mission, like that of the SEC, is to ensure and enforce a level playing field, but solely within these particular aspects of the investment markets.

The CFTC maintains regulatory authority over commodities, futures and derivatives, which are a form of futures contracts. They are responsible for everything from pork bellies to orange juice and coffee to grains and precious metals, as well as the oversight for "designated contract markets, swap execution facilities, derivatives clearing organizations, swap data repositories, swap dealers, futures commission merchants, commodity pool operators and other intermediaries."[40] Like the SEC, they protect customers and the markets from fraud, manipulation and abusive practices and ensure market integrity. The scope of their responsibility expanded considerably after the 2008 market crash when they were charged with safeguarding the OTC derivatives and swaps markets.

The Dodd-Frank reforms gave oversight of the OTC swaps/derivatives markets to the CFTC; however, securities-based swaps (derivatives) were assigned to the SEC. To add to the confusion, "the prudential regulators, such as the Federal Reserve Board, also have an important role in setting capital and margin for swap entities that are banks."[41] Determining which organization is responsible for which markets can be a bit tricky:

The CFTC and SEC share authority over "mixed swaps," which are security-based swaps that also have a commodity component. . . . In addition, the SEC has anti-fraud enforcement authority over swaps that are related to securities but that do not come within the definition of "security-based swap." These are called "security-based swap agreements." The Dodd-Frank Act provides the SEC with access to (but not authority over) information relating to security-based swap agreement in the possession of the CFTC and certain CFTC-regulated entities, such as derivatives clearing organizations, designated contract markets, and swap data repositories.[42]

WITHOUT A PADDLE: THE SROS

Self-regulatory organizations are essentially public-private partnerships between the government and the financial industry. The SEC relies heavily on SROs to police their own. FINRA is by far the largest and maintains the most responsibility for regulatory oversight. As noted earlier, there are two additional SROs that engage in broker-dealer examinations: the Municipal Securities Rulemaking Board (MSRB), which initiated the use of CUSIP (Committee on Uniform Security Identification Procedures) numbers on customer confirmations in municipal securities transactions in the late 1970s to facilitate digital recordkeeping, and the National Futures Association (NFA), which functions as the FINRA counterpart for the CFTC while also supporting SEC regulation. The NFA and OCC established administrative and trading practices for those in the futures and options markets, respectively. Other SROs, including the Depository Trust & Clearing Corporation (DTCC), National Securities Clearing Corporation (NSCC) and the Options Clearing Corpora-

---

Drowning in Alphabet Soup?

The regulatory agencies and the organizations that they oversee are famous for creating acronyms. To better help you wade through the morass we have created a glossary of useful terms and agency descriptors. It can be found at the end of the book.

---

tion (OCC) were created to develop and implement rule interpretations for transaction clearing and settlement activities. Unlike FINRA, the MSRB and the NFA, clearing organizations do not engage in direct oversight of member firms. Similarly, exchanges are also considered SROs because they maintain a codified internal regulation structure. Unlike government regulatory agencies, SROs are corporate entities, often with not-for-profit status, meaning that they are not subject to Freedom of Information Act disclosure requirements and are transparent only to the extent to which they choose to be. All are charged, in one way or another, with ensuring that member firms operate within specified boundaries.[43]

The NASD made great strides in organizing the industry. One of its most revolutionary accomplishments was the creation of the Central Registration Depository (CRD), which maintains records of all brokers and other licensed persons employed by member firms, determines licensing requirements for all industry-related activities[44] and facilitates registration and examinations, maintains customer complaint data and conducts disciplinary hearings to determine and administer penalties (appeals are made to the SEC). The CRD also made possible communication about licensing and registration between state securities agencies, federal agencies and the SROs. The NASD's creation of standardized forms and processes in 1971—including forms to register brokers, broker-dealers and terminate brokers—paved the way for this leap in regulatory administration.

That the fox was running the henhouse created occasional problems for the NASD.

In the mid-1990s the SEC took some rather extraordinary steps to segregate regulatory functions from market activity. To put an end to the conglomerate's market dominance, they mandated that the NASD sell 78 percent of its ownership of NASDAQ. This divestiture resulted in a huge windfall for NASD member firms and provided NASD Regulation with a $500 million operating cushion.

In 2007, after years of complaints from member firms about the duplication and complications of competing regulations, the NASD merged with the mem-

Ever wondered about the difference between a broker and a broker-dealer?

Turns out you're not alone—the use of the terms are confusing especially because their meanings change depending on whether you gained your knowledge from the industry side, the regulatory side or somewhere else. To set the record straight, here is a handy cheat sheet:

- *Broker-Dealer*: a regulated entity that engages in securities transactions and is comprised of employees (and sometimes independent contractors) who exercise trades and monitor accounts on behalf of their organization and its clients. Broker-dealers must be registered with the SEC, FINRA and the states in which their customers reside at a minimum, in order to conduct business.
- *Broker*: A person registered to buy and sell securities for his clients—who must also be clients of the broker-dealer with which he is registered. Examination, licensing and registration is completed through FINRA. In addition, brokers must be registered and licensed in all states in which their customers reside.
- *Registered Representative*: See 'broker.'
- *Investment advisory firm*: A regulated entity that provides advice to customers about which investments they should buy or sell. Unlike broker-dealers, only firms with more than $25 million under management must register with the SEC. Those who do not meet this bar are only required to register in the states in which their customers reside.
- *Investment advisor/money manager/retirement planner*: Generally, a person who is registered with a broker-dealer or investment advisory firm and who advises customers about their investment, often with discretionary authority over their customers' accounts—meaning they can buy and sell for their customers without the customers' explicit consent for the trades.

For the record, when we use the term brokers throughout the book we are using it in the colloquial fashion. For those of you with a regulatory background, feel free to interchange it with the term "registered representative" or "registered rep."

ber regulations operations of the NYSE to form the non-profit organization, Financial Industry Regulatory Authority, or FINRA. FINRA has come a long way from its OTC roots. Its scope of responsibility more closely resembles that of the SEC than the mission set out for it in the Maloney Act. Its responsibilities include ensuring basic investor protections, including product disclosures and suitability, licensing and testing securities brokers and broker-dealers, and regulating advertisements, in addition to auditing over 4,000 member firms and investigating sales and trading practices toward prosecuting infractions.[45]

BEYOND THE BUTTONWOOD TREE: THE EXCHANGES

The nation's first and preeminent stock exchange was started in the late 1800s as owners of government debt gathered around a buttonwood tree, near what is now Wall Street, to trade ownership of these securities. However, the dominance of the New York Stock Exchange (NYSE) as the primary trading venue and regulatory arbiter has long since gone by the wayside. Battles with the SEC, affiliations with the NASD and NASDAQ and acquisition by global partners, as well as the proliferation of new exchanges, in part to accommodate the meteoritic rise in algorithmic trading, have reduced the iconic institution to that of merely a figurehead.

Other exchanges have expanded considerably to reflect the proliferation of products and trading activity. For example, in 2005 the Chicago Mercantile Exchange was the first exchange in the country to go public; its stock is listed on the NYSE. It merged with the Chicago Board of Trade in 2006 and subsequently launched the world's leading derivatives exchange.[46] Over the last decade mergers and acquisitions have been a staple of the exchanges as well as the firms that trade on them, fueled in part by technological advancements, algorithmic trading and innovative payment and recordkeeping advancements.

Globally, exchanges have traded hands at break-neck speeds. In the last ten years in the US alone, the NYSE merged with Paris-based Euronext (2007), while NASDAQ and Nordic OMX combined to then acquire the Boston Stock Exchange. A year later CME acquired NYMEX, the world's largest futures market and NYSE Euronext bought the American Stock Exchange. A few years later NYSE Euronext merged with the Intercontinental Exchange Inc. (ICE) ending the independence of the New York Stock Exchange, once and for all. At the same time, BATS Global Markets, Inc. merged with Direct Edge Holdings to form the second largest US Stock exchange.[47]

There are currently eighteen exchanges registered with the SEC, each of which is considered an SRO in its own right as they retain the right to regulate their members. Still, eleven of the primary US stock exchanges have outsourced some of their regulatory responsibilities to FINRA. However, it appears that the exchanges are becoming disenchanted with that relationship.[48]

The exchanges have their own challenges in keeping up with technological advancements. In June 2015 the NYSE was forced to stop trading mid-day because of system problems brought about by a computer update. This four-hour shutdown was unprecedented in the history of the exchange.[49]

THE US TREASURY

There are a host of additional federally chartered oversight entities with varying degrees of responsibility for investment market activities—the most significant of which is the US Treasury. As part of its mission to ensure the country's financial stability, the Treasury plays a significant role in financial markets regulation. Its primary focus is commercial banking activities and regulation; however, it is also responsible for oversight of national banks' investment holdings as well as banks and brokerage firms that offer banking products and services, such as interest-bearing investments, commercial paper, repurchase agreements and government securities.

The Office of the Comptroller of the Currency (OCC) is a branch in the U.S. Treasury. Like the other regulatory agencies and SROs, the OCC performs on-site examinations of banks and investment firms. In the 1990s the Treasury began branching out, developing the Financial Crimes Enforcement Network, successor to the Office of Financial Enforcement (FinCEN), whose regulatory scope focuses on illicit use of customers' funds and securities and money laundering—writing and enforcing rules and reporting requirements to which all investment firms must adhere—as well as intelligence gathering. In addition, the Treasury's Office of Domestic Finance (ODF) oversees the nation's financial markets. The ODF is comprised of the Office of Financial Markets, Office of Financial Institutions and Office of Fiscal Service. Its scope of authority includes "legislative and regulatory policies as they relate to retail financial services by banks and nonbank financial services companies . . . including responsibil[ity] for the President's Advisory Council on Financial Capability through its Office of Consumer Policy."[50]

If it seems to you that this job description is similar to that of the SEC, you are not wrong. There have been claims within the securities industry of overreach by the Treasury, particularly by its Financial Stability Oversight Board (FSOC) as it turned its attention first to the insurance markets and then to investment advisors. Support for this 'overreach' also appears to have sources in the US. House of Representatives' Committee on Financial Services, which is not surprising since FSOC was created by Congress as part of the Dodd-Frank reforms.

BUT WAIT, THERE'S MORE!

The Financial Stability Board (FSB) is a globally oriented version of the FSOC. Like the other high-level groups, the FSB coordinates "national financial authorities and international standard-setting bodies as they work toward developing strong regulatory, supervisory and other financial sector policies. It fosters a level playing field by encouraging coherent implementation of these policies across sectors and jurisdictions."[51] And, as noted earlier, the Department of Labor regulates employment (for many firms, brokers are independent contractors rather than corporate employees) and retirement security (ERISA). As noted, DOL's definition of 'fiduciary' is causing havoc in the industry.

In addition there are the legal institutions, both domestic and international (including the US Justice Department but also state attorneys general), that are charged with investigating and prosecuting regulatory violations.[52] State securities regulatory commissions and agencies tend to follow the SEC's lead, but also play significant roles in monitoring practices and prosecuting fraud. There are no universal state regulations; rather firms are subject to the varying requirements of each state in which they are licensed to do business, and they run the risk of being audited by each and every one. Many states have taken a more proactive stance by banding together to develop comprehensive state regulation through the North American State Securities Association (NASSA).[53]

*   *   *

With all these moving parts, it should come as no surprise that most efforts to discuss the full breadth of the securities markets always end with an incomplete picture. Even the most recent Congressional Research Report, prepared for just that purpose, falls short of accomplishing its task.[54] For starters, disentangling commercial banking oversight and activities from those pertaining to investment banking, brokerage and trading is a complicated exercise. Within the securities markets alone, the list of regulators and regulations is extensive and their roles conflicting and convoluted. The regulators themselves are responsible for creating and enforcing their own (often conflicting) regulations, regardless of how that might affect other regulators, regulations or the firms themselves. And with their increasing reliance on SROs, regulators have become more like spectators.[55] The result is that too-big-to-fail has long been synonymous with too-big-to-regulate.[56] For investors, arbitration favors the firms and makes a mockery of the concept of investor protection. Case in point: the merger of the NYSE and NASD arbitration units eliminated investors' ability to leverage competing venues to help give them an advantage in arbitration.

Some at the University of Chicago[57] have suggested that the solution to the too-big-to-fail problem is to nationalize the largest commercial and investment banks, arguing that for these corporations "'bigness' and competition could easily become mutually exclusive."[58] Should we institutionalize a failed system?

In the early 1960s, as the NASD and the NYSE flourished in their roles as industry regulators, the SEC released its own quasi-independent, *Special Study of Securities Markets*. Their findings called into question the effectiveness of self-regulation and the ability of exchanges to adequately protect investors. It criticized the SEC's passivity in supervising exchanges and found that the SEC had not adequately enforced rules against large securities firms. Subsequently, Harvard Law School Professor Louis Loss and a multitude of advisors spent the 1970s reducing the complex body of conflicting laws and duplicate regulations to a 700-page Federal Securities Code in an effort to increase regulatory efficiency and investor protection. While it ultimately failed to get any traction, for the first time, the new code identified and endeavored to plug all the holes in the dike.[59] In the next section we explore what that might look like today.

Notes

1. The Chicago Board of Trade opened in 1848 and standardized the first commodities futures contracts in 1865. As of 2000 the CBOT was the fourth largest commodities market in the world. In 2006 the CBOT merged with the Chicago Mercantile Exchange. See Chicago Board of Trade, *Illinois Online Periodicals*, http://www.lib.niu.edu/2000/ihy000454.html (2000) and CME Group, http://www.cmegroup.com/company/history/timeline-of-achievements.html.

2. *The Memoirs of President Herbert Hoover* are available online at the Herbert Hoover Presidential Library and Museum (2009), http://www.ecommcode.com/hoover/ebooks/browse.cfm.

3. Securities and Exchange Commission (n.d.), http://www.sec.gov.

4. The almost 60-year span between major stock market crashes may be correlated with the country's robust economic growth. From the advent of market regulation in 1935 to the year before Black Monday annual GDP growth was often in double or high single digits, with average growth for the period of 20 percent per year. After the 1987 crash and throughout the subsequent major downturns, GDP economic growth slowed considerably, with annual changes in GDP ranging in low single digits and annual average growth of just 5 percent. See http://www.multpl.com/us-gdp-growth-rate/table/by-year.

5. Joel Seligman, *The Transformation of Wall Street: A History of the Securities and Exchange Commission and Modern Corporate Finance, 3rd Edition* (Aspen Publishers, 2003).

6. "The use of 'bull' and 'bear' to describe markets comes from the way the animals attack their opponents. A bull thrusts its horns up into the air while a bear swipes its paws down. These actions are metaphors for the movement of a market. If the trend is up, it's a bull market. If the trend is down, it's a bear market." Investopedia, *Bull Market*, http://www.investopedia.com/terms/b/bullmarket.asp (2016).

7. *The Memoirs of President Herbert Hoover*, Herbert Hoover Presidential Library and Museum (1952), vi, http://www.ecommcode.com/hoover/ebooks/browse.cfm.

8. Ibid., 14.

9. For some scholars, "The origin of the blue-sky laws is . . . a matter of some historical interest. There is, moreover, a normative element to the analysis. Proponents of mandatory federal disclosure rules cite the adoption and enforcement of blue-sky laws

prior to 1933 as evidence that securities fraud was a major social problem in unregulated markets. The argument for mandatory disclosure rules would thus be weakened if it were shown that securities fraud was not, in fact, a pervasive problem prior to the advent of specialized securities regulation. "The standard view among historians is that the blue-sky laws represented a response by the political system to serious 'abuses in securities markets.'" See Jonathan R. Macey and Geoffrey P. Miller, "Origin of the Blue Sky Laws," *Texas Law Review*, 70 (1991), 2.

10. According to US Senate records, Senate Resolution 84 (1932) "authorized the Committee on Banking and Currency to investigate 'practices with respect to the buying and selling and the borrowing and lending' of stocks and securities." Senate Resolution 56 (1933) expanded the investigation to include "private banking practices" and included a new chief council, Ferdinand Pecora. The investigation, known as the Pecora Investigation and later as the Pecora Committee, was chaired by Peter Norbeck (R-SD) and later Duncan Fletcher (D-FL). The committee issued a 400-page report on June 16, 1934, that "offered careful analysis of a variety of banking practices, though it stopped short of making concrete legislative recommendations. This was in part because Congress had already passed major legislation in 1933 and 1934, aimed at curbing some of the more egregious abuses uncovered by Pecora and his investigative team." More information is available from the *Art and History* section of the United States Senate website, https://www.senate.gov/artandhistory/history/common/investigations/Pecora.htm.

11. Ibid.

12. Joel Seligman, *The Transformation of Wall Street: A History of the Securities and Exchange Commission and Modern Corporate Finance, 3rd Edition.*

13. Ibid.

14. Securities & Exchange Commission Historical Society (2014), http://www.sechistorical.org.

15. Legal Information Institute (LII) (n.d.), https://www.law.cornell.edu.

16. Securities & Exchange Commission Historical Society (2014).

17. Legal Information Institute (LII).

18. andre douglas pond cummings, "Still 'Ain't no Glory in Pain'": *How the Telecommunications Act of 1996 and other 1990s Deregulation Facilitated the Market Crash of 2002, 12 Fordham J. of Corp. & Fin. L. 467* (2007).

19. Securities & Exchange Commission Historical Society. For more information, see the transcript of SEC Commissioner Philip R. Lochner, Jr.'s speech, *The SEC's New Powers Under the Securities Enforcement Remedies and Penny Stock Reform Act of 1990* at https://www.sec.gov/news/speech/1990/100490lochner.pdf.

20. The GLBA came into being essentially to accommodate a regulation-violating merger between Citibank and Travelers Insurance. Citibank, a bank holding company, merged with Travelers, an insurance company to form the world's largest financial services company in 1998. Matt Murray, "Fed Approves Citicorp-Travelers Merger," *Wall St. Journal A3* (Sept. 24, 1998). When Citibank and Travelers announced their not-then-legal merger, they hoped that their lobbying power would persuade Congress to modernize the financial services sector. Robert W. Dixon, "The Gramm-Leach-Bliley Financial Modernization Act: Why Reform in the Financial Services Industry was Necessary and

the Act's Projected Effects on Community Banking," *49 Drake L. Rev. 671, 676* (2001). Their lobbying efforts were clearly effective.

21. The irony of Fannie Mae's inability to file accurate or timely financial documents, culminating in the years between passage of SOX and the 2007 mortgage collapse, and the failure of any and all regulators (including the SEC, the PCAOB, and the NYSE) is not lost here.

22. "Over the last decade, regulators have referred substantially fewer cases to criminal investigators than previously . . . in 1995, bank regulators referred 1,837 cases to the Justice Department. In 2006, that number had fallen to 75. In the four subsequent years, a period encompassing the worst of the crisis, an average of only 72 a year have been referred for criminal prosecution." Gretchen Morganson & Louise Storey, "In Financial Crisis, No Prosecution of Top Figures," *New York Times* (Apr 14, 2011).

23. Jennifer Johnson, "Securities Class Actions in State Court," *Univ. of Cinn. L.Rev., 70, 2* (Aug 2012), 350.

24. "A derivative is a security with a price that is dependent upon or derived from one or more underlying assets. The derivative itself is a contract between two or more parties based upon the asset or assets. Its value is determined by fluctuations in the underlying asset. The most common underlying assets include stocks, bonds, commodities, currencies, interest rates and market indexes." Investopedia, *Derivative*, http://www .investopedia.com/terms/d/derivative.asp?ad=dirN&qo=investopediaSiteSearch&qsrc= 0&o=40186 (2016).

25. "A swap is a derivative contract through which two parties exchange financial instruments. These instruments can be almost anything, but . . . the most common kind of swap is an interest rate swap. Swaps do *not* trade on exchanges, and retail investors do not generally engage in swaps. Rather, swaps are, for the most part, over-the-counter contracts between businesses or financial institutions." Investopedia, *Swap*, http:// www.investopedia.com/terms/s/swap.asp?ad=dirN&qo=investopediaSiteSearch&qsrc= 0&o=40186 (2016).

26. The Financial Stability Board, an international non-profit organization, "promotes global financial stability by coordinating the development of regulatory, supervisory and other financial sector policies" and provides reports on the "progress in its work to the Heads of State and Governments and the Finance Ministers and Central Bank Governors of the Group of Twenty." Their *Ninth Progress Report on Implementation of OTC Derivatives Markets Reforms* can be viewed at http://www.fsb.org/2015/07/ progress-in-implementing-otc-derivatives-market-reforms/. The SEC's progress on implementation of Dodd-Frank requirements for oversight of derivatives can be found at https://www.sec.gov/spotlight/dodd-frank/derivatives.shtml.

27. Securities & Exchange Commission Historical Society.

28. *Third Report on the Implementation of SEC Organizational Reform Recommendations* (Securities & Exchange Commission, 2011), https://www.sec.gov/news/stud ies/2012/sec-organizational-reform-recommendations-101712.pdf.

29. SIFMA, *Fiduciary Standard Resource Center* (2016), http://www.sifma.org/issues/ private-client/fiduciary-standard/overview/.

30. Christine Idzelis, "Wirehouses Escape the Worst of the DOL Fiduciary Rule," *Investment News* (May 22, 2016).

31. Ibid.

32. Liz Skinner, "Figuring Out Fiduciary," *Investment News* (May 9, 2016).

33. Christine Idzeli, "DOL Fiduciary Rule Could Spark Acquisitions of RIAs as Broker-Dealers," *Investment News* (Apr. 24, 2016).

34. Securities & Exchange Commission Historical Society.

35. Ibid.

36. Ibid.

37. "When crafting the 1975 Amendments to the federal securities laws, Congress extensively debated the role of competition in shaping market structure. There was concern that there might be areas in which competition would not act to create essential infrastructure for the markets and that regulation was therefore necessary to achieve Congress's goals. However, the legislators were equally mindful that unnecessary regulation not impede market forces in shaping market structure, and that the markets and their broker-dealer participants 'not be forced into a single mold.' . . . The statute vests the SEC with extensive authority to influence market structure. Indeed, in certain respects, under the Exchange Act it is not enough for the SEC to merely fill in gaps left by competitive forces or correct the course of natural market development. Rather, the statute commands the SEC to be an activist regulator and to take affirmative action to achieve certain specific market structure objectives." Larry A. Schwartz, "Suggestions for Procedural Reform In Securities Market Regulation," *Brooklyn Journal of Corporate, Financial & Commercial Law, v1, 2* (Nov 10, 2006), http://practicum.brooklaw.edu/sites/default/files/print/pdfs/journals/brooklyn-journal-corporate-financial-and-commercial-law/volume-1/number-2/cfcl_v1ii_4.pdf.

Schwartz goes on to note Congress' observance that: "In 1936, this Committee [on Banking, Housing and Urban Affairs] pointed out that a major responsibility of the SEC in the administration of the securities laws is to "create a fair field of competition." This responsibility continues today. . . . The objective would be to enhance competition and to allow economic forces, interacting within a fair regulatory field, to arrive at appropriate variations in practices and services. It would obviously be contrary to this purpose to compel elimination of differences between types of markets or types of firms that might be competition enhancing" (From *S. Rep. No. 94–75* (1975), 8 as cited by Schwartz).

38. Securities & Exchange Commission Historical Society.

39. See generally, Report of the Presidential Task Force on Market Mechanisms (Brady Commission Report) (1988).

40. Commodities & Futures Trading Commission (2016).

41. US Securities & Exchange Commission, *Derivatives* (2005), https://www.sec.gov/spotlight/dodd-frank/derivatives.shtml.

42. Ibid.

43. The difference between the smaller SROs and FINRA is that their scope is not as all consuming. A firm may be registered to sell stock and futures but not bonds, so they would register with FINRA and the NFA but not the MSRB. No matter what their line of business, however, all firms must register with FINRA.

44. The NASD/FINRA facilitates examination and continuing registration for all persons in the securities industry, including exams for activities that fall under the pur-

view of other SROs, for example, the Series 3 exam for sales of commodities and futures product, the Series 52 and 53 for municipal bond sales and supervision, respectively, and the Series 4 and 42 for options supervision and options sales representatives, respectively. For more about the exams, see http://www.finra.org/industry/qualification-exams.

45. Financial Industry Regulatory Authority (2015), http://finra.org.

46. CME Group (2014), http://www.cmegroup.com.

47. Securities & Exchange Commission Historical Society.

48. John McCrank, "NYSE to take back policing duties from Wall Street watchdog," *Reuters* (Oct 6, 2014), http://www.reuters.com/article/2014/10/06/ice-nyse-regulations-idusL2N0S12N020141006.

49. Lauren C. Williams, "The NYSE Shutdown Isn't Just a Glitch, It's A Glimpse into Our Chaotic Future," *Think Progress.* (Jul 9 2015), http://thinkprogress.org/economy/2015/07/08/3678076/new-york-stock-trading-halts-completing-trifecta-technology-betraying-us/. And, Kevin Cirilli, "Giuliani rips New York Stock Exchange for messaging," *The Hill* (July 8, 2015), http://thehill.com/policy/finance/247233-giuliani-rips-new-york-stock-exchange-for-messaging.

50. US Treasury, About Domestic Finance (2014), https://www.treasury.gov/about/organizational-structure/offices/Pages/Domestic-Finance.aspx.

51. Financial Stability Board, About the FSB, www.fsb.org/about.

52. While some state attorneys general appear to be more actively pursuing violators, others are part of the problem. Case in point, the Texas attorney general charged with securities fraud (see Manny Fernandez, "Texas Attorney General Faces Federal Securities Fraud Lawsuit" *New York Times* (April 11, 2016), http://www.nytimes.com/2016/04/12/us/texas-attorney-general-ken-paxton-faces-federal-securities-fraud-lawsuit.html?_r=0; and New York's Attorney General's active prosecution of Wall Street firms (see his press release, "A.G. Schneiderman-Led State & Federal Working Group Announces $5 Billion Settlement With Goldman Sachs" (April 11, 2016), http://www.ag.ny.gov/press-release/ag-schneiderman-led-state-federal-working-group-announces-5-billion-settlement-goldman.

53. A complete description of the roles of NASSA can be obtained at http://www.nasaa.org.

54. Edward V. Murphy, "Who Regulates Whom and How? An Overview of U.S Financial Regulatory Policy for Banking and Securities Markets," *Congressional Research Service* (Jan 30, 2015).

55. "The New York Fed categorically rejects the allegations being made about the integrity of its supervision of financial institutions," was posted to the Bank's website in response to tapes released by examiner Carmen Segarra about the deference paid to Goldman Sachs by the Bank. See Jonathan Spicer and Emily Stephenson, "Secret tapes of Fed meetings on Goldman prompt call for US hearings." Reuters (Sept. 26, 2014) For a party-line perspective, see Thomas Eisenbach, Andrew Haughwout, Beverly Hirtle, Anna Kovner, David Lucca, and Matthew Plosser, *Supervising Large, Complex Financial Institutions: What Do Supervisors Do?* (Federal Reserve Bank of New York, 2015), http://www.newyorkfed.org/research/staff_reports/sr729.pdf.

56. The *New York Times* writes about this as if it is something inherent to the 2008 market collapse. See their editorial, "Too Big to Regulate" (Aug 9, 2014), http://www .nytimes.com/2014/08/10/opinion/sunday/too-big-to-regulate.html?_r=0. Yet this perspective has been around since the 1980s. Karen was told directly by NASD supervisors that disciplinary actions would not be taken against the largest wire houses because of the potential negative impact that could have on the economy.

57. Gar Alperovitz, "Wall Street Is Too Big to Regulate." *The New York Times* (Jul 22, 2012). "Some economists in and around the University of Chicago, who founded the modern conservative tradition, had a surprisingly different take: When it comes to the really big fish in the economic pond, some felt, the only way to preserve competition was to nationalize the largest ones, which defied regulation.

"This notion seems counterintuitive: after all, the school's founders provided the intellectual framework for the laissez-faire turn against market regulation over the last half-century. But for them, "bigness" and competition could easily become mutually exclusive. One of the most important Chicago School leaders, Henry C. Simons, judged in 1934 that 'the corporation is simply running away with our economic (and political) system.'"

58. Ibid.

59. Securities & Exchange Commission Historical Society. It took Professor Loss and his crack team a decade to produce what we think of as one of the most important documents in regulatory reform. His entirely new, comprehensive yet streamlined securities code was developed through a 10-year, proactive, intellectually conceived research project by a team of academics. Almost a decade later, another equally significant reform document was produced. The Report of the Presidential Task Force on Market Mechanisms was the result of a group of Government and business leaders formed in reaction to the 1987 market crash and who were given 60 days to complete their task. What is interesting is that these two very distinct vantage points should produce very different documents, yet they agree that the current structure needs to be fundamentally changed.

Part II

WHOLE MARKET REGULATION

In the previous section we acknowledged that the current disclosure model and its patchwork regulatory structure are no longer effective. In fact, they have not been for some time. The occasions when markets are shut down due to technical difficulties—be it a Twitter feed, update glitch, or worse—are happening with increasing frequency. Regulators are ill-equipped to write regulation (even with "guidance" from industry giants), enforce the ones on the books or determine how to keep up with, let alone anticipate, new trends.

In this section we look at possible alternatives. How might we create an effective, efficient regulatory structure that is able to keep pace in an increasingly sophisticated environment? While we applaud the work done by Professor Loss in the 1970s, we have something more streamlined than his 700-page Federal Securities Code in mind. And while we agree with the 1988 report by the Presidential Task Force on Market Mechanisms that a whole-market perspective is essential, we are not convinced by their recommendation that the Federal Reserve should be tasked with leading such a charge.

Our exploration of alternatives does not stop with regulatory structures. We move beyond the very core of our current regulatory composition—the disclosure regime—to develop a paradigm that embraces whole market regulation, one that acknowledges the disaggregation of investment practices and develops the idea of securities as products as a means to offer actual investor protection.

CHAPTER 4

Variations on a Theme

We're all agreed, right? The current model doesn't work. So what's next?

Building a new levee requires consideration of all the available options, as well as what might be devised to accommodate new challenges and future growth. Similarly, we will need to consider different proposals to improve on our current disclosure-based securities regulation model. In this chapter, we talk about three of the leading contenders: (1) systemic regulation, also known as the markets model; (2) regulating the participants, or the participants model; and (3) the products model. However, we will tip our hand here—we are particularly fond of the products model, despite its flaws. As we argue below, each model has its strengths and weakness. As we talk about each one, we will also show the dangers of focusing on any one reform of the system in isolation.

The Markets Model

One alternative to the current regulatory structure involves shifting the emphasis to market-based regulation. This involves a sweeping change to the nature of regulation but could still be accomplished within the current administrative structure. In essence, a markets-oriented model uses a focused approach that looks at regulation with the exclusive goal of stabilizing markets.[1]

At its core, a markets model of regulation acts as a computerized formula that tracks and monitors the market as a whole with the sole goal of enforcing market stability. Under this model all of the trades in the market would be limited to a specific bandwidth[2] and no security, nor the market as a whole, could increase or decrease more than a certain percentage.

The SEC made minor strides in that direction in 2010 with the implementation of circuit breakers[3] to halt trading in the event of a market crash. As former Senator Edward Kaufman Jr. and current Senator Carl Levin note,

> After the flash crash, the Securities and Exchange Commission moved quickly to apply a Band-Aid in the form of circuit breakers to limit daily price moves. Then it proposed a long-overdue consolidated audit trail, to plug the gaps in reporting requirements that prevent the efficient tracking and policing of orders and trades. It spent months painstakingly using antiquated methods to reconstruct and study the trading data during the flash crash.[4]

In 2013 the SEC implemented two additional initiatives designed to preempt market failures. "One initiative establishes a 'limit up-limit down' mechanism that prevents trades in individual exchange-listed stocks from occurring outside of a specified price band,"[5] and the second "updates existing market-wide circuit breakers that, when triggered, halt trading in all exchange-listed securities throughout the US markets."[6] These replaced individual stock circuit breakers installed after the 2010 flash crash and the market-wide control installed after the 1987 market crash.[7] The arguments for implementation of these new structural limitations are that they "lower the percentage-decline threshold for triggering a market-wide trading halt and shorten the amount of time that trading is halted."[8] They are designed to make the response time immediate and the amount of down time shorter, but the problem is that they are still reactionary, rather than proactive.

The market-based model requires regulation of constantly changing, new, sophisticated technologies, such as algorithmic and high-frequency trading, tracking stocks, blockchain[9] transactions and other new developments in real time. The big question is: How? To be able to keep up with large volume trading, any new structure would have to be quick and nimble in order to be responsive to instantaneous bulk transactions. The circuit breakers referred to above are insufficient, in part, because they represent a delayed response when real-time action is required. Developing true market-based regulatory reforms requires more than the ability to react in real time; it requires a proactive, collaborative approach to stay abreast of innovative new technologies as they emerge.[10]

There are advantages to embracing technological innovation. The Internet has put stock market and company information, analysts' reports and even trading platforms at investors' and market professionals' fingertips. Broadband speeds are increasing exponentially and sophisticated computer systems are making human involvement in back office functions, such as order entry, exchange routing and execution, a thing of the past. "Financial engineers"—a term and occupation new to this century—have developed complex electronic models that purportedly make trading at the optimum price automatic. Proponents of high frequency trading also assert that technology intrinsically decreases information asymmetry and the costs of capital and trading. It also increases order routing and pricing stability, liquidity, and transaction and market efficiency.

This decade saw the integration of HFT and algorithmic trading as a way of life in the financial markets. Two more advances that are significantly impacting the industry are Bitcoin and Blockchain. Bitcoin is a digital "currency" that uses registration numbers for exchange and tracking instead of minted money and banks. It has brought about new thinking about types and uses of currency—to the extent that it has spawned a multitude of successors, including the multi-million dollar Ethereum and others such as Ripple, Peercoin, Namecoin and Litecoin—and has turned regulation on its head. Blockchain is a recordkeeping system initially developed to track Bitcoin ownership. It is also finding its way into the mainstream and would be a boon for regulation because of its ability to clearly and efficiently maintain genealogical records of electronic currency trans-actions, securities trades and other digital transactions. Both of these systems are already impacting global markets activity and regulation.

On the other hand, we are entirely dependent on technology to run our financial markets, here and abroad. Our increasingly interconnected markets make transactions instantaneous, but they are also a dream come true for in-creasingly adroit hackers. They are vulnerable to an electronic "run" on the market prompted by social media posts that are immediately re-tweeted instantly around the world. The market crash in 2013, precipitated by a tweet,[11] and the sophisticated intrusions into the SWIFT banking network illustrate how easily damage could be done to interconnected securities exchanges and clearing net-works, as well as multinational Wall Street firms. Advanced regulation would have to include coordination with exchanges and firms globally in order to reduce vulnerability to cyber threats and pranks.

This regulatory model would monitor execution speed allocations, dark pool transactions and alpha stream cross trades,[12] all things that the current oversight structure is incapable of doing. In doing so, it would have to enforce minimum standards for technology infrastructure and security to ensure that both regulatory and industry institutions keep pace with technological advance-ments in all aspects of the industry, to prevent cyber security breaches and to protect the vulnerability of interconnected markets.

Accomplishing all this while maintaining improvements in stability, effi-ciency and liquidity is a tall order. Particularly as some efforts, by their nature, would adversely impact others. For instance, requiring dark pools to disclose components and transactions and regulate data bandwidth to stabilize and equalize market access would improve transparency and stability. However, making large transactions visible to the public would likely increase costs and discourage trading, which, in turn, has the potential to reduce liquidity.[13]

Why is this not enough? First of all, the market-based model of regulatory reform, by itself, is nearly impossible to accomplish. Bringing the regulatory institutions up to speed, literally, would cost billions of dollars and many of the regulatory organizations, in particular the SEC, are already incapable of meeting current demands with current dollars. The SEC's fiscal history is one of unfunded mandates and inadequate budget allocations, exacerbated by the use of continuing resolutions and sequestrations that have served to further erode Congressional appropriations.[14] All of this has made keeping up with technological advancements virtually impossible. Aside from the cost, the simple act of keeping pace, from a regulatory perspective, with technologies as they are introduced into the market is daunting. Research by Pardo, Djoko, Sayogo, and Canestraro shows that

> in many cases the information needed by actors in financial markets, particularly regulators, is available but not accessible in a meaningful way. A massive amount of data is sometimes available, but extracting meaningful information from the data requires large effort that might not be economically or technically feasible.[15]

Second, focusing on market-based regulation comes at the expense of investor protection and product oversight. Regulators are barely keeping up with new product advances; directing their focus to market stability would divert already scarce attention from assessments of products and services. A market based regulatory model is also fragmented; concentrating on trading oversight while ignoring investor protection and product stability could allow fraud to run rampant.

Finally, this devotion to market activity and efficiency would have far-reaching consequences. It would, of its own necessity, shift awareness to high frequency and algorithmic trading and away from the (relatively) occasional independent investor transactions. In this way the model would benefit institutional investors and reinforce the existing power dynamics that contribute to income disparity and economic instability. Institutional and high-net worth investors have long benefitted from rewards such as dividends and capital gains tax advantages that are attributable to their influence on the markets and that are not available to the average investor. Jack Favilukis, at the London School of Economics, asserts, "Wall Street played a 'major role' in the surging income gap over the last 30 years. Through 2007, the top wealth decile (the wealthiest 10%) owned 72 percent of the market's *total equity*."[16] Clearly, moving forward with this reform model without taking other aspects, such as the participants and products, into consideration would exacerbate existing stratification issues.

The Participants Model

One of the other models that made our top-three is the participants model, which makes sense given that individual and institutional investors are the life-blood of the financial markets. Having a regulatory model that has as its primary focus those who participate in the securities markets would, by its nature, address a significant component of the financial markets. However, there is a big difference between institutional and individual investors.

Institutional participants include mutual funds, pension funds, foundations, wealthy individuals and traders who buy and sell thousands of shares daily, often through high-frequency trading models, although sometimes not. Of course there are also individual investors: the do-it-yourselfers or "home gamers"[17] as well as the millions of clients of wire-house brokers, financial planners and investment advisors across the nation. As a result, any participants model would by its nature need to address this diversity of participants.

As an alternative to the markets model, the participants model emphasizes regulation of these participants rather than the products or the markets themselves (the markets model). A complementary regulatory structure would focus exclusively on allowing or denying access to the market based on participants' status, education or training. Regulators act as gatekeepers to allow access to what by nature would be an exclusive club.

For instance, with regard to education, the participants model could build on the scenario of investor protection currently in place. In the current environment, FINRA maintains the country's education, examination and licensing for brokers and broker/dealers and offers investor education through its FINRA Foundation. The SEC and other regulatory and advisory bodies, including the CFTC and the US Treasury, the FSB, NFA, MSRB and others, also incorporate investor education in their missions. These educational orientations provide the building blocks on which this investor-orientation is developed.

Education in the participant's model contrasts with the current regime in that the focus isn't on education for enlightenment purposes only. Rather it would have as an end-goal a licensing structure for investors. In this model, all investors—retail and wholesale, large institutional investors, your grandmother, and anyone else interested in investing—are the subject of regulation. Anyone who has a brokerage account has to go through training and obtain a license in order to place trades directly. Institutional clients, brokers, traders, advisors and other industry professionals are required to undergo more extensive training. A structure like this is easy to conceive of in that it could work similarly to our current driver's license system. The SEC would be involved in training investors about what to look for when buying a security and the best ways to do so without becoming the victim of fraud.

Table 4.1. Comparison of Alternative Regulatory Reform Models

Reform Orientation	Markets		Participants		Products	
	Strengths	Weaknesses	Strengths	Weaknesses	Strengths	Weaknesses
Product & Technology Innovation	Makes interconnected national & international markets less vulnerable to cyber threats	Shifts focus away from investor protection orientation	Increases liquidity & transparency, more efficient executions	Increases potential for market manipulation & fraud	Increases consumer protection and decreases cyber vulnerability	Shifts focus away from investor protection and market efficiency
Trading Practices	Controls market movement and number of shares traded	Increases potential for market manipulation	Disregards markets and products	Increases potential for market manipulation	Pricing and market stability based on product supply and demand	Shifts oversight away from transaction and market oversight
Investor Safeguards	Increases cost efficiencies Increases transaction transparency	Shifts focus away from investor protection orientation	Levels playing field among participants Increases investor sophistication	One-size-fits-all training and regulation	Treats investors as consumers Increases information and consumer protection	Caveat emptor
Market Stability	Maintains stabilization Supports market and platform consolidations Prevents market failure	Increases potential for market manipulation	Encourages stability through educated investors	Disregards regulation of markets	Encourages stability through consumer protection oversight	Focus on product quality, not market stability

This model could evolve in one of two ways. First, a proactive structure could be implemented that requires anyone wanting to invest to undergo training and licensing before doing so. A second approach could have the SEC acting reactively by simply requiring participants to register or to have a pro forma registration with no training beforehand; this would then enable regulators to track participants after the fact should something go awry in the system. In either case, regulation would focus on creating more sophisticated participants and leveling the playing field among them, which would, in turn, increase market stability.

Why not? we ask. While there are variations to this approach, we find this framework to be the most problematic for a number of reasons. First, implementing this system would also require enormous resources that the SEC simply does not possess. Currently, there are over fifty independent state agencies nationwide that provide citizens with drivers' licenses. Imagine trying to accomplish a similar activity through one federal agency! The second disadvantage involves the training process itself. Consensus among all the participants about the composition of SEC training would be necessary before it could be implemented in order to resolve questions including: What does it mean to train? What essentials are included in the basics of training? How are investors trained to spot a bad investment? And, how would this impact brokers and advisors?

The participant model also raises the one-size-fits-all problem: should we really treat hedge funds that move hundreds of millions of dollars of shares every day in generally the same manner that we treat a young parent who buys a few shares of Disney for her newborn? Moreover, any licensing or regulation requirement of all market participants could have the effect of shutting out the smallest investors who can't afford to participate in the market with this new hurdle. Given the current national trend toward economic stratification, providing or demanding this additional regulatory hurdle would exacerbate the situation. Consequently, any advantages that could be gained, such as increased investor literacy, would be far outweighed by the negative consequences.

In a nutshell, creating more educated investors and one-size-fits-all training would make everyone a generalist, allowing for specialists in specific products to take advantage of investors and the markets. The role of FINRA (The Financial Regulatory Authority), an SRO made up of industry members, as provider of investor education through its FINRA Foundation is an inherent conflict of interest. And the emphasis on retail investors ignores the impact of institutions and intuitional investors on the market. The participant model creates a myopic regulatory view of the financial markets industry, ignoring products and the markets.

The Products Model

The 2008 financial crisis brought with it the stark realization that not all investment products are created equal. Derivatives and swaps are inherently much riskier than Treasury securities or blue chip stocks, for example. But it was also a reminder that the number and type of products offered in the financial marketplace has grown exponentially since the dawn of regulation.

When the first market regulations were passed in the 1930s, they were aimed at products that conformed to the basic parameters of a security: equity or debt positions with publicly traded companies and national and municipal governments. Since then, the product lineup has grown to include A, B and C shares of common stock, preferred stock and corporate debt, municipal bonds, commodities, currencies, options and futures contracts, variable annuities, swaps and derivatives. In addition, there are mutual funds, with a variety of clear and not-so-clearly articulated commission and administrative fee structures, that invest in all or any of these investment products, as well as funds that focus on products related to particular industries (e.g., technology or energy funds), types of products (e.g., government bond or high-risk bond funds), and social issues (e.g., renewable energy or socially responsible funds).

Customers can purchase products through their broker, as has been the case since before regulation, but also directly through on-line trading firms (e.g., e-Trade, Ameritrade) or through their investment advisor. Currently brokers and advisors are highly regulated but the products themselves are not. New issues—or in many cases just the advisor or dealer that brought them to market—are registered with the appropriate regulators (SEC, MSRB, CTFC) but there is no review or assessment process to determine the safety or validity of the security itself. Even for equity securities, which are registered with the SEC, the review process simply relates to adequate disclosure, not an assessment of the worth of the security. As such, financial markets operate on essentially a *caveat emptor* philosophy. Customers can raise questions about the suitability of a product, in relation to their investment goals and risk tolerance, but there is no venue for consideration of whether the product itself is "safe." For example, individual and institutional investors, including pension funds nationwide, lost millions of dollars as a result of investments in Washington Public Power municipal bonds and Enron and Fannie Mae corporate stocks. Local governments and their pension funds (case in point, that of the city of Springfield, Illinois) have lost millions of dollars from investments in derivatives alone.[18]

To counteract these current challenges, this model centers on regulating securities as products more so than market stability or investor protection. Admittedly the most ambitious plan, it involves not only a complete change in the regulatory structure, but also a complete retooling of the market itself. In this scenario we embrace, rather than ignore, the decoupling between purchasing stock as stock and investing in individual companies that the SEC endeavors to regulate. Instead, a stock would simply be one more product that a company produces, such as a car or toaster or knife. In turn, this product would be the subject of regulation, but from a consumer protection standpoint rather than an investor perspective.[19]

The reforms warranted by this model are more extensive than any of the alternatives; nonetheless, we believe that this model has the potential to be the most comprehensive solution to the current market instability. The best advantage of this model is that it provides an accurate reflection and targeted regulation of the market as it is now rather than what it was in 1933. It also represents the most flexible option of the three discussed because it can accommodate subsequent changes in market compositions and trading platforms.

As with the other models we ask, why not? This regulatory model, implanted by itself, would create a vacuum in the market structure that could leave investors out-gunned—unwittingly exposed to fraud, market manipulation and power disparities. The products model is by its nature a consumer protection model with the focus on the safety and security of the stock. Just as we don't want a car to explode after we purchase it, we don't want a stock to inflame the market or a consumer's wallet. Since that is the case, the bedrock of regulation under the products model would be determining the standards necessary to establish safe securities products. This regulatory structure would have to be informed by the stability of the markets as a whole as well as the involvement of the players. In short, you can't regulate products without looking to the markets as a whole.

*   *   *

This is an interesting exercise for thinking through how to retrofit the existing regulatory structure to better correspond to the securities markets in their current incarnation. But it is really nothing more than that. Trying to make any one of these models fit is like sitting on a see-saw: when one aspect is emphasized (the markets, the participants, the products), one or both of the other aspects tilt. All of the efforts over the years to keep regulation relevant to changes in the investment markets, culminating with those contained in the epic 14,000-page, 398 regulations strong[20] Dodd-Frank reforms, have been more struggles to catch up than responses to recent innovations. All of the "improvements" so far, including the models here, have been built on a terminally flawed base.

In order to develop a holistic approach to market regulation, *all* of these aspects need to be included. To be clear, in creating a whole market structure, each aspect of the market may be affected. Taking into consideration investor protection, for instance, without considering algorithm trading will lead to a regulatory structure that is lopsided. This is the current focus of the regulation now in place—a crisis hits and the politicians react. However, this reactionary, piecemeal regulatory framework is particularly ill suited for the fast-paced free market system that we now have.

Clearly, the disclosure model is outdated—it has been reformed endlessly and still is ineffectual. Reforms predicated on any of the alternative models, all developed in reaction to the disclosure model, won't work either. We can't change this piecemeal. All efforts so far to do so have failed. We can no longer be reactionary. So, what's the solution?

Burn it to the ground.

Notes

1. In fact, this conception of market regulation was initially bandied about in the wake of the Crash of 1929, during the Pecora hearings. We talk more about this in the following chapter.

2. This would also have the advantage—or disadvantage, depending on your point of view—of eliminating the spread created by algorithmic traders using proprietary state of the art technology to access the markets. See Michael Lewis, *Flash Boys: Cracking the Money Code.*

3. The SEC gradually implemented single stock circuit breakers—starting with the S&P 500, then the Russell 1000 before moving to exchange-listed securities—in response to the 2010 flash crash as a way to augment market-wide trading 'pauses.' According to the SEC, "a U.S. stock exchange that lists a stock is required to issue a trading "pause" in a stock if the stock price moves up or down by 10 percent or more in a five-minute period. The same pause will be in effect on all other US stock and stock option markets as well as the single-stock futures market, resulting in a uniform halt. After five minutes, the exchange that issued the pause may extend it if there are still significant imbalances between orders to buy and sell shares of the affected stock. After a ten-minute pause, other exchanges are free to resume trading in the stock, and, once that occurs, trading may resume in the over-the-counter markets." http://www.sec.gov/investor/alerts/circuitbreakers.htm. It should be noted that the rules do not apply to the first or last fifteen minutes of trading or to after-hours trading.

4. This also illustrates why circuit breakers alone are not enough. Access to state of the art technology to analyze data is an essential part of any monitoring system. Senators Edward E. Kaufman, Jr. and Carl M. Levin, "Preventing the Next Flash Crash," *The New York Times, The Opinion Pages* (May 5, 2011), http://www.nytimes.com/2011/05/06/opinion/06kaufman.html?_r=0.

5. US Securities & Exchange Commission, *SEC Approves Proposals to Address Extraordinary Volatility in Individual Stocks and Broader Stock Market,* Press Release 2012–107 (Jun 1, 2012), http://www.sec.gov/News/PressRelease/Detail/PressRelease/1365171482422.

6. Ibid.

7. Ibid.

8. Ibid.

9. Blockchains came about because of the popularity of Bitcoin: "from an application standpoint, blockchains enable users to own 'things' without the need (or ability) for a central party to secure the ledger. The list of 'things' that can be secured by the blockchain are varied but easy examples include company shares, game tokens, dollars, and of course, bitcoins . . . When users in a blockchain network 'own' a given item, they are the only ones who can transfer the right of ownership to another person. Each of these transfer operations, once issued by a User, are assembled into 'folders' called blocks. A blockchain is a progression of these folders over time." See Chris DeRose, "Behind the Ingenious Security Feature that Powers the Blockchain," *American Banker* (May 21, 2015), www.americanbanker.com/bankthink/behind-the-ingenious-security-featuer -that-powers-the-blockchain-1074442-1.html.

10. Partnering with Silicon Valley to develop innovative applications for the financial markets and their regulation is not new. See Ilya Pozin, "15 Fintech Startups to Watch in 2015," *Forbes, Entrepreneurs* (2014), http://www.forbes.com/sites/ilyapozin/ 2014/12/14/15-fintech-startups-to-watch-in-2015/2/#5e5aa6f76453.

11. 21st Century Wire, "White House Attacked, Obama Injured. AP Tweet Hoax Crashes U.S. Stock Market," http://21stcenturywire.com/2013/04/24/white-hoUse -attacked-obama-injured-ap-tweet-hoax-crashes-us-stock-market/.

12. Zura Kakushadze and Dr. Jim Kyung-Soo Liew note that hedge fund investors are shunning traditional managed funds for direct hedge fund investments, "employing next-generation managed account platforms, which allow investors to pick and choose their hedge fund investments . . . with the added ability to not only pick unique alpha streams (unique hedge fund strategies), but also the ability to 'cross' trades between alpha streams." In their paper, "Is It Possible to OD On Alpha," *The Journal of Alternative Investments 18,2* (2015), 39–49 (http://arxiv.org/pdf/1404.0746.pdf), they argue the benefits of crossing trades in managed hedge funds. ". . . combining multiple hedge fund alpha streams yields diversification benefits to the resultant portfolio. Additionally, crossing trades between different alpha streams reduces transaction costs. As the number of alpha streams increases, the relative turnover of the portfolio decreases as more trades are crossed. However, . . . as the number of alphas increases, the turnover does not decrease indefinitely; instead, the turnover approaches a non-vanishing limit related to the correlation structure of the portfolio's alphas." Regulating such advanced cross trading poses a unique challenge for market regulation, particularly in market activities that are in and of themselves not currently regulated.

13. "Dark liquidity—meaning orders and latent demand that are not publicly displayed—has been present in some form within the equity markets for many years. Traders are loath to display the full extent of their trading interest. Imagine a large pension fund that wants to sell a million shares of a particular stock. If it displayed such an order, the price of the stock would likely drop sharply before the pension fund could sell its shares. So the pension fund, assuming it could execute its trade at all, would be forced to sell at a worse price than it might have if information about its order had remained confidential.

"In the not-so-distant past, the pension fund might have placed the order, or some part of it, with a broker-dealer, which would attempt to find contraside interest (whether on the floor of an exchange or by calling around to other traders), preferably without giving up enough information to move the market against its client. Information leakage about a larger order was a serious problem, and the 'market impact' of large orders would impose a major cost on investors." From "Testimony Concerning Dark Pools, Flash Orders, High Frequency Trading, and Other Market Structure Issues," by James A. Brigagliano, Co-Acting Director, Division of Trading and Markets, US Securities And Exchange Commission: *Testimony Before the Senate Banking Subcommittee on Securities, Insurance, and Investment* (Oct 28, 2009), https://www.sec.gov/news/testimony/2009/ts102809jab.htm.

14. In "The Recent History of Congressional Resolutions" (Outside The Beltway, 2013), http://www.outsidethebeltway.com/the-recent-history-of-continuing-resolutions/, Steven L. Taylor notes that "it had been 14 years since the House, the Senate and the president have all agreed on a bill to fund the government for an entire fiscal year. In the past 26 years, Congress and the president have agreed to a year-long budget only three times, in 1989, 1995 and 1997." Congressional resolutions have continued to be the mainstay of government funding. In "Continuing Resolutions: Overview of Components and Practices," *Congressional Research Service* (2012), Jessica Tollestrup notes that continuing resolutions require spending levels to continue as they were for the most recent enacted appropriations bills (which could be several months to several years ago) and prohibit any spending for new projects. So if the SEC is spending money on a program that has become obsolete and wants to initiate something more applicable to today's issues instead, it cannot. Further, sequestration, enacted in efforts to reduce the deficit, has resulted in reduced discretionary appropriations for most agencies. See Megan S. Lynch, "Sequestration as a Budget Enforcement Process: Frequently Asked Questions," *CRS Report* (2013), https://www.fas.org/sgp/crs/misc/R42972.pdf. As it is, there is often a disparity between SEC budget requests and allocations. See Sarah N. Lynch, "Senate, House unveil dueling budget plans for SEC, CFTC," *Reuters* (Jun 24, 2014).

15. Theresa A Pardo, Djoko Sigit Sayogo, and Donna S. Canestraro, *Computing and Information Technology Challenges for 21st Century Financial Market Regulators.* M. Janssen et al., Eds. Electronic Government: 10th International Conference, EGOV 2011, LNCS 6846 (2011), 198–209.

16. Jack Favilukis, "Inequality, stock market participation, and the equity premium." *London School of Economics* (2012), http://personal.lse.ac.uk/faviluki/inequality.pdf.

17. Jim Cramer uses his show, *Mad Money*, http://www.cnbc.com/mad-money/, to help "homegamers . . . people like you, who own stocks and feel like they're on the outside looking in, become better investors. That's the mission statement, plain and simple. My job is not to tell you what to think, but to teach you how to think about the market like a pro."

18. Warren Buffett has publically referred to derivatives and credit default swaps as weapons of mass destruction. See Robert Lenzer, "Warren Buffett Predicts Major Financial Discontinuity Involving Too Big to Fail Banks, Derivatives," *Forbes* (Apr 30, 2014), http://www.forbes.com/sites/robertlenzner/2014/04/30/seking-shelter-warren-buffett-limits-receivables-from-major-banks/.

19. The genesis for thinking about financial products from a consumer protection standpoint comes from Oren Bar-Gill and Elizabeth Warren's groundbreaking article "Making Credit Work" in the *University of Pennsylvania Law Review, Vol. 158, No.1.*, https://www.law.upenn.edu/live/files/112-bargillwarren157upalrev12008pdf. In that article, the authors applied the consumer protection analogy to a non-traditional venue: consumer credit products (such as credit cards, mortgages and payday loans). While our idea marks a substantial move forward (in that, to our knowledge, no one has previously advocated that securities regulation decouple corporations from their stock) we believe that, with some adaption to the financial markets, the analogy can be used here.

20. Davis Polk & Wardwell. *Dodd-Frank Progress Report* (2015). http://www.davispolk.com/Dodd-Frank-Rulemaking-Progress-Report/.

CHAPTER 5

Securities as Products

(A TOASTER BY ANY OTHER NAME)

Securities as products. It seems like such a simple idea. And if done right, it can change everything.

This concept goes hand in hand with our thoughts on regulating the market holistically. It combines the best of the alternative regulatory models offered in the last chapter to create cellular change on every level. The indisputable centerpiece to that change is how we conceive of securities. It is to this matter that we now focus our attention.

As noted earlier, we identified contemporary investing/trading patterns as characteristic of disaggregation, where investors focus their attention on the stock, not as a proxy for the company, but rather as a product in and of itself that can be bought or sold. Our whole markets model of regulation would embrace this disaggregation and in fact institutionalize it by divorcing the stock from the company.

If we are to treat securities as products, then stocks and bonds become just things that companies and municipalities—and yes, even the Treasury—produce, in the same way that GM produces Jeeps and Apple produces computers. In this model, issuers are, by and large, free from the onerous requirements of the disclosure framework, and yet they are still able to capitalize and benefit from their products—perhaps even more than they currently do.

Conceiving of securities as products may seem controversial, but doing so allows us to recognize the way securities have come to be valued, which, in turn, adds transparency and stability to investment practices and markets. Let's consider, for instance, the toaster and the dollar. The value of the toaster is predicated on its need and its intrinsic value—for example, how quickly and efficiently it makes toast, whether or not it is likely to start a fire if left unattended, and the appeal of the design to the consumer. All of these are intrinsic to the toaster. As a result of this intrinsic value, the manufacturer may bring the toaster to market with a specific price—the manufacturer's suggested retail price—in mind. Some customers will buy the toaster simply because of the manufacturer's reputation; they may have even purchased other products made by the same company. Ultimately, the toaster's price, or value, will be determined by the nature of the toaster and the need of that particular consumer.

In contrast, the value of the US dollar is, by its very nature, extrinsic. The worth of the product itself is nominal at best, limited to the cost of the paper it is printed on (or in the case of a coin, the metal on which it is struck). Rather, it's worth is conceptual and determined by external forces; it fluctuates in relation to other currencies as well as significant changes in the financial markets, economic conditions and political activity. For example, when, after the 2008 crash, Moody's announced that it planned to downgrade its rating of US Treasury debt, that perception negatively impacted the value of the dollar.

Similarly, determining the value of securities products has long been based, in part, on the financial condition of the underlying organization. Securities come to market at an established price, which then fluctuates according to demand. It is the basis for these fluctuations that has changed, thanks to the algorithms created to direct trading activity, from reliance on the company data and the industry within which it operates, to a composite of economic, industry, social, political and other data. No longer do investors look to the company for their determination of value. The rise of algorithmic trading has relegated that to a supporting role at best in this computation. Our model acknowledges this shift and builds on this new concept of value.

In addition, regulation by disclosure does not allow for determinations of whether securities are "safe" for investors. Most securities must currently be registered with the SEC or CFTC, but that requirement does not extend to all investment products. Some are exempt from registration. Others, such as derivatives and swaps, are not subject to registration at all—although sales of these products will become subject to regulation in 2017, assuming that the operationalization of that portion of the Dodd-Frank Act moves forward as planned.[1] Treasury securities, such as notes, bonds, bills and securities backed by governments and municipalities, such as municipal bonds, are exempt from regulatory registration. While municipal bond products themselves are exempt from registration, issuers and advisors are not; in fact, SEC Rule 15C2–12 subjects all issuers to disclosure requirements.[2]

> Of primary importance is the question of who, or what, is being regulated. The model currently in place emphasizes oversight of corporate disclosure, which allows for easy identification of who is being regulated, but it limits oversight to a very narrow spectrum of market participants.[3]

Registration requirements are, in essence, little more than a notification process. Evaluation and assessment of the products being brought to market are not part of the registration system or any other aspect of the disclosure paradigm, for that matter. Brokers and advisors may be charged with fraudulent behavior, companies may be delisted due to failure to meet financial or reporting requirements, and if a product is bad—if a company is found (often through class actions) to have materially misstated its financial condition, for example—"oversight" amounts to investor recourse through the court system. These are all-after-the-fact options that can only be initiated after the damage has been done.

A Consumer Protection Perspective

To be sure, transitioning to a product-centered system would not mean a safety-less system. In fact, just the opposite would occur. Maintaining a product perspective would at once orient us to a financial system that is based on safety in the same way that it is for more tangible products. In short, just as manufacturers are not allowed to put a car on the road that they know would explode, issuers should not be allowed to put a stock on the market that they know could lead to a market catastrophe.

Senator Elizabeth Warren, the leading proponent and architect of the Consumer Financial Protection Bureau,[4] has long thought about financial products in a safety framework. She and her co-author, Oren Bar-Gill, write, "Nearly every product sold in America has passed basic safety regulations well in advance of being stocked on store shelves."[5] Similarly, the idea of a product regime is one where investment products would be safe for investors. In fact, if done correctly, securities product safety would allow retail customers to enter the market in a way that has been dwindling in the last several years. Restoring a basic confidence to the market—which was largely diminished after the wave of corporate accounting scandals that began in the early 2000s and proceeded through the 2003 recession and then the 2008 market crash and recession—along with providing additional ease of access,[6] would actually benefit the market as a whole. This would also incorporate the leading benefit of a disclosure system into this model. As discussed elsewhere, proponents of disclosure note that it allows investors to have a baseline of confidence regarding the information a company must disclose, even if the investor herself doesn't look at the information specifically. Having a product safety regime would accomplish that same objective, arguably even better than the current system.

In their seminal article, Warren and Bar-Gill argue that the advantage of treating credit like products is that it will allow them to be safer. We agree.[7] However, for Warren, the solution is to develop regulation for credit products.

In contrast, for financial products, per se, regulation has not been the solution so far. Rather, developing the *right* type of regulation, one that alleviates the mismatch between the regulation and the market, is the most desirable framework. As such, the additional advantage to regulating securities in this way, which did not seem to be present with credit products, is that it can, if implemented correctly, produce less burdensome regulation than we currently have. Instead, regulation would be streamlined, targeted and efficient.

Our 'securities-as-products' orientation has additional benefits that the current markets for other, tangible products, do not. For instance, given the ease of access to the markets, there is no need for a structure of wholesale versus retail purchasers. Rather, everyone would have access to the markets at the same time.

It is typical in the current retail products structure (i.e., clothing, electronics) for wholesalers to set a discount for buying in bulk. Manufacturers who want to attract volume sales will offer incentives so that wholesalers can receive a profit when they re-sell to front-line consumers. Part of the reason for this is because manufacturers do not want to expend the time or energy in working with retailers directly. One of the advantages of our proposed securities market system is that the infrastructure necessary to deal with all the purchases, regardless of volume, should be the same. In that way, unlike the market system outlined in chapter 4, there is no distinct advantage to high frequency and algorithmic traders.

How does this differ from what we have now?

Life as We Know It: Secondary Markets

If you're reading this book then, you've likely dabbled in the market in some way, probably through someone else such as a broker, or by investing in a mutual fund, or through your 401k. Doing so might make you feel qualified to talk about the stock market with some confidence, after all, you are an investor . . .

Given that, you may be surprised to learn that the stocks that you bought most likely did not come directly from the company. Instead, they would have been considered secondary-market transactions. When a new issue is brought to market—whether it is a stock, or bond or other investment vehicle—the securities are sold through a pre-order method to ensure that they will be purchased at the stated price—the manufacturer's suggested retail price, if you will. Once the market opens, on the first trading day for these securities, the shares or bonds or contracts are subject to the same demands and data as all other existing products. This secondary market is where the vast majority of shares, bonds and contracts are currently traded.

Corporate securities—class A, B[8] or C and preferred shares, bonds and other such means of corporate equity or indebtedness are bought and sold on the

NYSE, the NASDAQ, and the numerous other stock exchanges. An easy way to understand this is to think of eBay—where you sell products that you acquired and then grew out of, or tired of, or simply want to resell. Similarly, we buy and sell investment products through brick-and mortar or on-line brokers, who take our orders into the marketplace (the exchanges) to fill at the best possible price. Each customer buy order is matched with a corresponding customer sell order.

As such, ongoing purchases and sales of a company's stock do not, by and large, directly impact the company.[9] We have made such a big fuss about the stock market and how corporations live and die by their stock prices, but the truth is, these numbers rarely affect their bottom line. To be more concise, if GM's stock price goes down by $2.25, that does not generally change the amount of money in GM's bank accounts, or how much disposable income the company has. It only affects people's perception of GM.

You would think that the price of a stock, for example, would also change significantly based on how the company is doing overall—the reputation of the CEO, his or her management style, what new products or acquisitions are planned for the future—and especially the company's financial condition— their "fundamentals." In keeping with the SEC's disclosure requirements, every public company files quarterly and year-end financial statements and related information about their current condition. The investing public is encouraged to pay special attention to quarterly "earnings seasons" to see how their stocks have done over that quarter. Good or bad earnings, especially if they are greater than predicted by the analysts, are often perceived as the basis for a significant price change: for instance, Google stock rose over $100 a share right after its summer 2015 quarterly earnings announcement. But algorithmic traders would tell us that phenomena of this sort are already priced into the security through daily news and demand.

There was a time when people worked their entire lives at one company. Company loyalty influenced everything—including what stocks we bought. Oftentimes investors purchased stock because they wanted a say in that par-ticular company's operations, or at least the illusion that they had a say.[10] Now, things are different. We don't buy AT&T, for example, because we love the company and want to own a piece of it to keep forever. HFT and algorithmic trading and financial engineers have changed that investment model for good. Instead, securities are bought and sold based on a market-basket of variables that are entered into a computer that then initiates orders based on changes in the programmed variables.

And what does this have to do with you? Well, quite a bit actually. Once again it emphasizes how very little what you are paying for has to do with what the company is selling or what they are required to show in disclosure. Perhaps you bought GM stock because you had a really good experience as a 16-year-old with a new driver's license or maybe you bought GM stock because you think the car industry is stronger than ever. Or maybe you are the rare person who bought GM stock because you diligently read through their 10Qs and 10Ks (quarterly and annual SEC filings) and their fundamentals and decided that the company was a good investment. Regardless of the reason, when you bought your GM stock you likely did not invest in any real sense in the governance of the company, despite any voting rights that may come with the stock.[11]

Since that is the current reality, we may as well admit it. If we recognize that we are buying a company's stock (or government's bond or country's currency) as a product, nothing significant would change in the transaction. We would still be buying it from someone else, we would still not have a say in the governance of the company, and the company's direct financial health would still not be affected if[12] we sell the shares to someone else. The difference is that, in our model, no one would be under any illusions to the contrary.

If you have dabbled in more than a few stocks in your time, then maybe you are one of the select investors in America who has invested in an Initial Public Offering (IPO). If, however, you are like the rest of us, allow us to explain what it means to buy an IPO.

Life as We Know It: New Issues

Whether we are talking about corporate stocks, municipal bonds or the myriad of other investment products, bringing new securities to market begins with registration and underwriting. These activities are entirely disclosure-based, although not all disclosures are required or made to the same regulatory agency and not all disclosures come from the entity issuing the security. Take stocks, for example. When a company decides to "go public" it prepares to offer shares of its company to investors.

They hire an advisor, perhaps an investment bank, such as Goldman Sachs or a consultant such as PricewaterhouseCooper (PWC) to help them, and the advisor does so by preparing the company's registration statement and filing it with the SEC.[13] "The SEC concerns itself with the thoroughness and clarity of the registration statement and the prospectus to ensure that these documents adequately inform potential investors. Keep in mind that the SEC only regulates the vehicle used to offer a security. It evaluates neither the company nor the quality of the security."[14] Its focus is to ensure that the registration documentation is complete, that all questions have been answered—it does not evaluate the information contained in the answers.

The end result is that if the company makes widgets (for example), and it has no idea if those widgets are going to work as described, as long as they dis-

"Going Public . . ."

Going public is the "process of selling shares that were formerly privately held to new investors for the first time." The term often refers to "a private company's initial public offering (IPO), thus [making] it a publicly traded and [publicly] owned entity." "Businesses usually *go public* to raise capital in hopes of expanding; venture capitalists may use IPOs as an exit strategy—that is, a way of getting out of their investment in a company." There are several advantages to going public: "it strengthens [the company's] capital base, makes acquisitions easier, diversifies ownership, and increases prestige." But there are also disadvantages. Going public "puts pressure on short-term growth, increases costs, imposes more restrictions on management and on trading, forces disclosure to the public, and makes former business owners lose control of decision making." From Investopedia (2015) http://www.investopedia.com/ask/answers/04/061704.asp.

close that they don't know if the widgets they make will work, their registration will be approved and their shares can be sold to the public.

In theory investors rely on disclosures—SEC filings for corporate securities, prospectuses for municipal bonds and mutual funds and variable annuities. There are no registration requirements for commodities—just firm and broker registration with the CTFC. For options, the options disclosure documents simply outline the risks of investing in options or currencies or derivatives. None of these offer a determination of whether the company or government or underlying asset actually has value. In fact, there have been any number of IPOs that have come to market with a history of no profits, sizeable annual losses and no foreseeable profitability (consider Twitter and Facebook for starters). Hedgeable's online blog notes that

> Even though tech and internet IPOs have matured quite a bit, a new breed of startups is taking their place—biotech ventures. Much like the dotcom surge, biotech startups are promising huge returns to public investors before they make any money. In 2014, 71 percent of IPO companies had no earnings (meaning they lost money) and most of those were biotech firms aiming to produce some sort of wonder drug. That's the highest percentage since 2000, when the internet bubble burst.[15]

Analogous to investing in the secondary markets, with IPOs you are still buying a product, usually with no real voting rights in the practical sense, and no long-term impact on the company, regardless of whether you hold your shares for 10 years or 10 minutes. In fact, for many IPOs, how shares trade on that first day will have *no* impact on how much money companies collect from that offering. Why? Because many IPOs are firm commitment offerings, where the underwriter essentially purchases (or guarantees) the security at a certain price and then immediately resells it to investors. On the one hand, the issuer gets a guaranteed sales price. On the other hand, the issuer does not recoup any additional money if the first day stock price goes up.

As mentioned above, a typical path for a security is for it to be registered with the SEC, thereby allowing the company to go public. However, in some cases, securities are exempt from registration. Oftentimes, exempt securities are sold to accredited investors—those investors who have some financial experience (where net worth is used as a proxy for experience) and can withstand some degree of loss—without the company having to comply with the same level of disclosure as those that go through the IPO registration process. The SEC also allows for registration exemption for intrastate offerings. In those instances, the securities must be (1) sold by a company located within the state; (2) sold within the state and; (3) sold to customers who reside within the state. Both of these exemptions (as well as others) allow privately held companies to forego the registration requirements normally applied to new issues. This is a great advantage for start-ups as it allows them to raise capital with fewer restrictions than traditional public offerings. Finally, a new method of raising capital is through the use of Crowdfunding venues. This is the ultimate in disclosure-based, buyer-beware investing, with regulators weighing in on none of the particulars. Like other exempt products, investments are limited to a percentage of the investors' annual income and net worth. Similar to lemon laws, investors may request a refund if they change their mind within 48 hours of making the investment.[16]

Investing in the New Paradigm

Fundamentally, there is no difference anymore between buying a stock or bond or pork belly or toaster. As we embrace this concept of openly treating securities as the products they are, how might it look in practice?

SECONDARY MARKETS

For investors, there is little change. Buyers and sellers continue to exchange what are essentially older models of products. A good example of this is eBay, a continuously operating secondary market that matches buyers and sellers of particular items—similar to how our current stock exchanges operate. It illustrates how the values of pre-owned products can vary. Purchase and sale prices can be different for the same, identical product, illustrating how some retailers mark-up their products more than others. The prices also reflect the fact that the products—even if they are 'new in box'—have been around a while. For example, a toaster produced two years ago may not fetch as much as it was worth when it was first purchased, but a much older, "vintage" model may go for considerably more than its original asking price. Similarly, with securities products, a dividend-paying stock might fetch more in the secondary markets because the price factors in the value of the ongoing dividends that will be paid to the owner. Or, it could simply be that the company which produced the product is seen as not as valuable as it once was, but it may have long-term potential for increased worth. For example, the price of Facebook fell in the weeks after its IPO and remained low for some time, but the company has been increasingly profitable and the current price reflects that increase in worth.

COMPANY REGISTRATION

The existing SEC registration exemptions are an important part of the regulatory framework in this new regime. If a planned new offering does not meet the IPO registration requirements, the company, municipality or issuing authority[17] may qualify for an exemption, which will allow them to raise capital under certain conditions. When the company is ready to sell its shares to the general public, it will have to meet all registration requirements.

The current SEC exemptions and all applicable restrictions also remain a viable option for new entries to the marketplace who do not wish to undergo the IPO process. Intrastate offerings, crowdfunding and small business funding can be offered to accredited investors with minimal initial disclosures. Regulation A and D exempt offerings are often ownership opportunities as much as they are investments, often with real voting rights that have governance implications. In fact, these exempt offerings are proving grounds for future IPOs.

There is no place in this new system for the traditional IPO disclosure requirements—in which company documentation is analyzed *not for the value of the product or the company but for the adequacy of the disclosure.*[18] As the regulatory structure shifts from disclosure to product safety, regulation of the IPO shifts with it. Under this new regime the IPO process is a place to rigorously review the proposed company to see if they adequately (and accurately) represent a company's material information. There is in fact some precedence with this on the state level. For instance, many states, including California, have a "merit review system" for securities, where the California Commission has considerable authority to pass on the viability of the securities. Specifically, the Commissioner determines "whether the terms and manner of the sale under the proposed offering are 'fair, just and equitable.'" One of the things within the Commissioner's discretionary authority is to deny qualification status if a company hasn't produced a profit in over 2 years.[19]

Why register the company and not the securities? Because, even though we recognize that the company's securities are a product separate and apart from the corporation itself, unlike a toaster, stock as a product is *initially* intrinsically linked to the company itself. At birth, a stock relies on the company for a significant portion of its characteristics. Once on the market, the stock takes on a life of its own and begins the decoupling process from the company that issued it. The longer the stock is on the market the more it is imbued with the consumer paradigm, that is, being bought and sold for its own value as opposed to an investment in the company itself. In this sense the SEC is currently getting it wrong on both counts. First, during the IPO process, they register the securities right at the time when they should be looking into the company. Then, once the securities are in the market, they oversee[20] the company through their disclosure regime.

Under our new structure, the current aspects of the IPO review that do work would continue. For example, a company would not get approval to go public until it had been in existence for a specified number of years, has solid, audited financial statements and is generally deemed to be in good health by the regulator. This IPO registration process may also include visits by the regulatory agency to verify the strength of the company.

For example, when Twitter decided to go public, in this new paradigm its application would have been denied. The company had no income and considerable losses. There was no proven track record of solid earnings or other measures of success or any indication that the company would be successful and sustainable. Ideally, companies in that stage of development would use the pre-IPO, exempt registration option to raise capital and develop the requisite record to substantiate profitability.

Our new registration standards would use profitability as a proxy for stability. One of the biggest problems with the current disclosure process is that it gives investors a false sense of security (pun intended). It allows investors to feel as if there is a safety net because companies are supposed to tell the truth in their public disclosures. And there's the rub. Disclosures have often been used as a shield by companies engaged in financial shenanigans. Fannie Mae's disclosures in the years leading up to the subprime crisis are a prime example of this. The company filed erroneous financial statements and amended statements and lobbied (successfully) against any kind of regulatory enforcement as it skidded toward insolvency—but the company filed the requisite disclosure statements, so by SEC standards it was in good standing. Our new disclosure structure replaces the buyer-beware mentality with a genuine base line of safety for customers.

The registration process is designed as a one-time event. Well known, secondary issuer requirements would no longer exist. Companies would no longer have to file subsequent registrations or disclosures for additional issuances of shares after their IPO.

No matter how many subsequent products the company or government produces, once it receives approval there is no need for additional registration or disclosure—unless the company ceases to do business, or some major, life-altering event occurs within the company. What the company produces—whether it issues stocks or bonds or options or futures—is basically irrelevant. What is essential is that the company is stable and that its products are safe.

Our idea of product safety involves a balancing test that weighs the product and its potential benefit against any possible harm. For instance, just as we would not expect a pill to go on the market without having a proven safety record for fear it could unnecessarily harm people—even though the medicine could benefit them—we should not allow securities to go on the market without assurance that the issuer has a proven record of success. In this case, that track record would be demonstrated profitability of the source of the product, namely, the company.

One of the current issues, and without a doubt one of the reasons for the 2008 market crash, is that while regulators were busy collecting (not reviewing) corporate disclosure documents, no one was looking at the products the companies were producing. Hence, the proliferation of "toxic assets."[21] We are clearly not alone in thinking that transparent product review and assurance of product safety would substantially reduce the occurrence of market failure.[22]

As mentioned earlier, a number of states, like California, already subject new offerings to "merit review." This takes the form of "review by a state official of a proposed offering of securities to determine whether the deal included provisions that were 'unfair, unjust, inequitable or oppressive' and whether it offered 'a fair return.'"[23] While there have been numerous arguments listing the potential problems resulting from merit review (such as rent seeking, corruption, and paternalism, to name a few), it is our contention that some steps to ensure that investments in securities products are not harmful to customers are essential. These mainly focus on assurances that the products are competitive with those currently in the marketplace, that all information about the company and the product is accurate and substantiated, and that the product is available to any and all members of the investing public.

As with many other products, companies may want to offer a warranty as a demonstration of stability and to engender customer loyalty. What would be considered guaranteeing a client against loss in the disclosure structure would be customer assurance in the new paradigm. Warranties would not be required, but companies would be allowed to sell their products at a premium because they include a warranty. It essentially tells the customer, "This is how much we believe in our company . . . if the product price goes down in the first year, we will guarantee against loss."

Under this structure of regulating IPOs from a product perspective, we share Senator Warren's concerns regarding the safety of products that consumers use. In this sense, the IPO process should be the initial gatekeeping by which sham products do not get into the market. However, once products are in the market, then the market should do what it is doing now: trading with respect to a consumer orientation, based on a host of factors that often have very little to do with the company and without interference from unnecessary and frivolous regulation.

VOTING RIGHTS

Historically, when you bought stock you received a certificate with your name and the number of shares embossed. Now you get a monthly or quarterly electronic statement that shows you how many shares you own.

As we mentioned previously, traditionally, purchasing a stock might also get you dividends—annual payouts from the company of a share of the profits that they made. And typically, it would get you voting rights—the chance to vote your number of shares on any matter that the corporation put to a vote (amending their bylaws or adding or changing directors, for instance).[24] What's more, most of the time your vote as a shareholder did not even get you that. For instance, many proxies (corporate ballots) for director seats—arguably one of the biggest rights a shareholder has—specifically have only two options (1) voting for the director or (2) abstaining from voting.

If you are keeping up with the math, you will notice that unless the company has a majority voting rule, even if one shareholder votes for Director x and a million abstain, the proposal still goes through. How is that for corporate democracy at work? And one final caveat is that this applies only to typical, Class A common shares. Different share classes generally provide even fewer rights than this. But on the bright side, at least you get something. With all other securities, you do not even get that.[25]

To be a shareholder implies that an investor owns a piece of the company. But that is no longer the case in our paradigm. We no longer buy the company (as noted, we really haven't done so before); we buy a product it produces. To be clear, investors are no longer shareholders, they are product owners. And because you are no longer a company shareholder, the dilution of shares that results from a stock split or when a company issues additional shares no longer matters. It is no longer a dilution of ownership interest, and because of that, it does not matter how many shares are on the market. A stock split would occur simply to make the price point more attractive to buyers. And like traditional stock splits, you would simply own more of the product, but the value would not change.

Companies may want to issue shares with voting rights, and under certain circumstances they will have the right to do that. For the most part, inclusion of voting rights will be limited to companies that are exempt from registration. Start-up companies need help raising capital and allowing for ownership participation is a way to encourage that. In this new paradigm, the ownership equity offered with an exempt product will constitute the cap on voting shares, making them a limited-edition product. Later, when the company becomes more profitable and qualifies for registration, the IPO (product) could not dilute the original ownership shares; new issues will have to be for non-voting shares. If during the IPO process the company wants to trade ownership shares for product shares, then the company has the right to determine the exchange ratio. This structure allows for a finite number of owners rather than number of shares.

How does adding this dual layer of owner and non-ownership rights affect state corporate governance? Currently, most states give the right to elect a corporation's board of directors exclusively to its shareholders. In states where that is the rule, companies could offer a separate product with limited voting rights, perhaps with one vote per owner, regardless of how much of the product (how many shares) someone owned. This could also encourage customer patronage because, unlike today, the voting rights that accompany that product would be undiluted, and thus truly worth something.

LABELING, RECALLS AND RATING AGENCIES

Another way companies can encourage patronage is by providing comprehensive information about their products in ways that are user friendly. Have you ever tried to assemble something using instructions that are unclear, incomplete or incomprehensible? If so, you surely know the value of complete, accurate information.

Being able to be an informed consumer is important, whether you are buying cars, toasters or securities. Most products provide descriptive information about the products they sell. Some have labels attached to the product itself, like pillows, while others provide information on the packaging, like groceries, where information is printed on the box or container, and still others provide online specifications that can be used to compare them to other, similar products, like computers.

For securities, one of the primary features of the new product labeling process is that it would place the onus of information disclosure in the hands of experts, where it belongs. The SEC's mantra is a perfect example of why this is important. For instance, the SEC frequently notes that "an informed investor is a protected one." However, given the sophistication of the products now entering the securities markets, that is often simply not true. The SEC's disclosure model places the onus on the investor (retail or otherwise) to sort through the voluminous amount of filings and documentation to divine their meaning and discern how they will affect the buyer's investment decision. Just as we do not ask consumers to understand the fundamentals of thermodynamics to purchase an automobile, we do not place the burden on the investors to learn the basics of accountancy and financial regulation to purchase a stock. Instead, companies would be required to make specific information available for all products offered to all customers, from your grandmother to pension fund and mutual fund managers to Warren Buffett. It would certainly level the playing field when it comes to buying securities.

Imagine if you could walk into a store and peruse a selection of stock. Offerings may be categorized by type, wherein aisle 4 has growth stocks, and aisle 6 has blue chips, or they may be sorted by sector, with technology stocks and options in aisle 2, medical and biomedical securities in aisle 3 and derivatives in aisle 4. There are sales associates to assist you with the various products offered. They can tell you the different price points and write up your purchase or sale. Alternatively, if you would like to keep all your purchases in an account—the practical choice as it keeps track of your products and makes buying and selling easiest—you could still buy securities products through a broker-dealer, advisor or bank. And if you would rather do it yourself, you can still buy or sell securities online. In all instances, information about the product and the underlying company would be readily available through company websites, consumer reviews, the ubiquitous *Consumer's Report* and similar magazines, professional reviews and blogs.

Product labeling would include specified information to encourage smart shopping. These disclosures, similar to a cross between *Morningstar* ratings and grocery nutrition labels, would all include, at minimum: [26]

- Company information, including founding date, contact phone number and website details;
- Issue specific identification;
- Industry identification (i.e., technology, medical, financial)
- Number of shares outstanding
- Suitability and risk profile (i.e., perhaps a *Morningstar*-type matrix indicating the ideal type of consumer/investor)
- Information about social issues

What might the details of these labels look like? Imagine the nutritional labels on food products in the grocery store. They break down basic information about the product into bite-size details that help you determine if this product meets your nutritional needs. Similarly, for securities products, labeling requirements begin with the name of the company and basic contact information. Then, depending on the type of security, it would include a product identification number of some kind. For bonds, that might be a CUSIP[27] number and link to government financial information; for corporate securities, it could link to the issuance details including the number of shares in that offering and the year; or in the case of management/director stock, perhaps it would indicate that it was restricted stock from the IPO of a specified year. Currencies labels could contain the issuer, country and internet link to the country's financial/economic information and historical values; commodities might provide breed and/or agricultural information or mine and mineral information; insurance company and policy information might be provided for variable annuities; and pertinent details and information about the underlying asset would be identified for commodity and currency futures.

Other information disclosed about the stock itself is whether it pays a dividend or is the result of a split, or in the case of a bond, its call features,[28] if applicable. Stocks that had applicable options chains would have them no longer—we are shipping options off to Las Vegas.[29] Further, labels would include general suitability information, again, similar to the Morningstar rating platform, such as whether the investment is suitable for persons with a conservative orientation, or for those with a tolerance for high-risk investments or whether it is suitable for retirement planning.

Rating agencies, as we know them now, would no longer need to be registered in our model.[30] Their role in the securities markets would be limited to assessing a company's potential growth or spotting failures (e.g., poor management or potential product recalls) and perhaps rate the viability of the products the company produces. And, to make sure that they're on the right side of the evaluation, they are no longer allowed to have any of their revenue linked to the products that they rate or the companies that own them.[31] Their customers would be consumers and broker-dealers who provide those products to consumers. We envision their value to be in production of an investment products version of *Consumer Reports*.[32] That isn't to say that *Consumer Reports* couldn't do the same thing; however, we suspect that in doing so the rating agencies' focus will be more on the stock products themselves. They could review securities products produced by automakers, for example, and provide a product comparison for consumers' use.

These reviews would also help inform the public with product recalls and lemons. Yes, we would extend the Lemon Law[33] to securities products. If you buy a stock and within a week you discover that something about it has been materially misstated (but not intentionally, because that would be fraud, which we discuss later), you can take it back for a full refund. As with all products, getting your refund may be simpler depending on where you bought it. If you bought the stock from a broker-dealer, the company would go to bat with the firm to get you your refund. On the other hand, if you bought it from an unlicensed seller (on eBay, for example) you may be on your own to work out a settlement with the seller or the company that is recalling the product.

Products are also occasionally subject to recalls. Recently, air bags in some cars have been found to have a flaw that keeps them from living up to safety requirements and expectations. Similarly, a particular stock or bond may be found to be defective in some way. For example, a bond guarantor may go bankrupt, leaving the bond owners without assurance that interest, and ultimately principal, payments will be made. The bond issuer—the company or municipality—could replace the bond with identification of a new guarantor or even omit the guarantor entirely. You would not get a brand new bond from the issuer, in the same way you wouldn't get a new car to replace the defective airbag—you would receive a corrected bond. This differs from buying a lemon in that these flaws are not necessarily the fault of the issuer and may occur over the life of ownership of the product.

What might trigger a recall? In the case of a municipal bond, for example, a reduction in the bond insurance. Other material but non-deceptive changes could include mergers and acquisitions, bankruptcy or other actions which would no longer make the product "safe" by the original merit-review standards (such as non-payment of pension obligations or plan terminations) but could be corrected or contained. These would constitute recalls initiated by the company that issued the product (security). The defect would be corrected and security returned to the owner with revised product information that reflects the changes made.

Of course fraudulent activities that render the product "unsafe," such as fraud, embezzlement and other actions punishable by law would constitute a regulatory recall. The SEC in coordination with the Consumer Financial Protection Bureau would also ensure that consumers are notified of their rights under Rule 10b-5 and other anti-fraud provisions.

The idea of buying and selling securities products in the same way that we buy toasters and bicycles is the foundational component for our new paradigm. We envision a securities marketplace in which securities are bought and sold like any other product, toasters or cars or computers, for example, and consumer protection takes center stage. Product labeling ensures that customers are informed and rigorous registration requirements ensure that issuers are viable and products are deemed "safe for consumption" before being brought to market.

In the same way that this concept turns traditional investing on its head, shifting to whole market regulation completely re-envisions the regulatory context in which these products are traded. It gives us the opportunity to build our levee from the foundation to the top. And as in the shift to product-based investing, regulation in our new paradigm is simplified and streamlined. We move on to this regulatory component next.

Notes

1. *Practical Law's* "Statutory Construction: How Are Derivatives Regulated Under the Dodd-Frank Act?" provides a comprehensive discussion of current and pending regulation.

2. US Securities & Exchange Commission, *Sources of Municipal Securities Information*, http://www.sec.gov/answers/nrmsir.htm and WM Financial Strategies, *Municipal Bond Disclosure—History, Requirements and Services*, http://www.munibondadvisor.com/Disclosure.htm

3. Jena Martin and Karen Kunz, *Into the Breach: The Increasing Gap Between Algorithmic Trading and Securities Regulation*.

4. Elizabeth Warren & Oren Bar-Gill, "Making Credit Safer," *157 U. PA. L. Rev. 1, 4* (2008). This article offers a number of analogies between physical and credit products that are applicable. The chief benefit is highlighting dangers *for all products (financial or otherwise)*. However, the comparison is not a perfect one. For instance, one significant way in which securities product purchases differ from credit card purchases is that the amount of data that can be collected, compiled and mined for securities transactions is nowhere near the same as ones with credit cards. In addition, since issuers would presumably have a much smaller number of products to offer than banks do to customers, there would be less chance for them to target unsafe products to customers based on their needs and patterns. In the end, Warren's article is a very useful marker for showing how products come not just with associated tangible assets but also in more intangible ways.

5. Ibid.

6. Ibid., 7. As Warren & Bar-Gill write for the credit regime: "Today, consumers can enter the market to buy physical products, confident that they will not be deceived into buying exploding toasters and other unreasonably dangerous products. They can concentrate their shopping efforts in other directions, helping drive a competitive market that keeps costs low and encourages innovation in convenience, durability, functionality, and style. Consumers entering the market to buy financial products should enjoy the same benefits." We believe a similar benefit can come from providing a rigorous initial analysis of the products (aka, the stocks entering the securities marketplace).

7. Ibid., 6. In that sense, there are definite parallels between the current state of securities regulation and the state of credit regulation as described by Warren and Bar-Gill in 2008. As they put it "the current legal structure, a loose amalgam of common law, statutory prohibitions, and regulatory-agency oversight, is structurally incapable of providing effective protection. We propose the creation of a single regulatory body that will be responsible for evaluating the safety of consumer credit products and

policing any features that are designed to trick, trap, or otherwise fool the consumers who use them."

8. What generally distinguishes class A and B shares is the accompanying voting rights. One may have more or less than the other; there is no hard and fast rule that says that class A shares always have more voting rights than class B. Class C shares, on the other hand, typically have no voting rights. In fact, it is up to the company whether to issue non-voting (B or C) shares.

9. The market price of the shares makes a difference for companies unless they are buying back their shares or if they are planning to sell additional new shares.

10. The central trait of the publicly traded corporation is the separation between ownership and control. There are very few decisions in which shareholders have a voice.

11. In fact, for a growing number of companies, your purchase of a particular class of stock does not automatically come with voting rights. Class B & C shares, for example, may or may not have rights—it is entirely at the discretion of the company. When Google's stock split, for example, holders were issued one non-voting share of Class C stock for every share of Class A voting stock held. An investor who owned one $1,000 share of Google Class A stock before the split owned one $500 Class A share and one $500 Class C non-voting share afterward. Since their issuance, the Class C shares have been trading at a lower price point than the Class A shares.

12. More like when, since buy-and-hold is a long-gone concept.

13. The following information from PricewaterhouseCooper is useful in understanding the IPO process: "The SEC's Division of Corporation Finance reviews the registration statement and ultimately allows or denies an issue to 'go effective,' that is, sell shares. Registrants generally are assigned to the SEC's Division of Corporation Finance's review branches on the basis of standard industrial classification codes. Teams of government attorneys and accountants and, in some cases, industry specialists or engineers, review each filing. The chain of review leads up to the director of the division and the issuance of a 'comment letter.' . . .

The registration statement (Form S-1) consists of two principal parts. Part I contains the essential facts regarding the business operations, financial condition, and management of the company that are required to be included in the prospectus, including the company's financial statements. Part II contains additional information that is not required to be included in the prospectus."

PricewaterhouseCooper, *A Roadmap for an IPO: A guide to going public* (2010), 42–49, http://www.pwc.com/us/en/transaction-services/assets/roadmap-for-an-ipo-a-guide-to-going-public.pdf.

14. PricewaterhouseCooper, *A Roadmap for an IPO: A guide to going public*, 43.

15. Shane Hampton, "71% of IPO Companies in 2014 had ZERO earnings." *Hedgeable* (2015), https://www.hedgeable.com/blog/2015/02/71-of-ipo-companies-in-2014-had-zero-earnings/.

16. US Securities & Exchange Commission, "Investor Bulletin: Crowdfunding for Investors," *Investor Bulletins and Alerts* (Feb 16, 2016).

17. Yes, we said municipality and issuing authority (i.e., taxing district). More about that in chapter 8.

18. Many people have noted that the SEC's current IPO process is more than adequate to operate as a failsafe against sham companies going public. By and large they are correct. However, even under the current disclosure models sometimes sham companies get through. See, for example, SEC vs. AremisSoft Corporation. The company "claim[ed] to be a multinational software development and marketing company" but in fact, routinely and significantly misstated the sum total of its operations, allowing two of its chief officers to sell "over $175 millions of overvalued securities" before the scheme was stopped. During the course of the scheme, AremisSoft's market capitalization grew to almost $1 billion in the 2 years since its IPO. As a result of the SEC's investigation, the corporation was delisted from NASDAQ. See U.S. vs. Kyprianou et al. Indictment# S101CR1177.

19. Therese H. Maynard, "Commentary: The Future of California's Blue Sky Law," *30 Loyola L. Rev., 1573, 1577* (1977). Sally St. Lawrence (ed.), *Organizing Corporations in California* (Continuing Education of the Bar, Feb 2016 Update), §4.116(b).

20. We use the term "oversee" loosely here. The EDGAR system merely collects filings. The disclosure system mandates quarterly and annual filings but not review or verification of the information contained in the filings.

21. According to a commentary by *The Wall Street Journal,* ". . . one of the original causes of the financial crisis—the toxic assets on bank balance sheets—still persists and remains a serious impediment to economic recovery. Why are these toxic assets so difficult to deal with? We believe their sheer complexity is the core problem and that only increased transparency will unleash the market mechanisms needed to clean them up." Kenneth B. Scott and John B. Taylor, "Why Toxic Assets Are So Hard to Clean Up: Securitization was maddeningly complex. Mandated transparency is the only solution." *The Wall Street Journal* (July 21, 2009).

22. Ibid.

23. From Stephen Bainbridge's "Federal merit review of securities offerings? No thanks!." *Journal of Law, Politics and Culture* (Apr 2012), http://www.professorbain bridge.com/professorbainbridgecom/2012/04/federal-merit-review-of-securities-offer ings-no-thanks.html.

24. What your shares will not allow you to do is manage the corporation. What do we mean? Well, if you do not want Nike to use child labor, all you can do is request that they think about it. Shareholders are not allowed to force the company to stop using child labor. If you do not like that your chicken pâté is made by inhumane means you may *suggest* that the company put together an advisory group, but all you can do is suggest.

25. Remember, there is no hard and fast rule that says that class A shares always have more voting rights than class B. Class C shares, on the other hand, typically have no voting rights. In fact, it is up to the company whether to issue non-voting (B or C) shares. All other securities (corporate and municipal bonds, Treasury securities, commodities and currencies, options, futures, etc.) do not come with voting rights.

26. *The Morningstar Rating,* often referred to as the "star rating," is a quantitative assessment of a stock or mutual fund's performance over time. It is "based on 'expected utility theory,' which recognizes that investors are (a) more concerned about a possible poor outcome than an expectedly good outcome and (b) willing to give up some portion

of their expected return in exchange for greater certainty of return." http://corporate.morningstar.com/us/documents/MethodologyDocuments/FactSheets/MorningstarRatingForFunds_FactSheet.pdf.

27. According to the SEC's Office of Investor Education and Advocacy, "CUSIP," stands for Committee on Uniform Securities Identification Procedures. A CUSIP number identifies most financial instruments, including: stocks of all registered US and Canadian companies, commercial paper and US government and municipal bonds. The CUSIP system (formally known as CUSIP Global Services)—owned by the American Bankers Association and managed by Standard & Poor's—facilitates the clearance and settlement process of securities. It is commonly used to identify municipal bonds in transactions. http://www.sec.gov/answers/cusip.htm

28. The SEC's Office of Investor Education and Advocacy tells us that "Callable or redeemable bonds are bonds that can be redeemed or paid off by the issuer prior to the bonds' maturity date [and] . . . are often a feature of corporate and municipal bonds. An issuer may choose to call a bond when current interest rates drop below the interest rate on the bond. That way the issuer can save money by paying off the bond and issuing another bond at a lower interest rate. This is similar to refinancing the mortgage on your house so you can make lower monthly payments." http://www.sec.gov/answers/callablebonds.htm.

29. See chapter 7 for our discussion on this.

30. As it is now, rating agencies must be registered with the SEC, but consistent with the disclosure perspective, it is nothing more than a notification process. Their activities are not monitored or subject to discipline, hence the proliferation of pay-to-play arrangements with issuers. See Matt Krantz, "2008 crisis still hangs over credit-rating firms," *USA Today* (Sept 13, 2013).

31. For a fun discussion of how their intermingling became a big contributor to the 2008 crash see Michael Lewis, *The Big Short*. Or watch the movie. You'll get the idea.

32. Elizabeth Warren & Oren Bar-Gill, "Making Credit Safer." It's worth noting that they also discussed *Consumer Reports* within the context of credit reports. However, given the number of products that are available to credit consumers, they dismissed this as having significant impact. In contrast, because we are dealing largely with a much more limited number of products, the advantage of a *Consumer Reports* type function is more apparent.

33. According to *Consumer Affairs*, there are state and federal laws that generally protect buyers if they purchase a faulty automobile. "[1] The Magnuson-Moss Warranty Act . . . is a federal law that protects the buyer of any product that costs more than $25 and comes with a written warranty. The act prevents manufacturers from drafting grossly unfair warranties. It also makes it economically viable to bring warranty suits by providing the award of attorney's fees; [2] The Uniform Commercial Code . . . applies to all 50 states and covers contracts dealing with the sale of products. [It] gives the consumer the right to a refund or replacement of a lemon. The UCC, however, does not define a 'lemon,' so it's up to a court to decide if an auto company must give you a refund or a new car. The Magnuson-Moss act and many state lemon laws also provide for attorney fees under the UCC; and [3] State-Specific Lemon Laws

. . . specify that a manufacturer must provide a refund or replacement for a defective new vehicle when a substantial defect cannot be fixed in four attempts, a safety defect within two attempts or if the vehicle is out of service for 30 days" within specified numbers of miles driven or years owned. From "The Lemon Law—A Guide to State and Federal Consumer Protection Laws," by Stephanie Moore, *Consumer Affairs* (2015), https://www.consumeraffairs.com/lemon_law/.

CHAPTER 6

Whole Market Regulation

A product is only as good as the system that it is designed to work within. That's true for cogs on a wheel, bricks in a dam and, in this case, products in a securities market. Whole market regulation is our recognition of this fact and, thus, our effort to address all aspects of this new marketplace.

Ironically, the idea of whole market regulation is not a new one. In fact, the original conception for whole market regulation begins where it all began—after the stock market crash of 1929.[1] Recognition of the need for a regulatory system to prevent fraud and market manipulation spurred innovative solutions, despite protestations from the most influential money men of the time—the "banksters" as Ferdinand Percora, the New York District Attorney charged with investigating the crash, called them. After endless Congressional hearings, Pecora developed the most innovative, comprehensive regulatory structure of the time—thus the SEC and the disclosure system were born. Since then, the idea for whole market regulation has been lost amidst the din of disclosure. It has reared its head on rare occasion, such as in the Report of the Presidential Task Force on Market Mechanisms in 1988. But in actuality, all of the Congressional legislation, commissions and task forces have only served to pile on to the existing disclosure system, creating a reactionary structure lacking preventative measures. The result is a regulatory structure that resembles our tax code, amended so many times that it has become largely ineffectual.

The irony is, that many people at the highest regulatory level, recognize that a piecemeal approach is unwise. For instance, "Secretary of Treasury Timothy Geithner said the string of recent financial crises 'have caused a great loss of confidence in the basic fabric of our financial system,' and 'To address this will require comprehensive reform. Not modest repairs at the margin . . .'"[2]

And yet, we keep doing it anyway.

Given how vast and complicated our current markets are, the idea of regulating the system as a whole is one that is becoming increasingly crucial. Our whole market regulation model goes back to the future, back to the core principles of the 1933 and 1934 Acts and their intent to prevent fraud and protect investors. And yet, to be effective, there are a number of implications for our whole market model that we need to examine. The purpose of this chapter is to assess the effects on regulation and regulators, sales and supervision, trading (both high frequency and regular investments) and the exchanges, and broker-dealer operations and compliance.

A Word About Whole Market Regulation

Whole market regulation, at its core, focuses on systemic risk. Traditionally, the focus of regulation has been on the players involved in the markets. Within this disclosure-based framework, corporations long garnered the most regulatory attention, with other participants—brokerage firms, market makers, exchanges and the like—also being considered but less centrally so. The expansion of SRO responsibilities allowed for increased focus on the workings of the markets, broadening over time to include broker-dealers, exchanges, brokers, advisors and managers. Investors, for the most part, have been exempt from regulatory purview.

In contrast, under a whole market scheme, the focus shifts from the participants to the markets. Under this new schema, *any* party (participant) can be subject to regulatory intervention if they are seen as interfering with market stability. This is accomplished through a global view of the financial markets universe, with emphasis on the quality of the products available to the public and the platforms through which they trade hands. Implementation of a streamlined regulatory structure with clear lines of responsibility and enforcement allows the regulators to be more nimble and proactive. Regulators can engage in any action as appropriate in order to maintain fairness and integrity in the markets.

The idea that systemic risk should be at the heart of our analysis in the financial markets is a late addition to the legal academic literature. Now, however, there is a growing consensus in the field that systemic risk must be central to any analysis of legal responses to our corporate and securities structure; whether through changes to corporate governance[3] or through changes to the securities market. Nonetheless, in order to be transformative to our regulatory agencies, we feel the scholarship should examine three things: (1) the current trading patterns in the US; (2) the current holding patterns of stock in the United States and; (3) the current state of systemic risk and risk assessment in the securities markets in the United States. To our knowledge, there is no scholarship in the legal academy that addresses all three issues. [4]

In addition to scholars, practitioners are discussing systemic risk more and more. For instance, the regulatory community has recognized the importance of risk assessment. Specifically, the SEC had begun to dabble in that area, although, by the time the agency created a risk assessment division in 2009, it seemed a bit like closing the barn door after the horses had left.[5] So, while it is encouraging that risk assessment is being discussed in addition to a disclosure paradigm, the current nature of the conversation—both within academia and with the regulators is, we feel, woefully inadequate.

If nothing else, the most recent financial crisis has shown that risk assessment needs to include systemic risks, not just the risk of individual sectors or corporations. Rather, the meltdown in 2007–2009 highlighted just how interdependent the markets are. In the case of the crisis, the underlying assets that caused the crash—namely toxic mortgages and subsequent bets against their credibility (i.e., credit default swaps)—occurred in a segment of the economy that was traditionally unrelated to the world of securities. That is, until some clever financial originators (or aggregators) decided to package them together into a bundle that could then be labeled as a security and traded on the securities markets.[6] Real estate and stock, largely unrelated, became interdependent thanks to vagrancies with other people's investments and loopholes in our regulation.

Given then that risk assessment should be an integral part of the view of securities markets, how then do we quantify it? Many argue that the difficulty in calculating these risks means that this avenue should not be pursued. In the end though, uncertainty and unknowing are not the same thing. Thus, there are a number of tools that can be employed to project how the markets will act and in what way they need to be regulated beyond simply using information contained in disclosures. The sophisticated levels of prediction now predominant in trading securities, for example, indicate that there must surely be ways to apply those predictive powers to the development of risk metrics.

This new solution does not completely dismiss the role of corporate scandals and corporate mismanagement—of course there is validity to the truth that some of the hits that the markets have taken have occurred because of corporate mismanagement and that regulatory disclosure may in fact have prevented even more from happening. However, whether increased disclosure actually serves to prevent future fraud remains to be seen. The Dodd-Frank Act requires oversight and disclosure of executive compensation and swaps activity that exceeds specified limits. How either of those serves to deter fraud in practice cannot be determined until implementation is complete. And the extent to which these additional disclosures act as preventative measures when existing disclosures often go unobserved is doubtful. If a disclosure indicates or alludes to questionable management but no one reads it, does it really happen? Perhaps we could ask Fannie Mae . . .

As such, there are two responses to the "disclosure prevents corporate fraud" mantra: first, the market seems better able, as a whole, to recover when the damage is done by individual corporate scandals. Even after wave upon wave of corporate malfeasance,[7] bull markets rebounded quickly. Second, there is no reason to assume that with other types of regulation—such as one that focuses on the market as a whole instead of on individual entities, as we are suggesting —we could not have achieved the same or an even better result than we did under the disclosure model. In short, an alternative regulatory structure could not only achieve many of the same ends as a disclosure-based system, but also build on those achievements to get to something greater.

What Then for the Regulators?

As mentioned earlier, the SEC is not the only regulatory agency on the block. In fact, Appendix A illustrates the crazy patchwork of regulators and regulatory responsibilities under the disclosure system. There are so many hands in that pie that it is even challenging for regulators to tell where the lines of authority and accountability lie. The beauty of whole market regulation, and particularly our model with its product-based orientation, is that oversight can—and should—be streamlined. Doing so allows regulators to focus on a specified range of products and related exchanges, trading patterns, registrations and sales practices and administrative functions. It also provides a clear path for all those on the receiving end of the regulatory structure (we will get to them in the next section).

Our model, as shown in table 6.1, streamlines the convoluted oversight structure illustrated in Appendix A by eliminating the SROs and other redundant organizations and marking clear lines of responsibility for those remaining. We propose three primary federal regulatory bodies—a regulatory triad—each with responsibility for particular aspects of the securities markets. Comprising a financial markets regulatory commission, the members are jointly responsible for oversight of the markets on a broad scale, and they may coordinate market regulation with the Federal Reserve fiscal policy to ensure economic stability. They may also solicit advice from industry leaders, currently members of the Financial Securities Oversight Commission (FSOC)[8] as needed. In that way, our whole market system will be in balance, significantly less expensive than the whole market framework we outlined in the previous chapter.

The regulatory divide in our model follows current lines of responsibility. Severally, the SEC maintains authority over equity, debt and related products—stocks, bonds, options, mutual funds, variable annuities, as well as investment manager (mutual funds) and advisory (hedge fund) activities. Commodities, currencies and specific futures remain the domain of the CFTC. And the US Treasury is responsible for government securities and interest bearing investments as well as the banking side of the financial markets, including commercial banking, enforcement of money laundering prohibitions, the Basel accord,[9] the Volcker Rule[10] and other aspects of the Dodd-Frank Act that ensure that commercial banks (including those engaged in investment banking) are not allowed to continue to be too big to fail. As you may guess, we advocate reinstatement of the Glass-Steagall Act,[11] which would reinstate the bright line between banking and securities activities. Until then, keeping commercial banks solvent and out of investment banking would, in and of itself, be a full-time job for the US Treasury.[12]

Under our model, these three regulators are responsible for setting standards, registering products and personnel, overseeing examinations and audits and investigating possible violations within their realms of responsibility. Enforcement of violations, including fraud and misrepresentation, is the purview of the Department of Justice. Having clear delineations will enable each of the three regulators to help to provide market stability.

This is a very simple structure whose time has been long in the making. It allows each regulatory entity to focus on what it knows best, with the idea being that a specific scope will allow regulators to maintain a proactive stance when it comes to national and global technological advances in trading and investing strategies. In addition, it eliminates the need for SROs as extensions of the regulation structure. They may choose to continue to educate member firms and investors as professional associations within the industry; however, broker-dealer and broker registration and examination functions will be absorbed by the SEC, CFTC and US Treasury, as applicable. For example, a broker would register with the SEC—through her/his broker dealer—to sell corporate securities and municipal bond products, the CFTC to sell commodities and futures contract products, and the US. Treasury to sell government bonds and notes. This simplifies regulation for end users as well, including brokers and broker-dealers, as well as state regulatory agencies. Registration of US Treasury products is exempt, however, selling them is subject to SEC and Treasury regulation.

Currently, the securities market is where the majority of the action is. While the CFTC and the commodities and futures markets are seeing considerable growth, and the US Treasury's scope has expanded to ensure that those that are too big to fail, don't, the securities market is still the predominant setting for product registration, regulation and trading, and it is where the major market failures have occurred. For those reasons, we focus our attention on what this paradigm shift will mean to the SEC.

Table 6.1. Whole Market Regulation-Oversight Structure

	Financial Markets Oversight Commission				US Attorney General
	SEC	CFTC	US Treasury	CFPB	
Product Registration					
Stocks	X				
Bonds	X				
Options	X				
Mutual Funds	X				
Variable Annuities	X				
OTC Derivatives & Swaps	X				
Commodities		X			
Currencies		X			
Futures		X			
Non-OTC Derivatives & Swaps		X			
Treasury Bonds, Bills & Notes			X		
Commercial Paper			X		
Interest Bearing Accounts			X		
Exchange Registration	X	X			
Broker-Dealer Registration	X	X			
Customer Protection				X	
Enforcement					X

TOWARD A NEW AND BETTER SEC

Clearly, the challenge of regulation in a rapidly changing world is not confined to the SEC. Nonetheless, the sheer breadth of what the SEC must regulate is enough to give one pause. The securities markets are the heart of the financial market here in the US, which is, in turn, at the heart of American economic stability. In addition, the stability of the US financial markets helps stabilize global markets; conversely, instability in our markets detrimentally impacts international financial markets. As such, how the SEC regulates, or fails to regulate, has a direct impact on the stability of American lives, as the most recent financial crisis brought into stark light. What is more, it is the markets that are subject to SEC regulation which are arguably undergoing the most innovation in recent years. This is a potentially combustible combination, akin to a dodo bird watching over an android robot.

Flash trading provides a particularly stark contrast regarding the pace between regulators and the world that they regulate. Flash trading, a form of HFT, comes when, after an order is placed by an investor, the exchange flashes the order for a split second to its members within the exchange. This gives the

HFT firms a fraction of a second to decide and then execute the order.[13] If they choose not to do so, then the order will go out to the market at large. This type of trading is particularly advantageous to HFT because they can move through these orders with ridiculous speed.[14]

To many, this gives flash traders an unfair advantage because the practice could be considered front-running. It is unfair to the investors because they will not get the best price, and it is unfair to the market because the HFT firms can use this information edge to trade ahead of pending orders.[15] Others claim that flash trading provides liquidity to the market. One thing everyone agrees on, however, is that flash trading is, well, fast.

In contrast, the SEC works at a much slower pace. Given the nature of government agencies and their attendant bureaucracies, the regulator's response time to an event could be considered quick if it were within mere months. Even when confronted with fast moving issues, such as technology malfunctions in the market, the SEC's reaction speed is eclipsed by the speed with which the initial event—and resulting consequences—takes place.

The 2010 flash crash is one example of this. An SEC regulator, when talking about the flash crash, stated, "I don't think I found out about this in real-time[;] this was probably a half an hour later, or an hour later. There's nothing that one can do in the middle of the day, so there's no button that we can press that says hey, stop, stop what's going on[,] so the markets are going to move the way the markets move."[16] In a market with over one billion shares traded per day,[17] the losses that can occur when there is "no button to press" can be disastrous. However, moving beyond a disclosure-based regime to one that can track the markets as a whole and even respond with deliberate speed would move regulators much closer to matching technological advances.[18]

As we noted in chapter 1, in response to the Flash Crash, the SEC implemented a rule that gave it the power to engage in both single stock circuit breakers and market wide shutdowns. Although this is a step in the right direction, for the new market we are conceiving this would have to be done on a much more systemic and rapidly responsive basis. For instance, according to one article, mini flash crashes occurring throughout the day are incredibly common, numbering upwards of a dozen episodes daily. In one notable example, shares of Silica Holdings dropped 9 percent in less than two seconds before rebounding back to its pre-crash level. Surely, with today's technologies, the SEC should be able to figure out how to halt a slide like this.[19]

Internal technological problems have also plagued the exchanges, shutting them down for extended periods. For example, in August 2013 a 'software bug' shuttered the NASDAQ for three hours and again for six minutes less than two weeks later. Less than two years after that, the NYSE experienced a four-hour shut down—again the result of a software bug after running software updates.[20] These technological issues also wreak havoc with markets and investors, however the SEC and other regulators have yet to consider how best to handle these situations.

These problems illustrate what at least one scholar has noted: that not all market processes that affect the price of a security fall within the law's definition of "deception" in securities regulation.[21] This point in fact strengthens why regulation needs to undergo true reform. In addition, as mentioned earlier, many of the trading practices that relate to a disclosure system (i.e., were properly conducted within the disclosure system) were nonetheless the same practices that led to the financial crisis. If part of the SEC's mission was to protect the markets—something not currently a part of its mission—then the practices that right now are legal *but* still unstable would be analyzed from a completely different framework. Instead of asking "does this provide adequate enough disclosure to protect investors" the relevant query is whether this protects the market as a whole. As such, under this proposed framework, all of the unstable legal and technical market practices would be challenged and new ways would be designed to ensure market stability.

At its core a paradigm shift of this magnitude requires us to question, at the most fundamental level, what securities regulation should be about. For instance, when we discuss regulating the securities markets, we often use the adage of "protecting investors." What does that look like when investors themselves are causing some of the most severe problems in the securities markets? Having a regulatory model that acts as a backstop against *all* sources of risk (whether those committed by the investors, the corporations or the markets themselves) would provide for stability in an economically shaken arena.

Moreover, there is a strong need in the securities market for a comprehensive regulatory framework that takes into account not just the securities market as an investment paradigm but also the securities market as a consumer paradigm; a regulatory framework that takes into account the systemic risks of the markets rather than the individualistic risks of public corporations. Otherwise, we run the risk of continuing to leave untreated the causes that led to the financial crisis.

But once again, what does that look like? Currently, in our regulatory structure, we have many different models that we can draw from that would allow the SEC to function in this new paradigm. To our mind, the best role that we foresee for the SEC is as part arbiter, part crisis responder. There is precedence for both of these functions in our regulatory schema.

The SEC as Arbiter

The problems that precipitated the 1929 crash continue to plague us today, despite the mountains of regulation that have been implemented since then. So in a return to basics, we focus on the issues that Ferdinand Pecora identified back then: fraud and misrepresentation in the sale of securities. Our plan strips away all of the ancillary regulation that has been added over the years and moves the SEC's orientation back to that essential function: making sure the playing field is free from misleading and fraudulent practices. This provides the underpinning for the SEC's role as arbiter.

Ideally, the SEC, unburdened by disclosure requirements and reactionary rulemaking, becomes a much nimbler creature. Make no mistake, the SEC's rulemaking authority continues in this new paradigm, but in a limited and proactive orientation. One of the agency's primary responsibilities is to develop, implement and maintain a rigorous registration structure. In this structure, every company that wants to issue a security of any kind has to register or receive approval of exemption prior to being able to bring products to market. After that, no other disclosures are required unless there was a material change in the structure of the company or an update to the initial product label.

As part of the registration process, companies would be advised of product labeling requirements for the products they plan to sell. They would be required to notify the SEC of product recalls, new developments not disclosed in the product label and any other "problems" or material changes to the product. These 'truth in advertising' requirements currently fall under Section 10(b) of the Exchange Act regarding fraud, manipulation and misrepresentation and would be retained as a pillar of the new regulatory model.

The SEC's role as arbiter also extends to those who trade securities—for themselves and for customers—as well as the exchanges on which they are traded. Under our scheme, everyone involved in providing products to customers, including investment bankers and advisors, broker-dealers, hedge fund companies, exchanges and clearing corporations, must register with the SEC. Those with direct sales interactions are required to pass an exam, similar to the test you take to get a driver's license. And continuing the driver's license comparison, any broker, trader or broker-dealer found to be involved in deceptive practices would have their license limited or suspended by the SEC, pending prosecution by the Department of Justice.

Finally, the SEC works with exchanges to ensure market stability and equitable access, prevent manipulation and make sure users are fully aware of price variations. The SEC does not control prices; however, it monitors trade activity, pricing and quotations to make sure that all customers have the same information and opportunities. This eliminates the arbitrage 'advantages' for HFTs since they would have access to the same pricing schemes as retail customers.

The SEC as Crisis Manager

The focus on a market place free of fraud and manipulation also provides the foundation for the second of the SEC's roles: that of crisis response and prevention.

With a streamlined regulatory structure, the SEC is free to step back and look at market activity as a whole and decide where and how adjustments can be made to maintain market integrity and stability.

What does that mean? Well, for us, it means that whenever you want to buy or sell stock in Google, for example, you are able to do so and at publicly available prices. That does not mean that you will always get the best deal. At times there will be more buyers than sellers, or more sellers than buyers, depending on the degree to which exchanges will continue to take the other side of unmatched trades, so finding the stock—the product—at the price you want to pay requires a little comparison shopping. And because prices vary depending on the vendor, arbitrage continues to be a way for high-frequency traders and institutions to profit from quick turnovers. More price and availability transparency virtually eliminates the use of dark pools, and this, in turn, may impact liquidity at times in some markets.

The SEC's role in all this is to make sure that the markets are open and able to facilitate customer activity, five days a week, from the opening bell through after-hours trading. They are responsible for not only ensuring liquidity, through the use of circuit breakers and various carrot-and-stick inducements aimed at exchanges,[22] traders and companies and other end-users, but also for setting standards for uses of technology and sanctions when technology is the reason for a disruption in market activity. For example, in our scenario, the NYSE would have been penalized for the recent four-hour outage that resulted when they implemented a software-update.

In addition, in our framework, the SEC now holds the exchanges responsible for the technical proficiency necessary to preempt outages caused by hackers, malware, algorithmic trading, twitter rumors and other such technological efficiencies. The addition of oversight and reporting to ensure technological security, combined with trading activity monitoring and reporting requirements, replace, in large part, the exchanges' previous SRO responsibilities. This shift, especially in light of the ever-increasing consolidations and changes in ownership and advancements in technology provide added security benefits for the exchanges and off-market exchanges, as well as for their users.

The advantages of this model are that that they allow SEC regulation to become much more efficient and effective, both in responding to and implementing proactive measures to prevent market meltdowns. Shifting the focus from disclosure to market stabilization requires less and different resources and frees up the manpower currently expended to comb through filings of individual corporations.[23] Instead, the SEC would use sophisticated software (perhaps in partnership with Silicon Valley)[24] to monitor markets to catch and prevent manipulative or deceptive activities, as well as require exchanges to electronically report incidences of spooling, front-running and other manipulative behaviors. As such, while these proposed changes initially require significant resources, on balance they will allow for cost savings for the federal regulators as resources are better allocated and responding to wild market swings becomes a thing of the past.

This new framework involves a wholesale change to the current philosophical approach to regulation. Protecting investors is no longer a part of the SECs mission; instead, the revised mission focuses solely on maintaining market stability and preventing market failure. In essence, the SEC's efforts to control the markets and ensure stability, by definition, become a form of market handling. For those in favor of deregulation, this provides an additional advantage in that the SEC no longer regulates individual companies once they become public, except for instances of material misstatements and faulty products, as discussed above.

The Other Fingers in the Dike

As you may remember from the regulatory oversight table in Appendix A, there are quite a few participants yet to discuss, including the SROs, state regulatory agencies and the other organizations engaged on the periphery of the financial markets. Here we address their roles—or lack thereof—in relation to sales and supervision, trading (both high frequency and regular investments) and the exchanges and broker-dealer operations and compliance.

One of the advantages of our new paradigm is that the number of members involved in the regulatory structure is significantly reduced. With the SEC as the lead arbiter and emergency crisis responder for the securities markets, and the CFTC and US Treasury in those roles for the commodities and government securities and banking markets, respectively, the remaining quasi-regulatory organizations can be revamped or eliminated entirely. In the case of the PCAOB (Public Company Accounting Oversight Board), for example, their functions are relegated to the SEC and Department of Justice: verification of public auditors and the veracity of corporate financial information are incorporated into the SEC's registration process, and penalty aspects are funneled to the US Attorney General. Similarly, broker fiduciary standards, which are currently administered by the SEC and the Department of Labor, continue to be applicable to a limited extent but, for the sake of consistency, are directed by the SEC only.

The SROs undergo the most dramatic makeover within this paradigm. In chapter 3 we noted that the exchanges are already taking steps to divest themselves of their regulatory oversight relationships with FINRA. In the new paradigm, FINRA is fully divested of all regulatory activities, including examinations, investigations, licensing and registrations, and its Central Registration Depository is adopted, on a smaller scale, by the SEC. The organiza-

Table 6.2. Organizational Responsibilities in the New Paradigm

Current Entity	New Responsibilities
SEC, CFTC, US Treasury	Company/government registration Market stabilization Broker-dealer registration & oversight Broker, advisor registration Investigations Advise state agencies of investigations Fiduciary standards
SROs: FINRA, MSRB, NFA, NASAA	Professional associations Member education
Exchanges	Trade execution Technology innovation Monitor & report trading and market anomalies
State Agencies & Attorneys General	Oversight and enforcement of state requirements Report actions taken to SEC Advise US attorney general of actions taken
Department of Justice	Suspensions, Expulsions, Sanctions & Prosecutions Advise state agencies of actions taken
Oversight: FSOC, FSB, Working Group on Financial Markets	Members become ad-hoc advisors
PCOAB	None
CFPB	Customer complaints, fiduciary issues
SIPC	Account guarantees in the case of broker-dealer insolvency
Investment Bankers/Underwriters	Advise company/government initial registration Advise company/government on product development
Broker-Dealers	Supervise sales activities Initiate customer trades with exchanges
Brokers, Investment Advisors Investment/Hedge Fund Managers	Customer sales and service
Clearing Firms/Transfer Agents	Deliver products to customer or broker dealer Maintain blockchain/customer ownership history
Rating Agencies	Product research resource
Financial Analysts	

tion is then able to become what it truly is: an association of industry professionals, focusing on industry education, including customer product and broker education. The other SROs, including the NFA, MSRB and NASAA (see Appendix A for the comprehensive list) also revert to professional organizations with no oversight responsibilities.

Streamlining this oversight structure is made possible in large part by the dramatically reduced need for broker-dealer examinations and broker investigations. As the role of broker-dealers, advisors, fund managers and brokers shifts to product sales and service, many of the compliance-oriented and sales and sales-supervision requirements and responsibilities go by the wayside. Similarly, with exchanges and traders, the SEC ensures market stability and investigates those who engage in prohibited activities, with the help of the exchanges through periodic reporting, but beyond that the exchanges are also released from compliance and supervisor activity. And while the SEC investigates infractions, the Department of Justice takes on enforcement, including suspensions, expulsions and prosecutions.

Another way in which SEC oversight responsibilities are minimized is in the area of broker-dealer, broker, investment advisor and fund management regulation. As these entities shift to a product sales and customer service orientation, broker-dealer compliance and sales supervision as we know it undergoes significant change. Compliance and sales supervision continue to be an essential element of the broker-dealer experience, but from a different perspective. Brokers and advisors continue to work with customers to help them buy and sell investment products and those that maintain customer accounts and transaction records during the transition period[25] are subject to reserve requirements to offset SIPC guarantees until such time as they no longer hold customer accounts. Fiduciary oversight and investigation of customer complaints shift from the SEC and Department of Labor to the SEC, with help from the CFPB, which is currently charged with ensuring consumer safety. The biggest changes are in the way products are sold to and bought from clients, and the shift in regulatory orientation to prevention of fraud and misrepresentation.

Why Such Radical Changes?

There are many people who believe that the SEC's disclosure framework, despite its flaws, is still the best method for regulating the securities markets. Proponents of a disclosure regime assert that the regulatory environment has secured the rights for investors in such a way that the investors now have a baseline of accountability. The disclosure model makes it seem as if investors do not have to worry about rampant fraud or failing corporations.

This is a legitimate point. As mentioned previously, the theory behind disclosure is that it instills faith in the markets by providing a common denominator of information that all investors can access. However, the disclosure system only works if the disclosures are legitimate and if they are perceived to have value. The SEC does not review submissions for validity—in fact, the completeness of their own financial statements have come under fire by the Government Accountability Office.[26] In addition, companies are increasingly promoting non-GAAP financial information as proof of viability, often distorting earnings and other fiscal data.[27]

Another argument is that taking disclosure information away could breed inherent mistrust in the system and lead to investors discounting the price of securities (for the inevitable fraud that will occur) and/or leaving the markets entirely. One of the benefits of a holistic regulatory system is that it minimizes the need for corporations to engage in fraud. In fact, our model decouples the company from the security, eliminating the quarterly and annual earnings-induced market swings and reducing uncertainty. Essential to the success of this shift—and the maintenance of consumer confidence (something the current regime has had difficulty doing)[28]—is that investors understand that they are buying *securities as products* not investments in companies.

Allowing for this new framework of disaggregation provides another benefit: it frees corporations from the predominate profit maximization model and allows them the freedom to develop their corporate structure in any way that they would like without being beholden to shareholders. This perspective encourages development of other corporate forms that are more mindful of socially conscious ideas, such as the current rise of B-Corps or LC3 business entities.[29] At the same time, it also allows for more traditional corporate structures to take into consideration issues such as business and human rights without fear that it might result in a short term price drop that would then affect analysts' adjustment and, in turn, the price of the stock.

Finally, the underpinnings of our model—disaggregation, efficiency and whole market regulation—reduce, and perhaps even eliminate, the dominance of the big Wall Street banks and the need for industry lobbyists to "help" Congress write legislation to "safeguard" the markets.[30] Companies will appreciate, and likely lobby for, continuation of the new-found freedom that comes from the elimination of continual disclosures requirements. This will also change how commercial and investment banks underwrite, acquire and hold securities, which, in turn, will make aspects of the Volcker Rule and other Dodd-Frank rules—all industry authored—obsolete. Ultimately, this new structure will instill greater confidence in the business sector, in part by naturally fostering the interests of corporations without the lobbying that frequently comes at the expense of shareholders. In short, this new structure changes the paradigm from a zero-sum game, with winners and losers, to a securities framework where everyone can benefit.

The markets,[31] in their wisdom, are already stepping towards a "beyond disclosure regime." For example, "tracking stock," in the world of securities, is a relatively new and (still) underappreciated phenomenon. Tracking stock is stock that is issued by a company that relates (or tracks) to one particular division of the issuer.[32] The issuer (and, to some extent, the parent company's shareholders) still retain control over the division and the management of that division; however, the money that is generated from that corporate issuance is listed separately on the financial statements and allocated simply to that specific division.[33] In their article, Peter Huang[34] and Michael Knoll[35] present a number of different ways that tracking stock can be used including reducing agency costs by aligning investors with specific division incentives; separating out divisions whose financials are more opaque and therefore difficult to value; and allowing for specific stock-based incentives for managers of that unit.[36] Tracking stock has been found to have another, unintended consequence: the further separation of the security from the underlying asset, namely, the company as a whole.

We have talked in detail in this chapter about whole market regulation, how it differs from the current disclosure structure, and why this new paradigm is infinitely more effective and proactive than what we have now. We have outlined our vision, in broad strokes, of what it might look like and how we see the roles changing for all of the current participants. In addition, we have noted the importance of the shift to perceiving of securities as products, and, while we talked about what that looks like in the previous chapter, here we situated that concept into the larger context of our holistic model.

What we have not talked about yet is how we get there from here. The devil is in the details, as they say. In Part 3 we venture into those weeds—or in this case, the seaweed.

Notes

1. Michael Perion, *Hellhounds of Wall Street: How Ferdinand Pecora's Investigation of the Great Crash Forever Changed American Finance* (Penguin Books, 2011).

2. Treasury Secretary Tim Geithner, Written Testimony House Financial Services Committee Hearing, March 26, 2009, as cited in Robert J. Shiller's "Democratizing and Humanizing Finance," in *Reforming US Financial Markets, Reflections Before and Beyond Dodd-Frank* by Randall S. Krozner and Robert J. Schiller (MIT Press, 2011), 3.

3. Margaret M. Blair, "Corporate Personhood and the Corporate Persona," 2013 *U. Ill. L. Rev. 785* (2013); Lucian A. Bebchuk & Jesse M. Fried, "Paying for Long Term Performance," 158 U. Pa. L. Rev. 1915 (2010).

4. Brett McDonnell, "Dampening Financial Regulatory Cycles," 65 Fla. L. Rev. 1597 (2013). See also, Yesha Yadav, "Beyond Efficiency in Securities Regulation," *Vanderbilt Law and Economics Research Paper No. 14–8* (2014).

5. For information about the US Securities & Exchange Commissions' Division of Risk Assessment, see http://www.sec.gov/dera/about.

6. For one in-depth analysis of the financial crisis and its role in the current economic structure see Steven Ramirez's, *Lawless Capitalism: The Subprime Crisis and the Case for an Economic Rule of Law* (NYU Press, 2014).

7. E.g., Enron, WorldCom and Tyco. In an unpublished paper entitled, *Four Years after Enron Assessing the Financial Market Regulatory Clean Up* (2005), 2–3, authors Roy C. Smith and Ingo Walter note that "By December 2001, when Enron, the seventh largest company in America and one of its leading new-economy concept companies, filed for bankruptcy, the NASDAQ index had fallen 74 percent from its high of less than two years earlier. In 2001 there were 171 large corporate bankruptcies involving liabilities of $230 billion, more than twice the level in 2000, the previous record year for bankruptcies. In July 2002, WorldCom, the country's second largest long-distance telecom company with $107 billion in assets filed for bankruptcy after revealing recent instances of accounting fraud. Throughout 2002 bankruptcies involving liabilities of $338 billion occurred, thus establishing a three-year period in which American bankruptcies—the ultimate form of corporate failure—broke all previous records. In addition, instances of accounting failures (in the form of restatements of prior audited financial results due to accounting errors) nearly quadrupled in the four-year period 1998–2001 to 616 cases. Restatements continued to occur at a record level during 2002" (available at https://archive.nyu.edu/bitstream/2451/26432/2/FIN-05–029.pdf). The Dow Jones Industrial Average closed at its lowest point, 7,286.27, on October 9, 2002, and then steadily rebounded (with the exception of April 2003) to a high of 14,093.08 on October 12, 2007. See http://finance.yahoo.com/q/hp?s=%5EDJI&a=05&b=1&c=2007&d=10&e=30&f=2007&g=d for details.

8. Voting members of the FSOC include heads of the US Treasury, SEC, CFTC, The Federal Reserve, OCC, CFPB, FDIC, FHFA, NCUA and an insurance representative selected by the President. Non-voting members include Director of the Office of Financial Research, Director of the Federal Insurance Office, a state insurance commissioner, a state banking supervisor and a state securities commissioner.

9. According to the Federal Reserve, "The Basel Committee on Banking Supervision (BCBS), on which the United States serves as a participating member, developed international regulatory capital standards through a number of capital accords and related publications, which have collectively been in effect since 1988.

"Basel III is a comprehensive set of reform measures, developed by the BCBS, to strengthen the regulation, supervision, and risk management of the banking sector. The measures include both liquidity and capital reforms." http://www.federalreserve.gov/bankinforeg/basel/

10. SIFMA's Volcker Rule Resource Center tells us that, "after an initial proposal in the Fall of 2011, final Volcker Rule regulations were released and adopted . . . on December 10, 2013. The rules generally prohibit banking entities from the following:

engaging in short-term proprietary trading of securities, derivatives, commodity futures and options on these instruments for their own account; and owning, sponsoring, or having certain relationships with hedge funds or private equity funds, referred to as 'covered funds.'" http://www.sifma.org/issues/regulatory-reform/volcker-rule/overview/.

11. "From 1933 to 1999, there were very few large bank failures and no financial panics comparable to the Panic of 2008. The law worked exactly as intended. In 1999, Democrats led by President Bill Clinton and Republicans led by Sen. Phil Gramm joined forces to repeal Glass-Steagall at the behest of the big banks." From James Rickards, "Repeal of Glass-Steagall Caused the Financial Crisis," *U.S. News and World Report* (Aug 27, 2012).

12. Oh, wait—the former already is!

13. Ibid.

14. "The ability of HFT scalpers to create latency arbitrage opportunities makes trading more difficult and costly for traditional investors who lack access to sophisticated trading platforms . . . latency arbitrage not only reduces profits of the other market participants, but harms market efficiency . . . [and] front-running HFTs impose a speed tax on normal traders, making markets less liquid and prices less informative." Elaine Wah and Michael P. Wellman, "Latency Arbitrage, Market Fragmentation, and Efficiency: A Two-Market Model," Univ. Mich., Strategic Reasoning Group, Proceedings of the *14th ACM Conference on Electronic Commerce* (2013), 855–872, https://web.eecs.umich.edu/srg/?page_id=1383.

15. James J. Angel, Lawrence E. Harris & Chester S. Spatt, *Equity trading in the 21st century*.

16. Marije Meerman's *Money and Speed: Inside the Black Box*, film (2011), http://topdocumentaryfilms.com/money-speed-inside-black-box.

17. Even when the market is undergoing relatively mild trading losses, the sheer volume that this represents often ranges in the billions. See NASDAQTRADER.com, http://www.NASDAQtrader.com/Trader.aspx?id=DailyMarketSummary. When there are actual corrections or unusual volatility, the results are even worse.

18. To be clear, this would be a radical change from our present structure. However, it is not without precedent in our federal government. For instance, FEMA (the Federal Emergency Management Agency) has "quick response" teams.

19. Maureen Farrell, "Mini Flash Crashes: A Dozen a Day," *CNN Money* (Mar 20, 2013). Even more disturbing, these crashes have been occurring even after the SEC implemented its new rules. However, because of the formula used to calculate a crash, none of the crashes meet the criteria for triggering a circuit breaker.

20. John McCrank, "NASDAQ says software bug caused trading outage," *Reuters* (Aug 29, 2013) (http://www.reuters.com/article/2013/08/29/us-NASDAQ-halt-glitch-idusBRE97S11420130829); and Adam Shell, "NASDAQ: Tech glitch caused 'brief outage,'" *USA Today* (Sept 4, 2013) (http://www.usatoday.com/story/money/markets/2013/09/04/NASDAQ-reports-another-brief-outage/2762847/), as well as Nick Baker, "NYSE says software upgrade, not a hacking attack, caused outage," *Financial Review* (Jul 10, 2015), http://www.afr.com/markets/equity-markets/nyse-says-software-upgrade-not-a-hacking-attack-caUsed-outage-20150709-gi950u.

21. David D. Gruberg, "Decent Exposure: The SEC's Lack of Authority and Restraint in Proposing to Eliminate Flash Trading," *65 U. Miami L. Rev. 263* (2010), 272.

22. What would an inducement look like? Quite frankly, we don't know yet. But we're open to suggestions.

23. Not only has that been a resource consuming activity, it has been highly ineffective, as evidenced by Fannie Mae, Enron, WorldCom and even GAO reports that provide evidence that the SEC is unable to effectively monitor corporate financial filings.

24. Financial institutions have increasingly been engaging technology firms to move electronic payments forward. See, for example, Camilla Hall and Sarah Mishkin, "Wells Fargo Chief Turns to Silicon Valley for Potential Partners," *Financial Times* (Aug 26, 2014) and Jane Wild, Martin Arnold and Philip Stafford, "Technology: banks see the key to blockchain," *Financial Times* (Nov 1, 2015).

25. We disagree amongst ourselves on the disposition of customer funds and securities and how best to ensure fair dealings with customers. The contention is whether broker-dealers should be allowed to hold customer funds and products or whether a third-party custodian should be required. Either way, at minimum, regulatory requirements must be considered for broker-dealers who hold customer funds while the transition to the new structure is underway.

26. See GAO Report 15–387R, *Management Report: Improvements Needed in SEC's Internal Controls and Accounting Procedures* (Apr 30, 2015).

27. Michael Cohn, "SEC Questions Widespread Use of Non-GAAP Measures," *Accounting Today* (Apr 16, 2016), http://www.accountingtoday.com/blogs/debits-credits/news/sec-questions-widespread-use-of-non-gaap-measures-77832–1.html.

28. The Vix, also known as the consumer fear index, has ranged from a high of almost 60 in October 2008 (pre-crash) to a low of 10.62 in 2016. See http://www.cboe.com/micro/vix/vixintro.aspx. The CCI, or Consumer Confidence Index, fell from a pre-crash high of 144.7 to close at 92.6 at the end of May 2016. See https://www.confer ence-board.org/data/consumerconfidence.cfm and http://www.advisorperspectives.com/dshort/updates/Conference-Board-Consumer-Confidence-Index.php.

29. A B-Corp (or, another variant, a social benefit corporation) is a corporation that is not solely created to make profits for shareholders. We talk more about them in chapter 8. An LC3 has a similar vibe in that it is a low profit company (some would say a cross between a limited liability company, or LLC, and a non-profit organization). Since our focus is on corporations, we don't discuss LC3s anywhere else. But there is a lot of information out there on this if you are curious.

30. Daniel Wagner, Allison Fitzgerald, "Meet the Banking Caucus: Wall Street's Secret Weapon in Washington," *Citizens for Public Integrity* (April 24 2014), https://www.publicintegrity.org/2014/04/24/14595/meet-banking-caucus-wall-streets-secret-weapon-washington.

31. In addition to the markets, other government agencies have recognized that the financial regulatory system in the United States needs to be overhauled. For instance, in the initial wake of the current financial crisis, the Department of Treasury released a report entitled *Blueprint for a Modernized Financial Regulatory Structure*. Blueprint for a Financial Regulatory Structure, http://www.treasury.gov/press-center/press-releases/

Documents/Blueprint.pdf. Although the report contains sweeping and far-reaching recommendations, Prof. Seligman forecasted that the report will most likely not be adopted. Most critically, Prof. Joel Seligman stated that the *Blueprint* "lacks the serious, detailed policy analysis necessary to support many of its specific proposals." Joel Seligman, "The SEC in a Time of Discontinuity," *95 Virginia L. Rev. No. 4*, p. 673.

32. For a fuller discussion of tracking stock see Peter H. Huang & Michael S. Knoll, "Corporate Finance, Corporate Law and Finance Theory," *74 S. Cal. L. Rev. 175*, 187–188 (2000).

33. Ibid.

34. Ibid.

35. Ibid.

36. Ibid.

Part III

IMPLEMENTATION AND IMPLICATIONS

In this section we discuss the details of implementation, including the regulatory hurdles that will need to be overcome to implement our model. We also explore the very real issue of how we might achieve the political will necessary to accomplish such an ambitious result. Finally, this section provides some preliminary blueprints for establishing such a system both substantively—through legislation—and procedurally—by overhauling our current agency structure.

Here we offer an honest and critical assessment of the effect the new regime will have on the market. Here, we prognosticate on how the new market structure could affect everything from business and human rights issues to stabilizing global markets to assisting in capital formations before considering the potential unintended consequences that could occur from adoption of this model.

As we think about how we might best create this new oversight structure, we have to think about what, exactly, we want to regulate. What current regulations are effective and worth keeping? For example,

- Is it feasible to allow corporations to opt-out of this new system and maintain some variant of a disclosure protocol?
- How does the new structure provide the investor with at least the level of confidence engendered by the current disclosure model—and preferably more?
- What role does 10b-5 play in this new system?
- How does this new system mesh with the global markets?

In the previous section we talked at length—and in theory—about our model: a comprehensive new paradigm in which securities are treated as consumer products within a world of whole market regulation. In this section we operationalize our theories by looking at what it would take to make our paradigm a reality. In chapter 7 we illustrate the ways in which the new regulatory model, a collaborative agency structure, will reduce bloat and make regulatory agencies more nimble. With less to regulate on a micro level, we show how agencies will be able to devote their attention to forecasting and investigating weaknesses in the markets and developing proactive frameworks for building 21st century financial markets. Chapter 8 covers the corporate perspective, the new requirements for corporate and municipal entities in their quest to raise debt and equity capital by bringing new issues—new products—to market. And finally, in chapter 9 we show how these changes might be brought about by examining the political and legal roads to implementation. There we also briefly explore how this structure might help stabilize global markets.

CHAPTER 7

A Regulatory Triad

We have talked at length about the need to stop plugging the old, leaky dike. Let's finally replace it with a brand new levee—a new regulatory structure that accommodates our new product orientation within a whole market perspective. In this chapter we describe this new, improved levee and talk about how it will hold back potential future financial tsunamis.

What will the shift in oversight look like at the agencies under this new market structure? Here we provide a point-by-point discussion of how our model will impact our regulatory system. In doing so, we briefly revisit the current model of securities regulation to show where it is deficient by being both over- and under-inclusive. We then proceed to develop a new agency structure that is much more nimble and streamlined and argue that this new regime has significant benefits: (1) reducing the bloat will make it more nimble and (2) having less to regulate on a micro level means that it can devote its attention to monitoring and forecasting weaknesses in the markets and then act accordingly and proactively (in much the same way that banks currently perform stress tests). This chapter also describes what each regulatory organization would look like under the new model. So for instance, the NYSE's oversight parameters would focus on market manipulation rather than bogus products.

In this chapter we move from theory to practice as we sort out the new regulatory regime. We start with the creation of a three-member regulatory commission before moving to the functions of the SROs, exchanges and broker-dealers. We look at issuer registration, broker and broker-dealer licensing, 10b-5 and anti-fraud prevention measures and compliance requirements. We consider what it will take to get there from here, laying out the considerations, benefits and challenges of making this shift.

Toward a Holistic, Whole Market System

The idea of a single regulatory market overseer is not new. As mentioned in chapter 3, after the "Black Monday" crash of 1987, President Reagan convened a task force to determine the causes and put forth suggestions to prevent something like that from happening again.[1] Key among the recommendations from the taskforce was for a "single agency," a coordinated cross-market regulatory system. It also recommended a circuit breaker mechanism that would allow for price limits and synchronized trading halts in the face of market volatility.[2] The Task Force's initial assessment was that the Federal Reserve would be well qualified to take that role. In our updated, 21st century ideal, we envision a three-party commission, made up of the heads of the three pillars of the financial markets: securities, commodities and commercial banking.

A Regulatory Triad

Tackling systemic risk in most areas, of course, requires a broader program beyond any particular agency's jurisdiction and authority. Risks that could cascade through our financial system could impact a range of market participants, many of whom, for example, the SEC does not oversee.[3]

The current top-heavy structure of the SEC requires that it be all things to all aspects of the securities market: new issue registrar and keeper of annual, quarterly and structural disclosures for publicly traded companies; registrar, auditor, investigator and enforcer to broker-dealers, clearing agencies and transfer agents, investment companies and advisers, municipal advisors, the national securities exchanges, SROs such as the Financial Industry Regulatory Authority ("FINRA") and the Municipal Securities Rulemaking Board, and the Public Company Accounting Oversight Board; exchange and rating agency registrar; market monitor and risk-manager, rule-maker and Congressional whipping boy. Sadly, innovator is nowhere within that list.

While the SEC is responsible for the majority of activity that takes place within the securities markets, at least in Congressional eyes, their realm does not extend to all markets. The CFTC is responsible for commodities, futures, currencies and derivatives and swaps. The US Treasury has authority over Treasury bonds, bills and notes, commercial paper, interest-bearing products, including money market funds, certificates of deposit, checking and savings accounts and all other commercial banking products, and rulemaking, investigation and prosecution of money laundering activities.

The commodities and futures markets, and particularly derivatives, swaps and hedge funds, continue to grow. Even after the downturn of mortgage-backed securities and credit default swaps in 2008, the industry continues to produce mortgage-related derivatives as well as other innovative, unregistered derivatives products. In the fall of 2015 the London Stock Exchange launched Curveglobal, a short- and long-term interest rate derivative product,[4] and Wall Street is developing derivatives products based on peer-to-peer lending and the success of crowdfunding venues.[5] The CFTC is slated to become responsible for all OTC derivatives (not backed by securities) transactions in 2017, assuming plans to operationalize applicable Dodd-Frank rules move forward as planned. Spurred on by the combination of product growth and Dodd-Frank Act oversight requirements, the CFTC and US Treasury have become increasingly vocal about regulation and rulemaking. The Act gave the Treasury two more agencies and both the CFTC and Treasury more oversight authority, blurring the regulatory lines of responsibility even more.

As we pointed out in chapter 3 and again in chapter 6, the vast number of other regulators—SROs, exchanges and other groups—makes any real comprehensive, cohesive whole market regulation impossible, even within the current disclosure system. This increasing number of fingers in the dike over the years has cumulatively served to weaken the system to the point of failure. Case in point, the 2008 market collapse.

Our model dramatically reduces or eliminates the roles and responsibilities of the multitude of players involved in the regulatory process, leaving the job to a collaboration among the SEC, the CFTC and the US Treasury. And instead of having to be all things to all markets, the focus of this regulatory triad is limited to product safety, truth in advertising—from registration disclosures to sales practices—and market stabilization. Regulation can then be nimble, encourage innovation and embrace emerging technologies, perhaps on a global scale.

Creation of a collaborative commission charged with keeping the markets safe for investors, issuers and traders is a practical move. Instead of being relegated to their individual fiefdoms, as is currently the case, a cooperative structure allows the SEC, CFTC and US Treasury to focus on what each does best. But it also requires active engagement and communication, allowing for a whole market perspective when it comes to rulemaking and stabilization. When there is a catastrophe within the financial markets, every market is affected. The collapse of the housing market and the derivatives and swaps markets showed us just how interrelated the national and international financial markets and global economies truly are. A more severe crisis within the current structure could effectively shutter all activities—including depositors' access to local savings and checking accounts. A collaborative, communicative, agile oversight structure just seems to make more and more sense.

Getting the three entities to work together should not be as difficult as it might seem. Thanks to the Dodd-Frank Act, they already sit on the Financial

Stability Oversight Council (FSOC) together. FOSC, however, has ten voting members, including the Federal Reserve, the Federal Housing Finance Authority and the National Credit Union Administration Board as well as the SEC, CFTC and Treasury agencies (including the Office of the Comptroller of the Currency and the Consumer Financial Protection Board), and five non-voting members, including Treasury agencies and state securities and insurance regulators.[6] Getting a board that large and diverse to respond quickly to a crisis or opportunity would be like trying to get a warship to turn on a dime. Clearly it would be much easier for three individuals to meet, strategize and innovate together rather than a group of fifteen who represent very diverse interests. But what about all those other interests? Of course they need to be heard, but in the form of an advisory council, which would ensure that their insights and concerns are included but still allow for rapid response and proactive creativity.

Ultimately, all rules developed and actions taken for all aspects of the financial markets—securities, commodities, investment managers and advisors, traders, investors, exchanges, etc.—would be the result of cooperative decisions made by the regulatory triad. Given the current regulatory structure and the piecemeal way in which it has been developed, our promotion to a comprehensive, coordinated oversight structure may seem groundbreaking, particularly as we explore how that might come to fruition.

A NEW, IMPROVED SEC

The SEC's mission, as previously discussed, has three components: ensuring investor protection, facilitating capital formation, and maintaining fair, orderly and efficient markets. To fully embrace its role in the triad and accommodate the shift to product-oriented market regulation, the SEC must undergo comprehensive structural alterations. In its new incarnation these three pillars of market regulation are contained within the Commission's dual-roles as arbiter and crisis responder. Here we elaborate on those ideas before getting into the details of the agency's internal make-up.

The most significant change to the SEC's structure is a foundational one—the end of the disclosure system on which it has been based since inception. In its role as arbiter, the SEC's focus supports capital formation and investor protection through its oversight and approval of issuer registration. Companies and municipalities now must meet stringent criteria to complete an initial registration process, but, once accomplished, the only other information required would be notification of material changes, such as a merger, acquisition or divestitures, offshore relocation, or reorganization or bankruptcy. Investment bankers continue in the role of consultants, just like accounting firms or other advisory firms that assist companies in preparing registration applications and product packaging, and even those that work with municipal issues do not need to be registered.

For registered companies and municipalities, the requirement for periodic disclosure filings ends, making quarterly earnings reports and the accompanying market fluctuations a thing of the past. For those entities that are not ready for full registration but want to raise funds through equity or debt offerings, exemptions, such as Reg. A and D, are still an option.

As part of the registration process, companies must comply with product labeling requirements for the products they plan to sell. They also have to notify the SEC of subsequent developments that might impact the product such as recalls, new developments not disclosed in the product label and any other "problems" or material changes to the product. This is the closest the new system comes to resembling continued disclosure requirements. These 'truth in advertising' rules fall under the existing SEC framework: specifically, Section 10(b) and Rule 10b-5 of the Exchange Act. They cover material misstatements and fraud and continue to provide the foundational structure for all of these activities.

Specifically, Rule 10b-5 provides the framework for regulatory oversight.[7] Currently, the rule states:

> It shall be unlawful for any person, directly or indirectly, by the use of any means or instrumentality of interstate commerce, or of the mails or of any facility of any national securities exchange,
>
> (a) To employ any device, scheme, or artifice to defraud,
> (b) To make any untrue statement of a material fact or to omit to state a material fact necessary in order to make the statements made, in the light of the circumstances under which they were made, not misleading, or
> (c) To engage in any act, practice, or course of business which operates or would operate as a fraud or deceit upon any person, in connection with the purchase or sale of any security.

Retaining Section 10(b) requires that it be amended, however, to add the word "product" everywhere within the language that could trigger the antifraud provisions. Doing so allows the current enforcement structure to stay applicable to all companies and governments who sell securities (whether registered or exempt) and adds the new paradigm of products as aspects that could become the subject of investigation. In addition, the general market manipulation statute (Section 9 of the Exchange Act) is incorporated into the language of Rule 10b-5 to ensure its access as an antifraud tool for the SEC. But what does fraud look like under a market regime? Well, almost exactly the same as it does now.

It is still illegal to make a material misstatement or omission in connection with purchase or sale of a security (and now a product).

The most significant adjustment to Rule 10b-5 pertains to existing ideas of what constitutes a material omission. Right now, the idea of a material omission comes from a corporation's duty to disclose certain material information. Under this new, largely disclosure-less regime, companies are required to disclose everything of significance in the registration process and only substantive changes thereafter, which is designed to produce much fewer material omissions. On the other hand, a company is still not allowed to exaggerate or fabricate information about its products—whether that is the safety of its new car or the prospects of its business plan—and, therefore, its stock. Nor are they able to lie by omission. If they do discuss a product, it must be honestly and completely.

The importance of a marketplace free of fraud and manipulation—maintaining fair, orderly and efficient markets—provides the foundation for the second of the SEC's roles: that of crisis response and prevention. With a streamlined regulatory structure, the SEC is now free to step back and look at market activity as a whole to determine if there are any adjustments needed to maintain market integrity and stability.

The advantages of this model are that SEC regulation is now able to be much more efficient and effective, both in responding to and enacting proactive measures to prevent market meltdowns. Shifting the focus from disclosure to market stabilization requires fewer and different resources. This frees up the manpower currently expended to comb through filings of individual corporations for use in other, more proactive endeavors.[8] For example, the SEC may focus on developing and engaging sophisticated software to monitor markets to catch and prevent manipulative or deceptive activities and to communicate with exchanges to collect and analyze data regarding incidences of spooling, front-running and other manipulative behaviors.

In what ways will the SEC take on these new roles? Internally, the functionality of the SEC changes dramatically as well. According to the SEC website, they currently have five divisions, each charged with supervising various aspects of the financial markets:[9]

- Corporate Finance's mission is to "ensure that investors are provided with material information in order to make informed investment decisions";
- Enforcement is supposed to investigate and prosecute violations of the securities laws and rules adopted under these laws;
- Investment Management "regulates investment companies, variable insurance products, and federally registered investment advisers";
- Economic and Risk Analysis was created in 2009 to add financial economics and data analysis to the SEC's bag of tricks;

- Trading and Markets "establishes and maintains standards for fair and orderly markets"; and
- The National Exam Program, comprised of the Office of Compliance and Inspections and Examinations "regulates the major securities market participants, including broker-dealers, self-regulatory organizations (such as stock exchanges, FINRA, and clearing agencies."

In our holistic model, the entire alignment of the SEC changes to accommodate whole-market regulation. The product orientation of the new structure means that the Corporate Finance Division now reviews and approves new issue registration applications and Crowdfunding, Regulation A and D exemptions (see chapter 8 for details). The registration process is designed to initially be much more detailed than the current disclosure system, with issuers required to show evidence of profitability prior to approval. The responsibility to ensure that customers are informed would be limited to making sure issuers comply with product labeling requirements.

While the registration requirements are much more stringent on the front end, once a company or municipality (in the case of government bonds) has registered with the SEC, the Division's job is virtually done. There are no subsequent disclosures, except for material changes that could trigger a recall or lemon law. With no required quarterly or annual financial filings, earnings releases become voluntary. We get to finally say good-bye to the irrational volatility of earnings season.

In addition, the SEC takes on the role of registrar for debt securities other than those issued by the US Government or related entities.[10] That includes maintaining regulations and process requirements for registration—and exemptions—of companies that issue corporate debt, as well as registration of states, agencies and taxing districts that register municipal bond offerings. Currently issuers do not have to be registered. The increasing number of municipal bankruptcies and states with fiscal instability warrant due diligence similar to that required of their corporate counterparts.[11] More on that in the next chapter.

The consolidation of Enforcement, Investment Management and the National Exam Program ensures that there is one division devoted to safeguarding fair practices. Broker-dealers, investment advisors, clearing and settlement organizations and their employees must deal fairly and honestly with retail and institutional investors and traders and maintain accurate and complete records of all transactions and accounts. This new division is responsible for monitoring compliance activity relating to customer transactions to identify and investigate fraud and malfeasance. Their oversight stops there, however. Enforcement falls within the jurisdiction of the US Justice Department or State Attorneys General, as appropriate. Cases of rule violations are turned over to them, for prosecution. This allows for an end to the seeming reluctance of regulators to indict member firms or those deemed "to-big-to-fail," and the conflict of interest inherent in regulators who have been previously embedded in monolithic investment banks.[12]

Another of the SEC's roles that undergoes significant change is its oversight of trading and markets. First, in our paradigm there are significantly fewer types of investment products available for customers. Of course investors can continue to buy and sell corporate and municipal equity and debt and treasury securities, although there are various new ways to do so, as discussed briefly below and in more detail in the next chapter. Options and futures contracts, however, are no longer an option, at least not within the securities markets, as they are not truly a security—they have no underlying assets attached to them. They may be related to specific stocks or currencies or commodities, such as coffee futures or IBM options. But if you buy that coffee future or IBM option, all you get is the right to buy or sell the product, not the product itself. These futures and options contracts are essentially betting on whether the stock will go up or down or whether or not too much rain will wash out the coffee plants. In fact, you can even buy futures contracts on the weather![13] And that's our point. When it comes to these instruments, they are simply regulated gambling.

The US Commerce Clause and state statutes regulate other forms of gambling.[14] In our new regime, we move options, futures, derivatives, swaps and similar products to where we think they really belong—the Department of Commerce and state gaming commissions. We anticipate the emergence of a whole new gaggle of bookies for those who are insistent on betting on the future.

Second, the scope of exchange regulation also changes. The overarching function of exchanges in our new regime is to facilitate purchases and sales of securities, be that for broker-dealers, traders or institutional or retail customers. Exchanges continue to be registered[15] with primary responsibility for trade facilitation and market security. They are also required to monitor trading activity and report to the SEC any suspicious arrangements[16] or transactions that could give unfair advantage in some way to some participants over others, as well as any activity that might undermine market stability. This effectively puts an end to pay to play schemes and the use of dark pools.

Further, exchanges are required to keep up with technological advancements and incorporate those technologies in the facilitation of trades; they are also charged with preventing viruses and malware, hacking, digitally initiated runs on the market, impacts of social media and other electronic sources, such as that triggered by a Twitter posting, and any other technology or abuse of technology that could pose a threat or hold up their ability to effect trades. They will be penalized for shutdowns and failures to keep up with current threats, instabilities and inefficacies.

The Division of Economics and Risk Analysis and the Division of Trading and Markets continues to collaborate and collect and maintain trading and market data. There is no longer a need to maintain or analyze the EDGAR database simply because continual disclosure is no longer part of the regulatory scheme; however, the system may be used to catalog approved registrations, as well as those currently on file, for access by regulators and investors. Examining trading trends and patterns and developing descriptive data about registrations, investment activity, investigations and referrals to the judicial system, and analyzing data for management and decision-making activities by the regulatory triad and making that data available to the public are all functions within the scope of this division. This is designed to be a truly cooperative division, working with all other divisions to collect and disseminate data. In this way, it also enables the SEC to comply with other federal performance requirements, such as the Government Performance and Results Modernization Act (GPRAMA) and the Digital Accountability and Transparency (DATA) Act, which dictate that agencies collect data about their operations and make that data accessible by the public.[17]

Clearly the new make-up and purpose of the SEC is considerably different from what we know now. EDGAR and collection of ongoing disclosures would be a thing of the past. Investigations that warrant further action shift to the Justice Department or States' Attorneys for enforcement, a transition that has been happening for some time and which seems to be the most effective way to prosecute violators. And beyond keeping up with technological innovation, the agency would also anticipate emerging issues (i.e., blockchain and digital currencies) and potential problems, an emphasis not currently in their repertoire.

Some things never change. Registration continues to be the central pillar of the SEC's product-oriented market regulation. Our model allows the agency to retain and strengthen its commitment to preventing fraud and manipulation through enforcement of its 10b-5 regulations. And we have dusted off the focus on anti-fraud, which seems to have lost its gloss since the 1929 crash, despite the fact that it was seen as one of the primary reasons for the market failure.

THE SAME GOES FOR THE CFTC AND THE US TREASURY

The orientation of the CFTC and Treasury are similar to that of the SEC. For instance, the CFTC's mission, as stated on its website, is "to foster open, transparent, competitive, and financially sound markets, to avoid systemic risk, and to protect the market users and their funds, consumers, and the public from fraud, manipulation, and abusive practices."[18]

In our new paradigm the substance of their mission does not change substantially but the scope does. The CFTC continues to be responsible largely for market stability within commodities markets. Like the SEC, they are responsible for registration of those commercial and non-commercial traders that provide the various commodities for investment. Monitoring traders and investment firms for violation of anti-fraud regulations also continues to be a prominent aspect of their regulatory endeavors. In addition, they are charged with ensuring stability and fair practices; to that end they track actual or attempted manipulative practices, and any investigations that warrant prosecution are turned over to the Justice Department or relevant State's Attorney's Office.

Unlike the securities markets, farmers and others in the agriculture industry have used commodity and currency futures contracts to offset production risks.[19] Unexpected changes in weather or the emergence of farm pests, for example, have devastated orange groves, coffee plantations and corn and soybean crops, and severe currency fluctuations have wreaked havoc on the spot market,[20] all taking their toll on local farmers as well as industrial behemoths. There is no underlying asset for these investments, so by rights we shift them to the gaming industry for oversight. We may need to consider an exception for agricultural risk management, however, we leave that to better minds to devise.[21] Derivatives and swaps contracts, on the other hand, will join their former securities cohorts in Las Vegas.[22]

Similarly, the US Treasury continues its reign over government and government-sponsored-entity issued products, including Treasury bonds, bills and notes, GNMA securities and any other products backed by the full faith and credit of the US Government. They also continue to be responsible for interest-rate products such as money market accounts, and of course, retail and commercial savings and checking accounts, certificates of deposit, commercial paper and other such banking products. The Treasury is also charged with regulating virtual currencies, such as the now mainstream Bitcoin and its successors, and monitoring and regulating advancements made in that area.

The bright line between the Treasury and the SEC that was characteristic of the now defunct Glass-Steagall Act served to define the different areas of responsibility: Treasury was responsible for commercial banking and related activity, including the bank stress tests, and the SEC was responsible for investment banking, or registration advisors as they are more commonly known in this new regulatory world. All of the consolidations that have taken place since the 2008 crash blurred that line even more than the initial legislation in 1999. Coupled with the additional responsibilities given to the Treasury in the Dodd-Frank Act, it is easy to see how the overlapping regulatory authority has taken hold. We bring that bright line back, through a regulatory division of labor, preferably codified in legislation. But more about that in the next chapter.

The concept of a regulatory triad, even absent our shift to a product-oriented structure, would significantly change the way regulation is created, conducted and anticipated. Such a nimble partnering, with advice from others involved in various aspects of the markets, stands to encourage thoughtful, comprehensive, forward-thinking visions of the financial markets in the 21st century. So, what about all the remaining participants?

Where Do the SROs and Other Regulators Fit?

If you think back again to chapter 3 and the chart in Appendix A, you'll recall there are many other fingers in the regulatory pie right now. Everything from the SROs, clearing corporations and the exchanges to the Departments of Labor and Justice, to Treasury agencies such as the Office of the Comptroller of the Currency and FinCEN (Financial Crimes Enforcement Network), state securities and insurance regulators and attorneys general, and general oversight boards created by the Dodd-Frank Act.

THE ROLE OF SROs

SROs are member-firm organizations that are supported by revenue generated from registration fees and fines. Currently, firms and individuals wanting to do business in the securities markets must be registered with the SROs. SROs also interpret and enforce securities rules and regulations, meaning member firms police their own. There's a bit of a conflict of interest in that design, but the SEC, whose funding has not kept up with the demand for audits and investigations, has increasingly relied on these organizations to police the industry.

As noted before, the Financial Industry Regulatory Authority (FINRA) is by far the largest and most active of the SROs. The Maloney Act gave life to the National Association of Securities Dealers (NASD), FINRA's predecessor, in 1938 as a means to allow "national securities associations" to establish "a mechanism of regulation among over-the-counter brokers and dealers" under the supervision and oversight of the SEC.[23] The NASD was the first member firm organization, followed by the Municipal Securities Rulemaking Board (MSRB) in 1984 and the National Futures Association (NFA) in 2001.

The scope and organization of FINRA have blossomed over the years. It now conducts the lion's share of broker-dealer examinations, acts as the repository for licensing, customer complaints and disciplinary actions and investigates and takes action against rule violators. It also operates FINRA Foundation, which focuses on investor education. As a non-profit corporation, FINRA is unlike government regulatory organizations in that its records and activities are not available to the public or even subject to access through Freedom of Information Act (FOIA) requests. The MSRB performs a similar role for the municipal securities markets, as does the NFA for the futures markets.[24]

With the shift to a product-based regulatory system the SROs become redundant. Product regulation is now limited to initial registration of the issuing organization. Broker and dealer examinations and investigations are constrained primarily to issues of fraud and manipulation and enforcement moves to the justice system. The restructuring of the SEC allows it to focus more on what it was originally charged with in 1934—ensuring market stability and preventing fraud. This shift in orientation and reallocation of resources enables the SEC to maintain the limited registration and examination structure called for in our new paradigm, putting an end to their reliance on SROs to police their own.

As a result, FINRA is able to become a true professional association. Like most other trade associations, their emphasis would likely shift to member education. Seminars on product information, such as how to read product labels and product warranties or the impact of recalls and lemon laws, workshops adapting anti-fraud practices for advertising, communications and social media and networking events with exchange members to encourage working relationships could help brokers and broker-dealers best serve their customers. They could also offer workshops for compliance officers and personnel on records retention, implementation of technological innovations such as blockchain and digital currencies and understanding fair practice regulations. This new orientation would hold true for the other SROs, including the NFA and MSRB.

THINGS DON'T CHANGE MUCH FOR THE EXCHANGES OR CLEARING CORPORATIONS

While the SROs account for the majority of the regulatory activity in the industry, clearing and settlement organizations and exchanges are essential components now and in the new paradigm. The markets run on execution and settlement.

Like buying toasters or widgets, customers may take their new purchases home with them or have them delivered to a third-party holding institution if they choose. In addition, new technologies, such as digital currencies and blockchain, are making ownership history and transaction payments much more efficient and, in the case of crowdfunded pools, more complicated. Clearing organizations are required to devote the resources necessary to keep up with and forecast these options and technological advancements in order to implement advancements that enable them to process settlements efficiently and securely and remain proactive participants in the industry. They must register with the SEC by notification to ensure compliance with these directives.

The exchanges continue to be a marketplace for brokers, dealers, managers and customers to buy and sell securities products. They no longer have SRO responsibilities (something they are currently in the process of relinquishing), but, like clearing companies, they must be registered, also by notification, with the SEC, CFTC and Treasury, depending on the types of products they offer. In addition, exchanges are responsible for maintaining market stability, in part by making sure everyone has equal information and access. They continue to control trading volume through the uptick rule and other automated mechanisms as warranted and maintain order to prevent market closures and collapses, runs on the markets and electronic instability. They are required to monitor activity to prevent market manipulation, including participants' use of high-speed cables, lasers or other technologies for pricing advantages, front running, and other types of malfeasance, and report such incidences to the regulators.

The exchanges also have to remain technologically agile and fluent with new technologies and methods developed to infiltrate and disrupt market activity and must advise regulators periodically of their efforts to do so. No more software installations shortly before the market opens without ensuring first that doing so will not shut down trading. In addition, the exchanges must be able to communicate with each other and maintain contingency plans to seamlessly route activity to other exchanges in the event of a power outage, electronic failure or technological sabotage.

AND WHAT ABOUT THE STATE AND FEDERAL REGULATORS?

The volumes of binders and pages that make up the Commerce Clearing Corporation's state securities manuals attest to the numerous unique statutes developed by each and every state to regulate securities and insurance transactions within its borders. Currently, federal securities law takes precedence over state law, leaving states no real latitude to create unique rules. This continues in our model. In addition, a number of state regulators work with local companies to raise capital. Our paradigm encourages them to continue that engagement, replacing securities regulation activities with a focus on corporate governance.

In many ways, the concept of whole market regulation is not new to most states. What might be challenging are the product orientation mindset and the no-longer-required disclosures once the initial registration is approved. The emphasis on monitoring broker, dealer and advisor activities for fraudulent customer activity may become more labor-intensive for some state agencies, although they have the option of adopting federal structures and relying on those regulators to oversee securities activities within their borders. We encourage the North American Securities Administrators Association to work with the states to develop a comprehensive regulatory structure that compliments the new paradigm.

Federal Actors

The Department of Labor has long had a finger in securities regulation in its consideration of broker-employee (such as those in Goldman Sachs or Merrill Lynch branch offices) vs. independent contractor (think Edward Jones). More recently it entered the fray again with the Executive Branch's decision that it should enforce broker compliance with its interpretation of fiduciary duty. While we concede that both issues fall within labor parameters, we believe the Department of Labor's involvement adds to the regulatory confusion, particularly since fiduciary standards are already contained in SEC statutes.

Other actors include the Financial Securities Oversight Council (FSOC) and the Financial Stability Board. The most salient aspects of the Council appear to be its mandate for shared information across all aspects of the financial markets (a first)—if nothing else, it gets the top SEC, CFTC and Treasury officials in the room at the same time—its affiliation with the also newly created Office of Financial Research at the Treasury, and its ability to designate non-banks for heightened supervision or reporting requirements. While the intentions of the Dodd-Frank Act were to include all relevant parties in oversight discussions, the boards are too big and too broad to effect substantive change and add to the confusion about who is responsible for what. The relevance of FSOC is also questionable. At House Financial Services Committee hearings to review FSOC reports, the Treasury Secretary has been peppered with questions about controversial policy decisions that have no bearing on FSOC's scope of oversight, while questions about the contents of the report appear to be an afterthought. The Financial Stability Board, on the other hand, is composed of the members of the G-20 major economic countries and other foreign ministries. Its purview is global in nature. While it is also so large as to be unwieldy, the focus on global markets oversight and stability is more relevant now than ever before and therefore it would stay in our regime.

The disposition of other actors under our framework is self-evident. The Treasury's recently created FinCEN is easily absorbed by the Justice Department, along with SEC efforts at regulating money laundering activities and enforcing violations, as part of a comprehensive data center on enforcement and prosecution of financial crimes. And, ideally, the Office of Financial Research moves out of the Treasury's offices and its jurisdiction expands to become an advisory organization for the triad, similar to what the Congressional Budget Office is for Congress. The development of a center for research on emerging trends and in product development, deceptive practices and, most importantly, technological advances, such as intrusion techniques, data manipulation, and systems management, promises comprehensive research across all securities markets platforms. In addition, it can model the proposed policy changes to estimate their effects across markets, projecting more comprehensive perspectives than the currently proposed legislation requiring cost-benefit analyses prior to adoption of subsequent rule implementations or policy changes proposed as part of the Dodd-Frank Act.

The orientation of the CFPB, another independent watch-dog agency created by Dodd-Frank, is charged with protecting consumers from fraud, manipulation and other forms of malfeasance within the financial markets. Its activities have centered around commercial banking and payday lending to date; however, our model expands the agency's reach to protect customers of securities products. The CFPB functions as a federally funded consumer advocate, working hand in hand with the SEC to identify and prevent deceptive practices and ensure consumer rights.

In our efforts to create singular, comprehensive regulation, our model curtails, consolidates and in select cases, expands the participation of these ancillary actors. Making any and all of these changes, however, requires legislative action. We talk more about that in chapter 9.

Brokers and Managers and Advisors, Oh My!

In our world, brokers and advisors continue to work with customers to help them buy and sell investment products, although customers now have other options. Fiduciary oversight becomes the domain of the SEC alone and investigation of customer complaints, particularly those involving fraudulent practices, may be shared with the CPFB, which is already charged with ensuring consumer protection in regard to other financial products.

For the most part, broker-dealers and brokers undergo some of the biggest changes. In keeping with the toaster metaphor, various companies sell slightly different toasters, all with labels that customers can use for comparison-shopping. But some companies put out better toasters than others; some customers are brand loyal, regardless of performance; and some customers can buy those toasters cheaper at some places than others. Where brokers and broker-dealers make their mark is in their commitment to their customers. It is in their best interest to be on the side of the customer, to be their advocates, their personal Consumers' Report. Simplifying the process in this way discourages market, currency and client manipulation.

When it comes to the role of broker-dealers in our new world order, for the first and only time, the authors disagree. We see the roles of brokers, dealers and advisors differently. We do agree that those who buy and sell products for customers must be licensed to do so. It is after that that we part visions. On the one hand, there are advantages to allowing broker-dealers to hold customer funds and products. Doing so facilitates sales and enables customers to see everything they own in one statement. On the other, however, breaking these functions out into separate entities eliminates the power brokers and broker-dealers have over their customers' funds and accounts through control of all of the customers' holdings. In this case, one broker-dealer is the retailer, similar to a boutique or big-box store, where you go to purchase or sell a product. Another broker is a "personal shopper"—your very own broker or advisor. Yet another broker-dealer is the place where you house your products, perhaps a bank or new type of holding institution of some type.

Our disagreement may become a moot point. This second scenario becomes increasingly feasible as transactions and payments become digital and portable. The advent of blockchain allows for life-time custody records, a genealogy of sorts, that can transcend the need for an account and trade documentation. The advantages of this technology have been recognized by numerous too-big-to-fail-sized wire houses, many of which are in the process of developing proprietary blockchain systems for use in-house and with customers. And after years of controversy over Bitcoin and the advent of Apple Pay and its competitors, digital payments and virtual currencies, and the advent of crowdfunded investment pools and similar digital, anonymous investment platforms, are quickly becoming the norm. As these technologies are increasingly embraced, the location of one's securities products or bank accounts are becoming totally irrelevant to the buying and selling processes.

The disassociation of these functions then begs the question of the need for SIPC. If broker-dealers no longer hold customer accounts, insolvency would not be an issue for them—however, similar safeguards would need to be applied to the custodial institutions.

LICENSING AND REGISTRATION

The vast variety of licensing available now (see Appendix C for the two-page list of licensing options, taken from FINRA's Form U-4 [uniform registration form]) would be replaced by a single exam that covers all products—securities, commodities and treasury securities—as well as advisory strategies, such as rules and requirements pertaining to fraudulent activity and examples of best practices and state regulatory information. Those who supervise individuals who work with customers to purchase and sell securities products, as well as the principal sales manager (CEO or other senior management), must also complete the exam. That's it. No special exams for principals or traders or currency specialists, etc. There is just one comprehensive exam for those who engage in and supervise customer-product interactions.

The purpose behind the licensing requirement is simple: brokers, managers, and advisors need to know exactly what actions constitute misrepresentation, manipulation, fraud and other forms of malfeasance so they know exactly what not to do and what the penalties are if they do. Remember the driver's license reference in chapter 4? Well, similarly, this is no different from knowing what the rules and then what the penalties are when, for example, you run a red light.

Right now, disciplinary action is generally handled by the SROs, particularly for securities. In our world, it is handled by the justice system. Either the US Department of Justice or a state attorney general, depending on the crime and jurisdiction. And make no mistake, defrauding customers is a crime. That was the consensus after the 1929 crash. After the 2008 crash, and particularly after the deceptions by brokerage firms regarding the composition and rating of some derivatives and their use of swaps to insure against loss when the they collapsed, it is important to re-emphasize the importance of that concept.

The focus of our 21st century broker-dealers shifts away from a myriad of compliance directives to this concept of fraud prevention. Now broker-dealers function as retail sales outlets, placing buy and sell orders for customers through exchanges and handling bundled products and return policies (see chapter 9 for details). They may choose to differentiate themselves through concierge services or other customer service orientations. The same holds true for investment advisors. For the firms themselves, the lengthy, elaborate registration process is also eliminated and replaced by a simple notification statement to the SEC. The simplification of the products themselves and elimination of the most speculative products from the realm of transaction possibilities makes the need for the onerous registration and licensing process irrelevant.

There is one other licensing requirement, however, and that is for compliance officers. Currently, these are the individuals charged with ensuring that the brokers and advisors employed by the firm, and the firm itself, engage in fair and honest dealings with all customers. They make sure transaction records and contingency plans are accurate and up to date, facilitate the transition to blockchain or other virtual recordkeeping and prompt and proper payment, via virtual currencies when applicable, and ensure that technical and electronic advancements are incorporated and protected. They are responsible for maintaining anti-fraud practices, including the use of appropriate advertising and communications, even through the use of ever-changing social media and Internet sites, reporting violations to the appropriate regulatory agency and coordinating on-site or electronic investigations with the regulators.[25] They will no longer, however, have to take all the individual compliance principal and FINOP exams—there will be just one compliance exam to meet compliance licensing standards.

Registration requirements for exchanges and clearing corporations are similar to those of broker-dealers. For exchange personnel, only those who facilitate trades for individual retail or institutional customers would be required to be licensed. Both exchanges and clearing corporations must have at least one licensed compliance officer to ensure that they are aware of their obligations regarding anti-fraud and market manipulation. But registration of the organization itself is simply by notification to the three regulatory authorities, with submission of data and periodic reports to assist the regulators in preserving market stability.

The minimal licensing and registration structure contained in our model makes the complex regulatory repository obsolete; however, we are not throwing the baby out with the bathwater. FINRA's Central Registration Depository, or CRD, has long been a well-developed system for registration and licensing. In our vision, the CRD continues its function as the repository for exam requests, exam development and testing and registration notification filings—but as a function of the SEC. Its activity is much more streamlined, however, than it is now. Instead of dozens of exam options there are just the two. Firms, exchanges and clearing corporations submit registration notifications[26] and periodic reports for purposes of review and data collection. This makes it possible for the SEC to monitor activity for fraud, misrepresentation, market manipulation and other such actions. Because the SEC is a federal organization, this data is required to be made available to the public through its website and by request.

Regulating Investors

By and large customers are expected to abide by and be held to the same anti-fraud standards as brokers and advisors, exchanges and clearing firms. Consumers buy and sell products directly with issuers, exchanges, broker-dealers, individual owners and other resellers. And while they do not have to be licensed to do so, they are subject to and have to abide by all of the 10b-5 anti-fraud provisions. How do they know about this? The requirements are spelled out on all of the regulatory agencies' websites, in plain language, so that every consumer could easily understand them. In addition, a boiler-plate reminder, in the form of a disclaimer, is printed on all product labels. If customers engage in misleading or fraudulent activities, they will likely find themselves the subject of a customer complaint, which would be investigated by the CFPB. Alternatively, a customer could be the focus of a SEC, CFTC or Treasury investigation and subject to prosecution by the Justice Department or a state attorney general. Findings of fault by the CFPB would also be subject to judicial action.

*   *   *

Our vision is a tall order. We're talking about radical structural changes to a system mired in dysfunction, power dynamics and politics. Changing existing laws and taking authority away from the SROs will certainly be an arduous uphill climb. Shifting the composition of FSOC to create a regulatory triad and advisory board or steering committee will surely engender resistance from current members. Restructuring the SEC, CFTC and Treasury to the new oversight configuration would require legislative action and likely prompt resistance from the SROs as they realize the extent to which their authority would dwindle.

While all that may take a miracle or more, the shift to a product-oriented market could possibly be easier to implement and more palatable to issuers and investors. The advantages are apparent—the elimination of disclosure requirements and clear, informative product labeling to allow for informed purchases and sales of investment products, to name just two. But that would also open up investing to more of the public and dramatically demystify investments and the need for complex and complicated licensing structures, something the Wall Street crowd may oppose.

The practical aspects of this new system place heavy emphasis on stable, sustainable markets, accomplished by a robust anti-fraud regulatory orientation and the strong commitment by all parties to keeping up with current and emerging technologies. In this way we can truly address the weaknesses that led to the market crashes in 1929 and 2008. Instead of trying to plug leaks while others continue to spring up, we can build the new levees necessary to prevent the next catastrophe.

Notes

1. What emerged from President Reagan's task force was a 396-page document entitled, "The President's Working Group on Financial Markets" (first mentioned in chapter 4). One of the Commission's recommendations was to "coordinate a few critical inter-market issues cutting across market segments and affecting the entire financial system; to monitor activities of all market segments; and to mediate concerns across marketplaces. . . . It must have broad expertise in the financial system as a whole," vi.

2. Ibid., vii.

3. Mary Jo White, *Testimony on of the Financial Stability Oversight Council.* Testimony before the Committee on Financial Services, United States House of Representatives (Securities & Exchange Commission, Dec 8, 2015), http://www.sec.gov/news/testimony/testimony-oversight-financial-stability-oversight-council-white.html.

4. London Stock Exchange Press Release, *London Stock Exchange Group Launches New Derivatives Venture-Curveglobal* (Oct 2015), http://www.lseg.com/resources/media-centre/press-releases/london-stock-exchange-group-launches-new-.derivatives-venture-curveglobal.

5. Tracy Alloway & Matt Scully, "Wall Street's Thinking About Creating Derivatives on Peer-to-Peer Loans." *Bloomberg* (Apr 15, 2015), http://www.bloomberg.com/news/articles/2015–04–30/wall-street-s-latest-craze-meets-small-short-in-new-derivatives.

6. Voting members include heads of the US Treasury, SEC, CFTC, The Federal Reserve, OCC, CFPB, FDIC, FHFA, NCUA and an Insurance representative selected by the President. Non-voting members include Director of the Office of Financial Research, Director of the Federal Insurance Office, a state insurance commissioner, a state banking supervisor and a state securities commissioner.

7. "Employment of manipulative and deceptive devices," *Cornell University Law School, Legal Information Institute, 17 CFR 240.10b-5* (n.d.). It can be accessed at http://www.law.cornell.edu/cfr/text/17/240.10b-5.

8. Not only has review of corporate filings been a resource consuming activity, it has been highly ineffective, as evidenced by Fannie Mae, Enron, WorldCom and even GAO reports that provide evidence that the SEC is unable to effectively monitor corporate financial filings.

9. US Securities and Exchange Commission, Division of Corporate Finance, http://www.sec.gov/corpfin.

10. I.e., Government National Mortgage Association (Ginne Mae), Tennessee Valley Authority bonds, GARVEEs (US transportation bonds, see https://www.fhwa.dot.gov/ipd/finance/tools_programs/federal_debt_financing/garvees/), and other organizations' offerings that are backed by the full faith and credit of the US Government.

11. Since 2010 there have been 51 municipal bankruptcies, nine for local governments, including Detroit, Michigan; Sacramento, San Bernardino and Stockton, California; and Boise County, Idaho. See "Bankrupt Cities, Municipalities List and Map," *Governing* (n.d.), http://www.governing.com/gov-data/municipal-cities-counties-bankruptcies-and-defaults.html.

12. Michael Lewis, "The Secret Goldman Tapes," *Bloomberg View* (Sept 26, 2014), http://www.bloombergview.com/articles/2014–09–26/the-secret-goldman-sachs-tapes. The article also references a number of related articles, videos and podcasts.

13. According to "How to get rich off the weather," *CNN* (Sept 2009), "You can actually make money speculating that the temperature in Sacramento, California, will be warmer than it normally is. If that's too dull for your portfolio, you can put money down on the inches of snowfall next winter in Boston, Massachusetts, or the strength of hurricanes in the Gulf of Mexico." Read the rest of the story at http://edition.cnn.com/2009/LIVING/wayoflife/09/14/mf.get.rich.off.weather/.

14. *Cornell's Legal Information Institute* details the differences in federal and state gaming requirements, https://www.law.cornell.edu/wex/gambling.

15. See Title 1 of the 1934 Securities Exchange Act, http://www.sec.gov/about/laws/sea34.pdf#page=671.

16. Scott Patterson, "High Speed Traders Turn to Laser Beams," *Wall Street Journal* (Sept 2014). High-speed traders are using fiber-optic cables, microwaves and laser beams to get an edge on trading execution. This would undermine fair practices, giving a few advantages over all others who access the exchange. In addition, exchanges would be prohibited from sharing their proprietary technology with select institutions or individuals who can afford to pay for them.

17. Federal agencies must collect and share data with the public as required by the DATA Act in 2017, http://www.datacoalition.org/what-is-data-transparency/data-act/.

18. CFTC website, Mission and Responsibilities tab, http://www.cftc.gov/About/MissionResponsibilities/index.htm.

According to the website, "The CFTC's predecessors in the Department of Agriculture dates back to the 1920s, but the Commission was formally created as an independent agency in 1974. The Commission historically has been charged . . . with regulatory authority over the commodity futures markets. These markets have existed since the 1860s, beginning with agricultural commodities, such as wheat, corn and cotton."

19. Eric A. Posner and E. Glen Weyl, "A Proposal for Limiting Speculation on Derivatives: An FDA for Financial Innovation," 1314.

20. A cash market where securities are traded and the transactions settled (paid for) immediately, or on the spot.

21. According to the USDA (2015) "Risk is an important aspect of the farming business. The uncertainties inherent in weather, yields, prices, government policies, global markets, and other factors that impact farming can cause wide swings in farm income. Risk management involves choosing among alternatives that reduce financial effects that can result from such uncertainties." The five types of risk in agribusiness are: production risk, price or market risk, financial risk, institutional risk and human or personal risk, http://www.ers.usda.gov/topics/farm-practices-management/risk-management/risk-in-agriculture.aspx.

See also, Eric A. Posner and E. Glen Weyl, "A Proposal for Limiting Speculation on Derivatives: An FDA for Financial Innovation."

22. We recognize that not everyone sees the purchase of every derivative as a form of gambling. *See e.g.*, Eric A. Posner and E. Glen Weyl, "A Proposal for Limiting Speculation on Derivatives: An FDA for Financial Innovation," 8; Lynn Stout, "Why the Law Hates Speculators: Regulation and Private Ordering in the Market for OTC Derivatives," *48 Duke L.J. 701* (1999) and Timothy Lynch, "Gambling by Another Name: The Challenge of Purely Speculative Derivatives," *17 Stan J.L. Bus. & Fin. 67* (2011). However, we believe that, with the exception of people in the agriculture industry, the line between social utility and socially problematic is not worth the cost of drawing—particularly because it would then allow others to find the loophole they so often crave. To our way of thinking, we would rather have a bright line to maintain order and integrity in the markets than an ambiguous one that can lead to turmoil and disruption again. That is not to say, however, that we would be against certain forms of insurance—as long as it is exactly that—insurance and nothing more.

23. *The Institution of Experience: Self-Regulatory Organizations in the Securities Industry, 1792–2010*, Securities and Exchange Commission Historical Society, http://www.sechistorical.org/museum/galleries/sro/sro04b.php.

24. Noticeably silent from our discussion in this chapter is the role of private litigation. That is because by and large we think the role will remain unchanged. In the same way that current private litigants can bring 10b-5 class actions, litigants in this new paradigm would be able to do so. However, given the changes to legislation for class actions discussed in chapter 3, whether these private litigants would be effective is another matter. We leave that debate to others.

25. Part of our disagreement about whether broker-dealers should hold customer funds and securities pours into the discussion of licensing. Some broker-dealers and clearing firms will likely hold customer funds and securities, at least through transition to our model. The integration of blockchain and virtual and digital currencies and other advances may eliminate the need for them to hold funds and products regardless of when and whether we make the transition. During the transition, however, any broker-dealers or clearing firms who hold customer funds and products would be subject to the reserve capital calculations currently required by the SEC.

26. For those of you in the financial services industry, think Form BD without the drawn-out approval process.

CHAPTER 8

Oh Captain, My Captain!

THE NEW MODEL FROM THE CORPORATE PERSPECTIVE

In order for us to build this levee, one thing is clear: we're going to need a lot of workers. In this chapter, we focus on those who can help get us there—the Captains of Industry—corporations and their executives. Many of them will have different reasons for wanting to build the levee—some want more freedom to use their corporate vehicle to make the world a better place. Others want more freedom to make better businesses, period. In either case, the structure that we outline has enough flexibility for both types of businesses to thrive. At the beginning of the chapter we talk about the current dilemma that industry, any industry, must face in trying to compete for capital. We then present portraits of two types of companies—those that are concerned about social issues and those that are focused purely on profit. We discuss how these entities can benefit from this new structure. Then, we move on to the details—a step-by-step analysis of how each of these corporations can bring their products (in this case *all* of their products) to market in our new system, providing a granular level view of structures and issues of corporate governance from this new perspective.[1]

The Problem Today

Traditionally, closely held businesses that want to become publicly traded corporations face a dilemma. On the one hand, registering their securities allows corporations to have access to a much wider audience for capital and markets for its products. Unfortunately, the initial startup costs to do so—to go public (to use the widely used but slightly inaccurate vernacular) are enormous. By some estimates, the costs to go from being a privately held to a publicly traded corporation range in the millions.[2] This makes the adage "it takes money to make money" ring true in regard to publicly traded corporations like nowhere else.[3]

Publicly traded corporations have tolerated the trade off, by and large, because often the benefits have been seen to be almost limitless, whereas the disadvantages amounted to little more than periodic filings. However, the weight of regulation has become more and more burdensome, prompting some to go so far as to voluntarily deregister their securities—in effect, "going private."[4]

What is the impetus behind such an extreme reaction? For some, it is simply a matter of not wanting to maintain the tedious, and some would say irrelevant,[5] filings that they need to satisfy regulation. The onerous reporting requirements prevent them from focusing on what really matters: the company itself. In addition, it seems that, apart from regulators, most people simply do not care what a company puts in its quarterly reports. As we have noted several times, these disclosures have no apparent bearing on whether or not investors purchase a security. Nor does it matter to regulators. Companies can, and have, simply amended an erroneous filing.[6] As long as disclosures are made on time, the stability of the business or the product offered is also irrelevant.

SEC filing and disclosure requirements—the type and frequency of reporting requirements and the content of those reports—are ripe for reform. Even the SEC admits it. In its 2013 report to Congress (required by the Jumpstart Our Business Startups or JOBS Act), the SEC reported that reforms are in the works. The SEC intends to solicit input from corporations about how to best restructure the requirements and work with the Financial Accounting Standards Board to "identify ways to improve the effectiveness of disclosures in corporate financial statements and to minimize duplication with other existing disclosure requirements."[7]

Their efforts come none too soon. The private sector has long argued that the requirements are impracticable and do not necessarily add value.

> Legitimate concerns have surfaced about the increasing volume, complexity and immateriality of corporate disclosure. Current and former SEC Commissioners have questioned whether investors are well served by the detailed disclosure about all the topics that companies currently provide in reports filed with the SEC. As disclosure documents become increasingly lengthy, legalistic, complex and repetitive, they may fail to clearly convey material information to investors.[8]

So, imagine for a moment that businesses could have it both ways: they could have access to the tremendous capital embodied in today's securities markets *without* having to account to regulators and shareholders, quarter after quarter, for how they make their money and what they plan to do with it. That is embodied in our new paradigm.

Of course, this new framework will not create a utopia for businesses. There will be costs of moving to this system, some different and less burdensome, and some—particularly for corporations initially going to market—that will be considerably greater than in the current structure (we talk about why at the end of this chapter). But we believe that, on the whole, our system will create better than a net win for businesses.

Consciousness Raising, Business Style

One of the most interesting trends that has occurred in the last few years is the emergence of two separate but, as Joanne Bauer and Elizabeth Umias state, parallel movements in the business community: (1) the business and human rights (BHR) movement and (2) the rise of the social benefit corporation.[9] These movements have some shared goals and ideologies. Their aim is to assist businesses in "maintaining a 'wide aperture' so that all impacts of a company on people and communities are understood and addressed."[10] Both the BHR movement and the B-Corp phenomenon have been touted as potential solutions to the classic, although some would say mythological, dilemma of the publicly traded corporation—namely the problem of shareholder primacy or, more specifically, being required to make decisions that are solely in the best financial interests of the shareholders to avoid, in the extreme, becoming a target of litigation.

Under our emerging market regulatory structure, you can buy B-Corp stock as a niche market, just like you would shop for specialty clothes at a trendy/sustainable/conscious boutique. These businesses, in turn, would be free from the burden of justifying their actions through a shareholder profitability lens. This, then, would allow them to truly do financially well and do good at the same time.

The trend toward incorporating business and human rights issues into the current securities regulatory framework has already begun. For instance, the Dodd-Frank Act requires the SEC to promulgate rules that require companies to

---

Business and human rights is not an oxymoron!

It is a growing field that emerged in the last decade. It is based on the ideal that as corporations are becoming increasingly global and increasingly involved in development, they have an enormous impact—both good and bad—on the communities in which they operate. To the extent that these impacts have been negative, there is a growing consensus that countries and corporations need to be part of the conversation about how to mitigate these negative impacts.

report on whether any of their products contain minerals from the Democratic Republic of Congo—an area rife with conflict. When the SEC did put forth such a rule, it was immediately challenged by businesses in court. Eventually, the measure was partially struck down. Ironically, a similar measure that the SEC promulgated regarding issues related to "the resource curse,"[11] and which was also challenged in court, resulted in a bit of whiplash. After the SEC lost the battle in trial court, they declined to appeal, stating that they would instead reword the rule. Then, in 2015, the SEC was subjected to *another* court order, this one stating that the agency wasn't working fast enough to rework the rule. Clearly, when it comes to securities regulation of business and human rights issues, contradictory instructions from legislators and the judiciary make progress almost impossible. Perhaps allowing those businesses that truly care about these issues to take the lead might be the best way to make regulators *and* businesses happy.

The goal of most corporations, however, is to act as profit driven machines that will grow based on and within the current legal structure. The "greed is good"[12] movement is still alive and well.[13] Since the 2008 crash, publicly traded corporations have continuously posted record-breaking profits.[14]

The beauty of our new system is that your businesses can be both (a socially conscious company and a profit maximizer)—or rather, what they want to be (within the bounds of the law) and still be able to access capital. If you want to be the next Patagonia and operate as a publicly traded B. Corp, you can do so without concerns of shareholder litigation or investors arguing that your decision to remain a "mission driven" company[15] prevents them from maximizing their profits. Similarly, if you are All About the Profits, Inc.,[16] you can exercise your right to maximize profit without having to worry about the impact that your profits will have on those who want to expand the reach of 10b-5[17] or, quite frankly, *any* shareholder who thinks they have the right to tell you how you run your business. Instead, since everyone knows that when you buy a share you are buying a product—think of it as the Wall Street Rule on steroids[18]—corporations finally get the relief of running their operations exactly how they see fit. This is feasible because the product labeling required for every issue would also be required to include information about social issues, therefore allowing the consumer to decide before investing.

Nowhere can this relief be seen more than in the disappearance of quarterly reports. This allows companies to focus on the things that matter instead of on periodic reporting that has analysts making mincemeat out of stock prices if earnings fail to meet projections by even a penny. Companies are no longer beholden to the whimsical nature of analysts' reports and investors quirks because neither investors nor analysts have any say in the nature of the company. The value of analysts' reports, you may recall, now resemble those from *Morningstar* or *Consumer Reports*. They provide consumers with valuable assessments of the products themselves, including pertinent information about the companies that offer them.

We understand why businesses may be reluctant to embrace our world. The current market regulatory system has created (either because of or in spite of) a system of wealth that, for the top 1 percent, is the greatest that has been witnessed in human history. Why change a system that has done nothing but make them rich beyond their wildest dreams?[19] Allow us to offer a reason. Or more specifically, a date: October 27, 1929.

That was the day *before* the beginning of the most devastating crash in the history of the stock market—the day before the origins of the Great Depression, where everything changed in America.[20] Now we are sure that if anyone had approached Charles E. Mitchell (of Citibank) on that day—and prognosticated that bankers were at a pinnacle of their wealth and power the likes of which would not be seen again for *the rest of their lives,* he would have scoffed.

Now, move a little closer in recent memory: September 17, 2008.

Many have argued that if the federal government had not intervened, the resulting carnage in the stock market would have made the Great Depression seem like a slight downturn in comparison. The truth is that the government intervening because industries are "too big to fail" can only work if the industries do not become so big that the government can no longer *stop* them from failing. Think back to chapter 1—how do you stop a tsunami with a crumbling dam? Even the Hoover dam isn't big enough if the water is bigger.

A comparison of the wealth of the government with the wealth of Wall Street in 2014 shows that the federal government brought in $3 trillion in revenue.[21] In 2012 the World Bank calculated US financial markets' total market capitalization at $18.7 trillion, with other sources estimating growth since then of about $3 trillion, bringing the current total to over $21 trillion. "Depending on which index you look at there are roughly 3,500 to 4,000 public, exchange-listed companies in the United States."[22] From the global perspective, in 2013 assets under management amounted to approximately $68.7 trillion, with more than half of that ($34 trillion) in North America alone.[23] An analysis of "global stock of debt and equity outstanding" in the OTC markets only, found that in mid-2013 investors held $62 trillion in unsecured lending, $50 trillion in equities, $47 trillion in government bonds, $42 trillion in financial bonds and $25 trillion in OTC derivatives.[24] Dam, meet your tsunami.

The current model for trading in our securities markets is not sustainable for two reasons. First, it is built on a model that privileges short-term profits over long-term gains and stability. When the markets are based on short-term earnings and, more specifically, reports of those earnings, the market becomes inherently more volatile as analysts' predictors frequently fail to align with a company's actual earnings. This is augmented by the increased reliance that the market places on these earnings reports. Volatility can also be increased by the rise of technology that, as we mentioned before, completely divorces the company from the stock. Therefore, to the extent that there are any traders left who focus on the fundamentals, they frequently execute trades that send conflicting signals to the market. Similarly, even among algorithmic traders, since formulas in quant shops are top secret, the market can again receive conflicting signals. Further, in the aspects where they are making the same trades (albeit based on different underlying determinations), they can create tremendous one-way activity that can shock the market as a whole. We call this the bandwagon effect.

The second reason the current trading patterns are not sustainable is the fundamental and slow moving nature of regulation. As the 2008 financial crisis so aptly demonstrated, our current regulatory structure is ill-equipped to deal with increasingly exotic products (such as credit default swaps) that are often times specifically created to evade regulatory oversight. Moreover, since these types of investments are frequently not tied to any underlying asset, there is no tangible (frequently corporate) investment that is being purchased. This, in essence, creates competition for corporate issues without any corporate skin in the game or the same regulatory scrutiny. In our system, companies have a much more level playing field in competing for investors' (or consumers) dollars.

As of this writing, there are approximately 3,700 corporations listed on US exchanges, less than half of that in the mid-1990s.[25] We certainly would not ask any of them to undergo an intensive registration process all over again, particularly since they have been submitting quarterly and annual reports since their registrations were first approved. As it is, the current regulatory framework does not have the capacity to audit those entities.

To be fair, we propose a short, less intense process for those companies that are currently listed on exchanges. Once our new structure is accepted, these entities would be grandfathered in, having only to provide current information through a simplified submission, similar in scope to what companies currently have to do for a WKSI offering. WKSI stands for Well Known Seasoned Issuer. A WKSI offering allows a currently listed public company to sell shares directly to the public without having to go through the voluminous paperwork suggested by an initial public offering. Similarly, as we make this transition to the new framework, those companies which have been on exchanges for the longest amount of time will still have to go through the initial process but on a much more truncated level then those which will go through it for the first time. Sure there will be some extra work initially, but then companies can fix their attention on being productive and profitable. For those companies wanting to go public, the new process is more rigorous initially but much simpler afterward.

What It Looks Like On the Ground, Step by Step

STEP 1: BUILD YOUR BUSINESS

Right now, if you want to take your company public, you must submit a number of filings to the SEC and provide extensive disclosure. As part of the process, the SEC reviews the registration application and provides comments on the *disclosures,* using only the information provided to determine whether or not the statements accurately and materially reflect the corporation's assets and its present and future viability.

In the new paradigm, extensive SEC review and auditing procedures remain in place, but the focus is markedly different. In addition to assessing the disclosure statements to ensure that the *information* is accurate, the SEC gauges the viability of the corporation. Specifically, they look for whether or not the current operations have generated a positive cash flow in the preceding years.

It should be noted that this structure also differs slightly from the current merit review system used by some states.[26] Under a merit review system, the regulator has the right to reject an offering if it believes that the underlying product is not commercially viable. Under our system, the market will have already signaled the commercial viability of the company through investment in and revenue generation, based on sales of the products or services offered. So, for instance, if Apple wanted to go public, the regulators would not have the right to pass judgment on the value of the personal computer. Instead, they could only examine the extent to which consumers believed in the product and whether the company has been able to effectively translate those sales into a stable, viable business model.

Start-up companies need not apply. Instead, companies that are not commercially viable but have promise have to rely on venture capitalists and sophisticated investors for sustainment until they become a consistently profitable corporation—one that can be bought and sold on the exchanges.[27] In this scenario, the SEC, through its rule-making process, provides clear, specific benchmarks for what it would take to qualify for an initial public offering. Companies that meet the criteria can apply for listing on an exchange, while those that do not would not be eligible to even apply.

As companies work toward meeting registration qualifications, they may employ exemption options to build capital and gain expertise. The SEC's Reg A, Reg D and Crowdfunding exemption options currently allow companies to raise funds from qualified investors. Those options continue to be supported—in fact encouraged—in our model.

For example, imagine for a moment that you are an entrepreneur with the *next big idea* (congratulations, by the way!). You have been smart with your business plan and have methodically worked through all the kinks. Initially, you used start-up funding to provide financing for your operation. That start-up funding may have come from various sources: through one or more of the many exempt crowdfunding offerings that the SEC allows or through traditional venture fund investing or even simple bank financing. Up to this point, very little has changed from our current regulatory practices. All the challenges and rewards that a start-up business faces today are still relevant in our new model. The biggest changes happen in Step 2 . . .

STEP 2: GENERATE A PROFIT

Here is where we separate the old from the new, the speculative from the stable. At this stage, Mark Zuckerberg would have waited on the sidelines a while longer before being able to bring Facebook to market. As would Jeff Bezos. And Steve Jobs. In the disclosure regime this is where venture capitalists—or the company executives—look at the promise and potential of a company and raise working capital by offering its securities to the public. The company may go public based on their big idea or business model but possibly before they have actually made a profit, or have even come close.

How to skip Step 2:

Let's say that you have made the best widget. We mean *the best widget*, ever. People are weeping over your genius and extolling your brilliance in song. Well, you might just be able to bypass this waiting game. How? Buy being bought out by a big (already registered) company.

Here's what it would look like on the ground:

In step two you secure funding through a variety of ways. If one of those ways is through a Reg A, Reg D or crowdfunding offering, then there is a strong likelihood that your idea has been noticed by "angel investors" (for a reminder of what that is, see the glossary in chapter 2). Angel investors have contacts, often very big contacts, with CEOs of publicly traded companies who might also be interested in your company. If you are lucky enough to attract their attention, to the point where they want to buy the company from you, then, just like that, you have fast-tracked your product onto the public markets.

In our paradigm, a company must be profitable, and have been profitable for some time, before it is permitted to go public. Going back to the example of the widget startup, now you know you have made the world's best widget. But the initial production costs were much more expensive than anticipated. Once the production hurdles were overcome, the company realized that it had a healthy demand for the widgets and was able to fill all the orders that were placed for your new stellar product. Six months later, you feel confident about your production scheme. Even though the initial start-up costs ate into all of your revenue (and therefore, all of your profit), you are absolutely *certain* that you have honed in on the best way to make a widget—one that will change the world forever. All you need now is to take your product to large scale production in order to take the world by storm. All you need now is to engage in an initial public offering. Except you cannot.

In fact, your company is not ready for the public market. Nor is the market ready for you. Under our framework, only proven companies are able to go through the initial public offering process. These are companies that have shown a profit for at least two consecutive years. For companies that do not meet this benchmark, that may mean that they have to scale back production, or focus on a regional market until they have developed a solid market and are able to demonstrate that the business is commercially viable.

This does not mean that the market will miss out on new, innovative products because we have to wait for companies to be successful. If the demand is there, all the market, and the company, will see is a delay. And, for those companies that could not maintain stable, profitable operations for at least two years, then it seems, the public markets—and investors—are better off without them.[28]

STEP 3: REGISTER YOUR COMPANY WITH THE SEC

For many companies, registration will be the hardest part of our framework. That is a tall statement considering that, under the disclosure structure, registration (i.e., going public) is already the hardest part for most companies. They must file volumes of documents with the SEC to support their request for registration. They must disclose (on form S-1) their financial condition, their business plan and reams of information about their executives. They have to produce letters from their auditors attesting to the soundness of their accounting under Generally Accepted Accounting Principles (GAAP) and support many of their statements with underlying documentation. In short, companies have to bare their souls for the SEC to review.

Admittedly, under our framework the process is even more extensive. The requirement for all pertinent information remains. But now, in addition, the company must provide a good faith analysis illustrating how its business model is sustainable. That must include statements showing that the last two year's profits were generated through sound policies, rather than accounting maneuvers or questionable practices. In short, companies have to justify, to the satisfaction of the regulators, that they have a way of continuing their success. Of course, no one can predict the future. However, having a sense of how the company plans to get there goes a long way to ferreting out the wheat from the chaff.

That is not all. In our model, the regulators have the right to visit company operations, to verify the information that was documented, and to make sure that the information provided can be backed up by what is happening on the ground. In short, the SEC conducts a forensic investigation of every company's application to make sure that everything truly is as described. Unlike the existing process, our registration requirements are intense, intrusive and thorough.

STEP 4: ENJOY YOUR STATUS AS A PUBLIC COMPANY

Now that the process is over—the registration has been approved—it is over for good! There are no ongoing disclosures. The company has been registered and the securities, complete with product labels describing their attributes, have been approved—but the securities are not the company. Rather, they are a product of the company, just like the widgets that are produced. Now you can simply focus on running a successful company. No more quarterly reports, annual reports or disclosures of any kind. Now the company's track record will be what sustains it.

This is where our paradigm becomes more advantageous for business. Once the initial benchmarks have been met and the disclosures have been made, companies are released from disclosure obligations. Of course, disclosure can still be an option for those companies that want to share their successes with the investing public. In fact, companies that want to provide increased transparency can link additional information to the product in a warranty system similar to that used for many of the products currently on the market.[29] In this way, companies may charge a premium for products that are linked to voluntary disclosures or warranties. All companies—including those that do not provide information updates or warranties, are still obligated to comply with regulatory anti-fraud requirements. So, just as with existing regulations, companies that choose to disclose additional information must be truthful about it. The major difference in the system we envision is that companies would not be compelled to share.

Taking the consumer concept still further, all securities are also subject to a federal version of the lemon law framework, similar to the one currently in use in the auto industry. Under this scenario a consumer who is faced with a bad product—a company that closed its doors or stopped production within 30 days of issuing a new line of stock for example—would have the right to return the stock for a full refund.[30] Admittedly this could be merely a paper right if the company is already failing; in that case, the consumer may have to stand in line with all of the other company's creditors.

BENEFICIAL OWNERSHIP

Another advantage of our schema is that corporations can say good-by to the SEC's Schedule 13D filing requirement. Schedule 13D is generally thought of as a "beneficial ownership report." A "beneficial owner" is any person or entity "who directly or indirectly shares voting power or investment power (the power to sell the security)."[31] When an individual or other entity is a beneficial owner of more than 5 percent of a company's securities, notification to the SEC is required.

This is no longer relevant in our regime. Owning 5 percent or 50 percent of a company's products gives the customer just that—ownership of a product. Because they no longer represent the company itself—unlike our current Class A shares of stock, for example—these investment products do not entitle most owners to voting rights or any other rights.[32] This can be liberating for corporations, as it eliminates the possibility of a hostile takeover and any need for poison pills or white knights.

ABOUT OTHER PRODUCTS

By and large all of the above applies to issuers and producers of other securities products including corporate debt, municipal securities, commodities and variable annuities. The process allowing these issuers and producers to bring products to market is similar to an IPO in that they all have to go through an initial registration. Municipalities—states, local taxing districts, airport authorities and all the other government bodies wanting to raise funds through debt offerings—must register with the SEC, unless they qualify for an exemption. Oil producers, mining and agribusiness and all other commodities producers wanting to sell their products will also go through an initial registration process, but with the CFTC.

Once registered, entities are able to bring other issues to market without having to reregister. And, as noted, there are no continuing disclosure requirements. However, they are all subject to labeling requirements, notifications of material changes and other anti-fraud requirements, as well as all the other stipulations applicable to those that issue corporate securities.

This could be particularly challenging for some state and local governments that have experienced fiscal instability. Those issuers that fail to keep up with pension contributions, fail to keep up with payment obligations (whether for debt service, social services or any other contractual agreement) or file for bankruptcy or reorganization relief would have to advise product owners and may find themselves subject to recall requirements. Similarly, commodities producers that benefit from government subsidies (grants, tax expenditures, price supports, etc.) would have to advise product owners of any change in those supports, and could also find themselves subject to recall.

Exchanging a Stock Market for a Stock Mall

Some of the most fundamental differences in our system are the modifications to the exchange structure itself and the relationship of corporations to these newly designed markets. Under the existing system, corporations are listed on an exchange based on market capitalization. For example, if a company's IPO is expected to generate over $10 million (IPO price x the number of shares issued) it would debut on the New York Stock Exchange; however, it would subsequently be traded on other exchanges as well. In our model, market capitalization no longer matters. Each exchange determines the products it wants to facilitate transactions for based on what customers it chooses to serve.[33] This is a complete re-imagining of the markets into marketplaces (or malls).

We envision different types of exchanges that choose to focus on whatever range of products they prefer, perhaps specializing in municipal securities or just corporate securities or commodities or the full range of products on the market. An algorithmic trader would likely choose an exchange that caters to high-speed trading needs, perhaps one that could ensure liquidity. On the other hand, a retail customer may want to buy and sell directly to other retail customers, using an eBay-like exchange to facilitate those transactions. An institutional investor might choose an exchange that can facilitate large orders, whereas a broker-dealer could choose one with whom it could develop wholesale arrangements. An example of this in existence already is IEX, a broker-dealer that matches buyers and sellers to effect off-exchange transactions through their alternative trading system (ATS). IEX's commitments to investor protection and transparency are what drove them to develop their ATS. They only facilitate transactions for broker-dealers, and their business model is solely subscription-based. They recently requested SEC approval to become an exchange, and plan to retain the same business model even after approval is received.[34]

We believe a tailored approach to the markets is advantageous for the exchanges. They are able to purchase products from various sources (directly from the corporations and/or from institutions, broker-dealers, customers, etc.) and structure their activity and price structures (e.g., fees, price spreads, a wholesale/retail structure) as they choose. The only caveat is that they may not structure compensation in a way that gives the payee an advantage over other similar customers. The days of pay to play—such as paying an exchange for faster fiber optic or laser lines in order to get quicker executions—are over.

In addition, they may charge broker-dealers directly for space on the exchange, similar to shelf-space in a store. Under this scenario, broker-dealers presumably charge their customers a higher price for products than a "retail direct" exchange, one that sells directly to the customers. Broker-dealers charge more because they can also provide the consumer with services or incentives not offered elsewhere. For instance, the broker-dealer might offer a return policy (e.g., additional protections beyond what the corporation would be offering). The customer simply chooses the type of broker she wants to interact with, similar to choosing to shop at Neiman-Marcus or Target or Macy's. Broker-dealers are able to offer concierge services and bundle products as long as those products or services do not provide some customers with an undue advantage over others.

Consumers have choices as well. Customers are able to purchase securities products from a host of other sources beyond broker-dealers. Some buy or sell directly from/to the corporation or an exchange, or through a private transaction with someone they know or through an auction arrangement such as eBay. Others keep their products in an electronic account with the broker-dealer or advisor,[35] or have them delivered to/from a bank or holding institution, or take them home and keep them under their mattress—and all the permutations in between—as they so choose.

Consequently, exchanges may choose to engage directly with retail consumers, similar to a mall or flea market structure. In this instance, they facilitate investor transactions between each other, act as a retailer in direct competition with broker-dealers or facilitate transactions through auction sales, again similar to the eBay model.

Other exchanges may choose to service algorithmic traders. Presumably these exchanges would see the greatest trading volumes. They also must pay constant attention to execution activity and the latest developments in cyber-technology and related protections since computerized trading happens at lightning speed, and these traders are always looking for ways to give themselves an edge on their competition. Like the other exchange structures, this group structures their profit network however they choose, such as flat transaction fees, fees or percentages based on the number of shares traded or percentages of the spread between transactions. They may also charge for ultra-high speed networks or other infrastructure or service accommodations. As noted in earlier chapters, algorithmic and institutional traders currently have an advantage on retail customers. The difference in our world is that the exchanges are responsible for monitoring market activity to make sure that traders do not use existing ploys or devise new ones to get a leg up on each other.[36]

Finally, the exchanges are required to develop a coordinated, comprehensive electronic system that allows them to communicate with each other and respond instantly to any market calamity. This will enable the exchanges to remain nimble and responsive to a run on a product for example, regardless of what marketplace that the run occurs on, and allow for an immediate, coordinated response. This can be accomplished in one of two ways—with some sort of supra organization coordinating the flow of the information (acting as a monitor) or via a liaison within each of the exchanges that is responsible for coordinating the information with counterparts at the other exchanges. Of course, each exchange retains the ability to "flip a switch" and halt trading on their own system. In addition, they are still required to monitor stability within their own exchanges.

Why are we structuring the exchanges this way? Part of the challenge for today's markets—and there are so many challenges—is that retail investors and institutional investors are playing in the same sandbox while playing different versions of the same game. Matching exchanges with trading preferences reduces those challenges and makes for a much more stable system. It also provides clear lines of demarcation for the different types of buyers and sellers. Finally, it may be that the exchanges can largely reorganize themselves to accommodate this new world order without too much legislative or regulatory change required. We consider that in the next chapter.

Investing vs. Gambling

Many of the products currently being touted as viable investment products are anything but. We are referring to options, futures, derivatives, and swaps. There is no underlying asset, nor have any of these products had to pass muster through any regulator. Customers, from individuals to pension funds, purchase them thinking they are investing when they are actually gambling. Yet, the current regulatory structure legitimizes these investment choices, leading to a false sense of security (pun fully intended) regarding the value of these assets.

These products have traditionally had a significant role to play in the investment markets, often allowing investors to hedge their bets (again, pun intended). Yet we argue that these instances often involve a gambling stance, such as "betting on the weather" when buying orange juice futures, or betting on foreign political leadership when buying currency futures. There is no dispute that these alternatives offer investors viable options, but, because there is no underlying asset, calling them a security is a misnomer.

Where do they fit in our paradigm? As noted in earlier chapters, they belong with all the other gaming activities—in the casinos—and are subject to oversight by federal and state gaming commissions. If you are able to place your bet on commodity futures or derivatives while staring over the Strip, at least then you'll know for sure you are gambling.

In our model, the registration process for companies wanting to bring their securities to market involves a much more thorough screening, including a vetting process that verifies the *information* contained in the disclosures. While more onerous at the start, it is a one-and-done process; no further disclosure is ever required. The only exception is if the company undergoes a material change, such as a merger or acquisition or reorganization filing. In keeping with the anti-fraud orientation of the new paradigm, material changes must always be disclosed to the regulators as well as consumers. Our paradigm also opens up a host of advantages for exchanges and customers in how they choose to buy and sell securities products, allowing them to facilitate transactions in the venue(s) and partners of their choice.

Notes

1. Parts of this chapter build on Jena's extensive work on business and human rights, including a two-day conference she organized in 2013 that brought together academics from across the nation and the world, as well as practitioners, government officials and people from industry.

2. According to one report, one-time costs alone are over $1 Million. See Price-waterhouseCooper, *PWC Deals Practice, Considering an IPO? The Costs of Going and Being Public May Surprise You* (Sept. 2012), https://www.pwc.com/us/en/transaction -services/publications/assets/pwc-cost-of-ipo.pdf. Not to mention the continued costs of disclosure now that the company is a reporting company with quarterly and annual reporting obligations.

3. Jo Confino, "Will Unilever become the world's largest publicly traded B Corp?," *The Guardian* (Jan 2015), http://www.theguardian.com/sustainable-business/2015/ jan/23/benefit-corporations-bcorps-business-social-responsibility.

4. Kerig Green Mountain Coffee, whose stock price has fluctuated between $40 and $140 in the last year, is the most recent of a number of companies to "go private."

5. More and more investors are saying that disclosures, as currently created, are useless. For instance, Brian Barnier, an analyst at ValueBridge Advisors says that corporations "'can use 1,000 words and say nothing' [and] they often 'disclose far too little of value to fundamental investors.'" Emily Chasan, "Investors: Filings are for Searching, not Reading," *The Wall Street Journal* (Jun 2, 2015), http://blogs.wsj.com/cfo/2015/06/02/investors-filings -are-for-searching-not-reading/. The SEC seems to be responding. In 2013, as part of rule-making under the JOBS Act, they began a project to increase disclosure effectiveness. See *Disclosure Effectiveness*, https://www.sec.gov/spotlight/disclosure-effectiveness.shtml. Again, it's the right problem but the wrong solution.

6. For example, Fannie Mae amended its financial filings several times during the 1990s.

7. SEC Staff Release, *SEC Issues Staff Report on Public Company Disclosure* (2013), 269, http://www.sec.gov/News/PressRelease/Detail/PressRelease/1370540530982.

8. Holly J. Gregory, "SEC Review of Disclosure Effectiveness," *Practical Law: The Journal, Transactions & Business* (Jun 2014), 29.

9. As Joanne Bauer and Elizabeth Umias state, they are not the same thing. Generally speaking, the B-Corp movement is a largely unified movement of primarily small and medium sized enterprises that provide companies with the flexibility to look at larger social policies rather than simply the financial impacts of its operations. The Business and Human Rights Movement, in contrast, requires companies to take into account how their operations may have negative human rights impact and (one hopes) minimizes those negative externalities—either voluntarily or through force of law. Joanne Bauer and Elizabeth Umias, "Making Corporations Responsible: The Parallel Tracks of the B Corp Movement and the Business and Human Rights Movement," *Social Science Research Network* (Aug 24, 2015), http://ssrn.com/abstract=2650136 or http://dx.doi.org/10.2139/ssrn.2650136.

10. Ibid.

11. Have you ever noticed that the countries (or even states) that have the greatest amount of resources are often the poorest and most disadvantaged? Yeah, that's the resource curse. There are many theories for why this is so—some blame corruption, others discuss weak governance systems. So much so that the SEC (through Congressional edict) has tried to get companies to disclose it. Want to know more? See Ben Geman, "The Resource Curse, Big Oil, and the Dodd-Frank Battle that Won't Die," *The Atlantic* (Dec. 11, 2015).

12. As a side note, when we originally typed this quote we realized that we had written it as "greed as god." We wonder now if that is the more accurate statement. The Gordon Gekko "greed is good" speech, from the 1987 movie, *Wall Street*, can be heard in its entirety at https://www.youtube.com/watch?v=PF_iorX_Maw.

13. The idea that we are acknowledging (and perhaps even encouraging) the profit at all costs ethos causes great trepidation for the authors. Jena, in particular, a firm convert to the BHR field, realizes that there may be significant backlash among her colleagues in the movement regarding what this will imply in the field. Her response is quite simply this: like it or not the business and human rights movement has gained widespread acceptance and recognition, including among some of the world's largest corporations. However, within this world of widespread acceptance, there is a huge divide regarding the *means* to achieve that. And all of those approaches are helpful. You need someone to advocate for legislation. And you need someone to work with the business community to develop best practices. And you need someone else to give voice to the voiceless regarding the negative impact some businesses are having on the community. Sometimes it can be the same person. Sometimes it can't.

14. A 2010 article noted: "Corporate profits have been doing extremely well for a while. Since their cyclical low in the fourth quarter of 2008, profits have grown for seven consecutive quarters, at some of the fastest rates in history. As a share of gross domestic product, corporate profits also have been increasing, and they now represent 11.2 percent of total output. That is the highest share since the fourth quarter of 2006, when they

accounted for 11.7 percent of output." Catherine Rampell, "Corporate Profits were the highest on record last quarter," *The New York Times* (Nov 23, 2010), http://www.ny times.com/2010/11/24/business/economy/24econ.html. And they just kept setting new highs. Two years later CNN noted, "In the third quarter, corporate earnings were $1.75 trillion, up 18.6 percent from a year ago, according to last week's gross domestic product report. That took after-tax profits to their greatest percentage of GDP in history." Chris Isidore, "Corporate profits hit record as wages get squeezed," *CNN Money* (Dec 4, 2012), http://money.cnn.com/2012/12/03/news/economy/record-corporate-profits/). And finally, in 2014, "Corporate profits are at their highest level in at least 85 years. Employee compensation is at the lowest level in 65 years . . . before taxes, corporate profits accounted for 12.5 percent of the total economy, tying the previous record that was set in 1942, when World War II pushed up profits for many companies." See Floyd Norris, "Corporate profits grow and wages slide," *New York Times* (Apr 4, 2014).

15. "Patagonia Becomes a California Benefit Corporation" (quoting from a press statement by Patagonia CEO Yvon Chouinard), http://www.treehugger.com/corporate-responsibility/patagonia-becomes-california-benefit-corporation.html http://ga-institute .com/Sustainability-Update/2014/11/24/benefit-corporations-and-the-public-markets -will-we-ever-see-a-public-benefit-corporation/.

16. Just to be clear, *All About the Profits, Inc.* doesn't really exist as a corporation. Yet.

17. As of this writing we are unaware of any case that has been successfully brought against a corporation for a 10b-5 violation based on failure to disclose negative human rights impacts. However, shareholders have used shareholder proposals in the past to bring to light corporate activities that may implicate human rights. *See, e.g.*, State Ex Rel. Pillsbury v. Honeywell, 191 N.W.2d 406 (Minn. 1971).

18. For those of you who are not familiar with the Wall Street Rule it is when a shareholder, unhappy with the policies or decisions of a corporation, decides to divest of the corporation's shares. For more on the Wall Street Rule and its effect on corporate governance, see Corporate Governance, *Ending the Wall Street Walk: Why Corporate Governance Now?* (n.d.), https://corpgo.fatcow.com/forums/commentary/ending.html.

19. Unless of course you just happen to have very *very* big dreams.

20. And which, not coincidentally, gave rise to some of the most exigent measures in the recorded history of the stock market.

21. The White House, Office of Management and Budget (OMB), *Historical Tables* (2015), https://www.whitehouse.gov/omb/budget/HistoricalsTable 1.1—Summary of Receipts, Outlays, and Surpluses or Deficits (-): 1789–2020, https://www.whitehouse .gov/omb/budget/Historicals.

22. The World Bank 2015. Data: Market Capitalization of Listed Companies (current US$), http://data.worldbank.org/indicator/CM.MKT.LCAP.CD. In "Where is the Money? World Market Cap and Sector Breakdown," *Wealthengineers* (Jun 2014). Jonathan Duong provides current estimates of the number of exchange-listed companies and market capitalization.

23. Boston Consulting Group, "Global Asset Management 2014: Steering the Course to Growth," *BCG Perspectives* (2014), https://www.bcgperspectives.com/con tent/articles/financial_institutions_global_asset_management_2014_steering_course_ growth/?chapter=2.

24. "Anatomy of the OTC Market," from *The Value of Derivatives* (International Swaps and Derivatives Association 2013).

25. Barry Ritholtz, "Where have all the public companies gone?" *Bloomberg View* (Jun 24, 2015).

26. And would hopefully prevent the rise of the now infamous rejection by Massachusetts authorities of Apple prior to its initial public offering.

27. Of course, under the SEC's current rule making for Regulation A and (in the near future perhaps) for Regulation Crowdfunding, this might in fact be an easier slog for some corporations than it is currently. However, that may very well signal that some of these new regulations may also have to be revised so that they do not amount to a giant loophole that a corporation can use to perpetually evade the onerous burden of an initial public offering.

28. Don't believe us? Think of all those wonderful, innovative companies that had IPOs during the dot.com phase. Those wonderful household corporations like Webvan.com, geocities, theGlobe and, of course Flooz.com. No? Not ringing any bells? There's a reason for that. For a list of the ten biggest flops from that era and a little bit of their backstory see http://money.cnn.com/galleries/2010/technology/1003/gallery .dot_com_busts/3.html. In reviewing the companies, CNN's assessment reads like an op-ed piece for our platform. These companies went bust because, among other reasons, their "business model wasn't sustainable" (Pets.com), the company's "customer base and margins weren't large enough to support all of the planned expansions" (Webvan.com) or simply because of the "stupidity of its concept." Our contention is that none of those companies (or at least, very few of them) would have made it to market (and into investor's portfolios) under our framework. Or, and this is also a possibility, they *would* have made it to market but under a much more stable model.

29. So for instance, if you want to provide a warranty to your stock, you would simply add that to your listing. It could even be indicated by a simple W at the end of the ticker symbol. In that way, consumers would know that this particular stock came with a warranty. The company (or re-seller) would then provide the consumer with the details of that warranty prior to purchase so the consumer could take that information into account in making her purchasing decision. Obviously, the company and then the re-seller would have the right to sell that particular W stock at a premium. Since no warranty lasts forever, when the warranty runs out, the W would disappear from the ticker symbol.

30. Similar to the right of rescission that is currently available to investors under Section 12 of the Securities Act.

31. SEC, *Schedule 13D* (2015), http://www.sec.gov/answers/sched13.htm.

32. As we mentioned earlier, there may be some corporations that still have shareholders with voting rights (either from when they were privately held corporations or as a special incentive for shareholders), however, this will not be the norm in our regime.

33. Keep in mind, under this vision penny stocks would go away because they would not be able to pass the IPO muster.

34. IEX operates an Alternative Trading System ("ATS") supporting displayed and non-displayed trading. IEX also operates a Smart Order Router ("SOR") to route unfilled portions of orders to trading centers displaying protected quotations . . . They

conduct compliance monitoring of all trading on or through the ATS [platform] and of the system itself. More at http://www.iextrading.com/about/.

35. Again, full disclosure: we disagree on this point. As we discussed in detail in the broker-dealer discussion in the previous chapter, we are of two minds: one in which funds and product may be held by the broker-dealer or advisor, and the other where product advice, sales and delivery functions are disassociated. For the most part we assume the latter; however, in transition from here to there and until the applicable technologies are more fully realized, we consider both options.

36. For a well-documented discussion of the phenomenon, see Michael Lewis, *Flash Boys: Cracking the Money Code.*

CHAPTER 9

Building a New Levee

We have described at length what our holistic market structure looks like in theory and in practice. In some ways it is a monumental leap from where we are now, in others it is nothing more than a small step forward. Where do we begin? How do we get there from here? We begin by getting the dialogue started.[1] But who should be included in those conversations and what parts will they play in moving the ball?

In this chapter we look at what it takes to start building a new levee. Not simply a dike this time, but a permanent yet flexible structure that can withstand any external force. Our model and suggestions for implementation are feasible because they are practical—they adapt regulation to current practices—and because they are designed to appeal to policymakers from all political parties. The reduction in regulatory requirements should appeal to conservative views and those on Wall Street, while freeing up more socially conscious corporations from having to answer the ever persistent call of profit maximization from shareholders should appeal to liberal perspectives. Both public companies and those planning to become one are likely to embrace our plan.

We also look briefly at how making the switch benefits global markets by examining threats posed to global economies from current practices and structures, such as those triggered by social media and electronic order activation, and ways that this new paradigm minimizes those risks. In addition, this shift provides the US with the ability to take the lead in developing a collaborative global markets paradigm and regulatory structure. The chapter concludes with a preliminary analysis of how this new system might be received by markets and market regulators worldwide.

Calling in the Army Corps of Engineers[2]

The culturally accepted definition of insanity is doing the same thing over and over while expecting different results.[3] Yet that is an accurate description of what reform has looked like over the last few decades. Even the Dodd-Frank Act's 2,300-plus pages call essentially for keeping the status quo—but with more commissions. An equally popular meme is that the first step toward change is admitting there is a problem.[4]

The securities markets have a problem. We all know it. The trick is in getting those who can truly effect change to admit it and then do something *different* (maybe read this book!) to develop solutions. And to do so before the next tsunami hits. It's a tall order, we admit.

The first step is to get everyone talking. By "everyone" we mean all those involved in the securities markets system. From brokers and broker-dealers, exchanges, and clearing corporations located throughout the country, to the regulators and policy makers, of course, but also representatives of publicly traded corporations, municipal issuers, and commodities producers, fund managers, individual and institutional investors, traders and others not noted here but who should be. Our system is not perfect, nor is it the only way, but it is a start. A truly holistic solution requires inclusion. All voices must be heard. Not just those in Washington.

Politics with a Capital "P"

It would literally take an act of Congress to change our entrenched regulatory structure. The Banking and Securities Acts of 1933, the Securities Exchange Act of 1934, the Maloney Act and the myriad legislation passed to accommodate the financial services industry as it has evolved have to be overcome to accommodate this new paradigm. To do that, indeed, requires Congressional legislation. That sounds daunting, but the idea is not completely without precedent.

Removing and rewriting portions of the foundational securities laws, originally thought to be sacrosanct, has been done to some extent already. In 1999, for example, President Clinton signed the Gramm-Leach-Bliley Act, which effectively repealed the Glass-Steagall Act.[5] Revising and removing out of date, ineffective and redundant requirements that were enacted over the decades and retaining those with applicable value to today's concerns would go a long way toward creating new regulatory capacity.

The establishment of open Congressional hearings, such as those conducted by Ferdinand Pecora when our current and then groundbreaking regulatory structure was being considered, is another way to begin the march forward.

Hearings such as these enable all parties to share their perspective of how our paradigm prevents or mitigates the next big crash and how they might tweak it to better suit their needs and concerns.

These hearings also offer an opportunity to develop consensus. Using our paradigm as a preliminary discussion blueprint is an effective way to begin because it touches on every aspect of the system—in it no one is immune from change. It also offers advantages for everyone in that it reduces regulation while making it more effective, largely eliminates disclosures and makes it easier for organizations to raise capital and protects investors.

A transition of this magnitude takes considerable time and money, especially at the start. Our plan is to begin with the SEC, in which portions of existing divisions are phased out or reconfigured to reduce, change and add functions to develop their new responsibilities. For example, we expand the division charged with registration to accommodate the more extensive application evaluation process. The staff allocated to processing disclosures and managing the EDGAR system, however, continue with the division but undergo extensive training to take on registration analysis. Consequently, the overall net result is not so much an expansion as a reorientation.

Other aspects, such as identifying, investing in and gearing up to use and monitor cutting-edge technologies, require a substantial investment, and, once accomplished, staying current with advancements and keeping security up to date to prevent cyber intrusion requires a steady commitment of funds. Working with SROs to absorb records, some functions and personnel where possible and absorbing or developing a proprietary version of the CRD also requires initial funding, but, once operational, the significant reduction in oversight and licensing activities, supported by user fees, enables the registration and records system to become self-supporting and ultimately provide cost savings. Similar conversions, transition costs and cost savings are anticipated for the CFTC and Treasury, but, because their scope is more focused than that of the SEC, their transitions are expected to be less dramatic and costly.

Once completed, this transition is projected to result in real cost savings for taxpayers. The expanded issuer registration process is more than offset by the efficient regulation and divesture of disclosure and enforcement responsibilities. As noted, these costs are covered by implementation of examination, licensing and registration fees.

What would prevent Congress from taking such bold action to prevent an inevitable future crisis?

No one likes change, and Congress is no different. And make no mistake, this is a big change. In addition, Congress is not inherently motivated to change existing law when it comes to the financial markets. Historically, it has been more expedient for them to point to the SEC and accuse it of falling down on the job.[6] Another reason for resistance to this change is the ability of Wall Street to influence policy-making and rule-making processes. One way they do this is by contributing heavily to lawmakers' election efforts. Contributions to the Chairman of the House Financial Services Committee and the Subcommittee on Capital Markets and Government Sponsored Enterprises topped $5.5 million between 2010 and 2015; the top financial industry donors were JP Morgan Chase and Citibank, respectively.[7]

> In the current election cycle, employees and political action committees of financial companies have donated nearly $149 million to congressional candidates, more than any other industry, according to data compiled by the Center for Responsive Politics. That's more than two-and-a-half times the $57 million donated by the health care sector, the second-most-generous industry.[8]

Also, Wall Street lobbyists are famous for their influential relationships with members and have been known to use those relationships to strong-arm regulators, especially those involved in development of rules and implementation policies for sections of the Dodd-Frank Act. "There are more than 2,000 lobbyists for financial firms and trade groups and many are spreading money around Washington, enlisting like-minded members of Congress to write letters, propose legislation, hold hearings and threaten agency budgets as they pressure regulators to ease up on banks."[9] So despite public clamor for Wall Street reform, lawmakers generally have no inclination to bite the hands that feed them.

> . . . if you follow the money, it's obvious why so much work remains to be done on financial reform. This year alone [2010], Wall Street spent a staggering $251 million fighting financial reform. . . . lawmakers who voted with Wall Street on both the bailout and reform received nearly *triple* the campaign cash of those who opposed Wall Street [between 2007 and 2010].[10]

In addition, some members have family ties to the financial industry, prior work experience or close personal friendships with individuals at Wall Street firms. The Banking Caucus, as it is known on the Hill, includes Chairman Jeb Hensarling (R-Tx.) and Subcommittee Chairman Scott Garrett (R-N.J.) as well as Reps. Shelley Moore Capito (R-W.Va.), Sean Duffy (R-Wis.), Jim Himes (D-Conn.), Blaine Luetkemeyer (R-Mo.), Gregory Meeks (D-N.Y), Ed Royce (R-Calif.), David Scott (D-Ga.), Steve Stivers (R-Ohio), and Ann Wagner (R-Mo.).[11] All have ties to Wall Street.

Consequently, industry firms have considerable sway over lawmakers when it comes to changing—and enforcing—securities laws. As Senator Elizabeth Warren points out in her discussion of the aftermath of the 2008 crisis,

As stories of illegal behavior in Massachusetts and across the country tumbled out, Wall Street plotted its strategy. Instead of owning up, huge financial services companies took a different approach: They set new spending records hiring an army of lobbyists to shift attention away from their wrongdoing.

The big banks and their allies followed a now-familiar game plan: Launch an offensive against anyone trying to enforce the law with rigor; work overtime to block serious investigation of illegal activity; and persuade the government to accept a slap-on-the-wrist settlement to absolve their violations of the law.[12]

These same Wall Street firms have also been very involved in writing legislation and interpretative administrative rules.

In a sign of Wall Street's resurgent influence in Washington, Citigroup's recommendations were reflected in more than 70 lines of the House committee's 85-line bill. Two crucial paragraphs, prepared by Citigroup in conjunction with other Wall Street banks, were copied nearly word for word. (Lawmakers changed two words to make them plural.)[13]

Conversely, Congress' relationship with the regulators has been anything but cozy. They have been loath to increase the SEC's budget for some time. In the last few years alone, the agency has used its budget justifications to make the case for increases needed to comply with additional auditing and reporting stipulated by the Dodd-Frank Act and also to adequately complete its mission. In their most recent request, the SEC notes, "stated simply, the SEC's jurisdiction is vast and its mission is critically important. The SEC needs substantially more in the way of resources to fulfill its mission to investors, companies, and the markets"[14] Yet between the constant use of continuing resolutions[15] and the rare passage of omnibus appropriations, the SEC continues to make the same case over and over with no success. Congress has no problem adding to the SEC's responsibilities without providing the wherewithal to do so—and the doing so enables them to pontificate about how the SEC is inadequate to its tasks. A change of the magnitude that we are proposing would require a corresponding budget—at least initially. Such a request would have to include illustrations of future cost savings and increased efficiencies, as well as some real convincing, to make it out of committee.

There are also entrenched interests within other agencies. Many of the bureaucrats at the regulatory agencies, the Treasury, the Federal Reserve, and the myriad commissions, "grew up" at the largest Wall Street firms such as Goldman Sachs, Morgan Stanley, Citibank and JP Morgan Chase. While their influence is not as great as the Wall Street moguls, many have provided Congress with expert testimony and advice. But not everyone is averse to telling the emperor he has no clothes, as a former SEC Commissioner notes:

> Rather than responding appropriately to the crisis, which would include developing a modern regulatory system with the flexibility to adapt to changes in the global financial system, we instead have been saddled with an increasingly prescriptive and inflexible regulatory environment that is characterized far more by *more* regulation than by *smart* regulation. Put another way, Congress, in fact, *did* let a crisis go to waste. The calls for proactive reform contained in the various reports I mentioned were ignored when the patient was on the operating table. Far from cured, things have, indeed, gotten even worse. To extend the analogy, under the surgeons' care, the patient's infection turned into sepsis.[16]

As such, accomplishing the shift to a different regime can only occur with buy-in from all constituents and agreement on the underlying implications: the legislative and regulatory hurdles to be overcome; the revised oversight structures and training needed to reorient the SEC, CFTC and Treasury; and the access to information—a new level of transparency—available to market participants. On a fundamental level, implementing this form of regulation is demonstrative of one of the tenets that the SEC has fought hard to guarantee: market stability—free from any and all forms of manipulation. In that regard, the SEC's role now shifts significantly from corporate focused regulation—which would be within its purview in the initial registration only—to product regulation and market sustainability.

How might we achieve buy-in? A first step is to ensure that all stakeholders are aware of the benefits for them in this conversion. For the most part, it is obvious. Corporations are big winners, with little or no regulation—other than the anti-fraud emphasis—once they have gotten past the initial registration hurdle. This is a real boon for the current 3,700 public companies who will be grandfathered in via a simplified initial registration during the transition. The elimination of ongoing disclosures (other than game-changing activities, such as a bankruptcy filing) also means better market stabilization (no more quarterly earnings fluctuations, for starters) which, in turn, means more stable securities prices. This also translates to a more stable market for commodities producers and municipal issuers as well.

Customers (retail, institutional, algorithmic, et al.) also come out on top. Segregating the issuer from the product is already being done to a large extent in practice. Our model simply acknowledges the obvious and ensures the advantages of that structure to all consumers. It makes product information and execution opportunities equally available to all consumers. And it creates more ways for customers to buy and sell products—an advantage to corporations and other issuers as well.

Further, our streamlined regulatory structure replaces the pile of confusing, conflicting regulation with a regulatory triad and simple, easy to understand requirements. It shifts the focus for all those in the financial markets back to prevention of fraud, manipulation and deceptive practices through the use of current technologies and proactive engagement with budding innovations. This allows the regulatory bodies to be more efficient with less, while still providing comprehensive coverage.

We understand that institutions prefer to preserve their power. Most fight to retain what they have. And we expect the same here. Our paradigm will not please the SROs or the host of other agencies and organizations who no longer have a role, primary or supporting, in securities regulation. There is hope, however: the regulatory bureaucrats have already acknowledged that they are not keeping up with investigation, enforcement or technological advancements, let alone able to develop proactive or innovative systems. Not only would refocusing allow it, it would require it.

Of course we could just wait for the next crash . . .

> . . . following a bust, there is often a regulatory backlash leading to new and tighter rules for regulators to enforce. This contrasts with the attitude in boom times, when there is often a push toward deregulation or business-friendly application of existing rules. It is paradoxical that, while the role of the regulator might well be to 'take away the punchbowl just when the party starts getting interesting,' the reality is that the punchbowl is only willingly ceded up when the party is well and truly over. This syndrome fuels what has been called a cycle of decay and growth of regulation[17]

Small "p" Politics

You will notice that we have not mentioned soliciting retail consumer buy-in—perhaps because retail consumers have no clout. Retail investors do not contribute to campaigns, run in the social circles with the 1 percent or hobnob with corporate and government leaders.

Less than half of Americans—48 percent—own investment securities. That's down from 65 percent in 2007. And of those, only 14 percent actually own shares in a company, such as Apple or Google. More people own cats than stock. More than twice as many own dogs, or tablets or cigarettes. "One is more likely to encounter a daily tea drinker in the United States than someone with money invested in the stock market—and that includes so-called non-direct investments like mutual funds held in 401(k) accounts."[18]

Many, if not most of the population, are too busy with survival issues to care or know what happens on Wall Street. Wage stagnation, rising health care costs, child care and other debt keep many out of the market. And then there are the "post-recession jitters."[19] People think the market is too risky, opting for safer choices such as real estate or cash. And if they do follow the markets, they do not have the faith in economists and analysis that was there before the crash. "There's a growing sense that the world of investing is for highly specialized, rich professions. . . . In the eyes of most people, this is an extraordinarily difficult game in which the average person is underprepared, under-provisioned."[20]

There are advocates for the disenfranchised and those taken advantage of by the financial markets, such as Warren Buffett, Robert Reich and Elizabeth Warren, to name just a few. Senator Warren's Consumer Financial Protection Bureau (CFPB) has certainly been a step forward in both protecting average Americans and enabling them to participate in various aspects of the financial markets (although, so far it is limited to commercial banking and pay-day lending). We include the CFPB in our paradigm so that it can expand its mandate for consumer protection to those who buy and sell securities products. Since there will be little difference between a stock or bond or toaster, having the CFPB handle customer complaints—a job currently done by an SRO run by investment firms—seems to be a perfect fit.

From Here to There

So, how is it then that reform legislation ever passes? In crises, including market crashes, political entrepreneurs gain attention and electoral success by exploiting popular discontent.[21]

As with most other change that requires legislative action, probably the *second* most effective way to get members of Congress—our representatives—to truly change the structure of the financial markets will be through our votes. Some argue that the smaller, more motivated interest groups are more likely to be successful in the long run.[22] A small strongly motivated group can even dominate a majority.[23] These groups can, and often do, champion their legislators' reelection efforts and can use that strength to help him or her build a coalition to support an idea or legislation. "Ideally, political entrepreneurs can unite and sustain a political coalition of investors, enabling them to resist better-funded special-interest groups."[24]

Or we could simply wait for another crash (the *most* effective way to get representatives' attention). There is no doubt that without substantive change, history will repeat itself—it is simply a matter of time. Crisis breeds an opportunity to overcome legislative inertia.[25]

Global Impact

What happens in America no longer stays in America. Our financial crisis is now the rest of the world's financial crisis, and theirs are ours. Greece, Portugal, China, Italy . . . with every fiscal hiccup our markets responded in kind. Just as our market collapse in 2008 resonated through their economies and markets.

Until recently, the US dominated the global financial markets. We raised more money through more IPOs and saw more money flow through exchanges than anywhere in the world. We set the standards for development and regulation. That is no longer the case.

> Due to its sheer dominance in the global capital markets, the US financial services industry for decades has been able to manage the inefficiencies in its regulatory structure and still maintain its leadership position. Now, however, maturing foreign financial markets and their ability to provide alternate sources of capital and financial innovation in a more efficient and modern regulatory system are pressuring the U.S. financial services industry and its regulatory structure.[26]

Across the global markets, exchanges and regulation have become more sophisticated. The institutionalization of capital markets worldwide is providing added "liquidity, pricing efficiency, and risk dispersion and encouraged product innovation and complexity,"[27] to a world formerly dependent on the US for them. The challenge with that, however, is that "these institutions can employ significant degrees of leverage and more correlated trading strategies with the potential for broad market disruptions . . . [In addition] the convergence of financial services providers and financial products has increased over the past decade."[28] Global collaboration was essential in the development of the Dodd-Frank Act simply because, "for the five biggest U.S. megabanks, about 80 percent of their foreign operations are subject to the jurisdiction of the UK."[29]

The expansion of investments in emerging markets and the advancement of global capitalization and trading capacity brought increased prosperity to many parts of the world. It brought new technologies as well, interconnecting us in ways and at speeds never imagined before. Our new proximity has brought with it advantages and concerns that are a direct result of these technological advancements. Electronic trading, funds transfers and instant communication and news through internet and social media sources have increased the speed, efficiency and liquidity of the markets but have also increased exposure to hacking and other forms of cyber sabotage. As noted earlier, there have been a number of instances that illustrate the global vulnerability of the world-wide securities markets.

Other issues resulting from our 'one-world' perspective sound like a rehash of the assessment of the 1929 crash.

The increasing interconnectedness of the global capital markets poses new challenges: an event in one jurisdiction may ripple through to other jurisdictions.

In addition, improvements in information technology and information flows have led to innovative, risk-diversifying, and often sophisticated financial products and trading strategies. However, the complexity intrinsic to some of these innovations may inhibit investors and other market participants from properly evaluating their risks.[30]

What is important to understand is that we are no longer the regulatory leader. New emerging markets are more technologically proficient, making them more able to take advantage of advancements and opportunities as they arise and also anticipate and respond to market deviations. They are looking at the future of regulation while we are still responding to what happened seven years ago.[31] We had hoped to talk here about how the US could lead the way in coordinating a globally comprehensive, innovative global financial markets paradigm, but without a substantive shift—be it to our paradigm or adoption of other equally forward-thinking strategies—that conversation will be more bluster than substance. And with the global consolidation of the securities markets, our backward approach is more evident every day.

There are reasons to move forward and to do so now. We prefer taking the initiative—at the very least getting the conversation started (and getting the life boats prepared)—*before* the next tsunami.

Notes

1. The idea for starting a conversation is not ours alone. For instance, "The Obama Administration proposals that were embodied in this [Dodd-Frank] Act, by their own admission, 'do not represent the complete set of potentially desirable reforms in financial regulation.' The Act is in fact only a beginning of a dialogue on how to move our financial system into the twenty-first century." Randall S. Krozner and Robert J. Schiller, *Democratizing and Humanizing Finance, from Reforming US Financial Markets, Reflections Before and Beyond Dodd-Frank* (MIT Press, 2011), 4, http://www.library.fa.ru/files/Shiller3.pdf.

2. You know, the folks who come in and build the structures after a flood.

3. See Daniel D'Addario, "'The definition of insanity' is the most overused cliché of all time," *Salon* (Aug 6, 2013).

4. Our thanks to Bill W. for the definition.

5. Depending on who you listen to, the extent of the repeal was significant to non-existent. Robert Reich, President Clinton's former Secretary of Labor, told Bill Moyers that the impact was significant, calling it the cause of the financial crisis. See his article on the *Moyers & Company* website, entitled "Hillary Clinton's Mistake with Glass-Steagall,"

(Jul 15, 2015), http://billmoyers.com/2015/07/16/hillary-clintons-mistake-on-glass-steagall/. Conversely, Yaron Brooks and Don Watkins, writing in *Forbes* ("Why the Glass-Steagall Myth Persists" [Nov 12, 2012]), contend that it had no relationship to the 2008 crash and subsequent bailout of the banking industry. See http://www.forbes.com/sites/objectivist/2012/11/12/why-the-glass-steagall-myth-persists/.

6. Of course this accusation is true, but as noted, the SEC has been asking for the money necessary to complete the ever-increasing Congressional directives for decades.

7. Daniel Wagner & Alison Fitzgerald, "Meet the Banking Caucus, Wall Street's secret weapon in Washington," *Center for Public Integrity.*

8. Ibid.

9. Ibid.

10. Zach Carter, "Crony Capitalism: Wall Street's Favorite Politicians," *Huff Post Business* (Sept 28, 2010), http://www.huffingtonpost.com/zach-carter/crony-capitalism-wall-str_b_742460.html.

11. Ibid.

12. Elizabeth Warren, "Where is Wall Street Accountability," *Politico* (2011), http://www.politico.com/story/2011/12/where-is-wall-street-accountability-069994#ixzz3khnxYSLE.

13. Eric Lipton & Ben Protess, "Banks' Lobbyists Help in Drafting Financial Bills," *Dealbook* (May 23 2013), http://dealbook.nytimes.com/2013/05/23/banks-lobbyists-help-in-drafting-financial-bills/?_r=0.

14. SEC, *FY 2015 Congressional Budget Request,* http://www.sec.gov/about/reports/secfy15congbudgjust.pdf.

15. A Continuing Resolution (CR), allows Congress to fund government at the same levels as were designated in the last passed appropriations bills. In some cases, the most recent budget bill could be 3 or 4 years old. In addition, CR's prohibit the elimination of existing programs, even if they are completed or no longer needed, as well as spending on any new initiatives. Section 23 of the OMB Circular on apportionments under continuing resolutions spells this out, https://www.whitehouse.gov/sites/default/files/omb/assets/a11_current_year/s123.pdf.

16. Daniel M. Gallagher, "Emerging Challenges for Regulating Global Capital Markets," US Securities & Exchange Commission, *Harvard Law School Forum on Corporate Governance and Financial Reform* (2013), http://corpgov.law.harvard.edu/2013/03/27/emerging-challenges-for-regulating-global-capital-markets/.

17. E. Gerding, "The Next Epidemic: Bubbles and Growth and Decay of Securities Regulation" *38 Conn. Law Review* (2006), 393. Quote and text from Jeremy Cooper, "The Regulatory Cycle: From Boom to Bust," contained in *The Future of Financial Regulation,* an edited collection of papers presented at a major conference at the University of Glasgow in Spring 2009. Edited by Iain G. MacNeil, Justin O'Brien (Bloomsbury Publishing, 2009).

18. See Cole Stangler, "As Market Mayhem Grips Investors, Fewer Americans Have a Stake In What Happens On Wall Street," *Int. Business Times* (Aug 25, 2015), http://www.ibtimes.com/market-mayhem-grips-investors-fewer-americans-have-stake-what-happens-wall-street-2067673.

19. Ibid.

20. Ibid., 304, quoting Richard Wolff, Professor of Economics at The New School. Also, Victor Reklaitis & William Watts, "Wall Street will always crush the little guy, but the stock market could be fairer," *Market Watch* (Jul 16, 2015), http://www.marketwatch.com/story/why-the-stock-market-is-unsafe-for-the -average-investor-2015–05–21.

21. John C. Coffee, Jr., "The Political Economy of Dodd-Frank: Why Financial Reform Tends to be Frustrated and System Risk Perpetuated," *97 Cornell L. Rev.* (2012), 1022.

22. Mancur Olson, *The Logic of Collective Action: Public Goods and the Theory of Groups, 2nd Ed.* (Harvard University Press, 1971), 33–36.

23. There are 60 members of the Tea Party in Congress, vs. 535 that make up the combined House and Senate

24. Cole Stangler, "As Market Mayhem Grips Investors, Fewer Americans Have a Stake in What Happens On Wall Street," 304.

25. Mancur Olson, *The Logic of Collective Action: Public Goods and the Theory of Groups, 2nd Ed.*, 309.

26. Henry Paulson, *Blueprint for a Modernized Financial Regulatory Structure* (The Department of the Treasury, 2008), as quoted in Daniel M. Gallagher, "Emerging Challenges for Regulating Global Capital Markets," 302.

27. Ibid.

28. Ibid.

29. Mike Konczal, "Sheila Bair: Dodd-Frank really did end taxpayer bailouts," *The Washington Post* (May 18, 2013), https://www.washingtonpost.com/news/wonk/ wp/2013/05/18/sheila-bair-dodd-frank-really-did-end-taxpayer-bailouts/.

30. Ibid.

31. The DavisPolk, *Dodd-Frank Rulemaking Progress Report,* tells us that "As of the end of the third quarter of 2015, a total of 271 Dodd-Frank rulemaking requirement deadlines have passed. Of these 271 passed deadlines, 193 (71.2%) have been met with finalized rules and rules have been proposed that would meet 45 (16.6%) more. Rules have not yet been proposed to meet 33 (12.2%) passed rulemaking requirements. In addition, 249 (63.8%) of the 390 total required rulemakings have been met with finalized rules, and rules have been proposed that would meet 58 (14.9%) more. Rules have not yet been proposed to meet 83 (21.3%) rulemaking requirements." More at http://www .davispolk.com/Dodd-Frank-Rulemaking-Progress-Report/.

Conclusion

This book is a start toward a real solution. We admit there is a problem and offer a solution that embodies an entirely unique structure: a whole-market solution to a fragmented system. Ours is a truly product-oriented investment framework that acknowledges the shift that is already taking place. And it includes an emphasis on technological fluency in order to not only keep up with, but move beyond advancements and cyber threats that are already becoming old-hat.

We do not think this will come easy for anyone, nor do we think it will be fast. In addition to the structural adjustments, educating broker-dealers and exchanges, corporations and other issuers, consumers and the general public and, of course, Congress will be an ongoing process. Our best guess is that it could take between five and ten years to complete the transition. In the meantime, we anticipate a period of life in a parallel universe. But we can't go back to this:

> Across most of the financial regulatory agencies, the deep-seated preference is to depend upon bureaucratic oversight and case-by-case monitoring in preference to more prophylactic rules. But, as prior market crashes show, the same cognitive limitations that blind market participants also cloud the vision of regulators. More objective, market-based tests are possible and desirable, but they have no supportive constituency. As a result, the same regulators who missed the Long-Term Capital Management crisis in 1998, the IPO Bubble in 2000, the Enron and WorldCom failures in 2001–2002, the market timing scandal involving mutual funds in 2004, Bernie Madoff and the Lehman and AIG collapses in 2008 seem likely in time to do it again in the future. Sadly, the inevitability of bounded rationality, . . . implies that eventually we will face another systemic risk crisis.[1]

* * *

The structure as we envision it is really very simple—and largely dependent on emerging technologies. A largely automated structure would make market stabilization easier to ensure, with electronic executions, monitoring and reporting and built-in triggers to respond to disruptions as they happen. It would also provide the means for transparency and knowledge sharing, making insider trading a thing of the past. And virtual records and payment solutions would make fraud and misappropriation easier to detect.

But such systems are expensive to create and maintain, and constant updating to include new innovation will continue to require devoted resources. In addition, these systems are vulnerable to external cyber disturbances—everything from low-level hackers looking for data to sell, to cyber sabotage, to a full-blown terrorist attack. Within the system, dishonest algorithmic traders or hackers could dominate the market for an unpredictable amount of time, putting other investors at a distinct disadvantage. As we, in essence, embrace the machine, we have to continually think long and hard about the potential for how it might be misused and develop solutions. On the other hand, keeping up with innovation will demand equal attention. For example, virtual currencies and recordkeeping, both unfathomable a decade ago, are now ubiquitous.

This new approach is not without its challenges. Because of the fundamental shift that would need to take place, there are many trials that will inevitably rise when this amount of disruption is put into the system.

At its core, a paradigm shift of this magnitude requires us to question, at the most fundamental levels, what the premise of securities regulation should be. For instance, when we discuss regulating the securities markets we often use the term of "protecting investors." But what does that look like when it is investors themselves who are causing problems in the securities markets?

Translating these issues within the current regulatory environment would require an examination of our current structures from a critical, indeed a surgical, standpoint—something we have never done before. For instance, the impact of whole market regulation goes to the heart not only of what we regulate but, moreover, the process by which we regulate. Currently, the general approach to regulation can be seen as a top-down patchwork. Some scholars have reflected on the inadequacy of this approach, commenting that current financial market regulatory structures often reflect limited voices. "Sources of financial market risk, however, may go much deeper in organizations, including down to the level of individual traders embedded in highly complex networks."[2] Similarly, the intended beneficiaries of the financial regulation that is being produced are often much more deeply embedded in the economy and the community than the promulgators of this top down approach are aware.

Finally, something to keep in mind is that very little about what caused the 2008 financial crisis can be connected back to the things that the disclosure regime is designed to regulate. In large part the crisis was caused by bad securities (and the bad actors who developed and sold them). But without a comprehensive process to review products before they go to market, we are left to wonder what does "bad securities" actually mean? Is it the way in which they are packaged? Or the value of the underlying asset and industry? Our new regime treats securities as the products they are and ensures that all customers are given comprehensive information, through a labeling system similar to those used on packaged food, prior to purchase. In addition, issuers are required to advise regulators and customers of any material change to the substance or value of their products, and failure to do so puts them in the sights of the Department of Justice. This emphasis on knowledge sharing is specifically designed to counter the possibility that "bad securities" could trigger another such crisis.

Change is hard. Whether it is adding a new exercise routine or changing your investment profile, even the most basic change comes with risk, uncertainty and ambiguity. And of course, the more radical the change the more intense the reaction and the fear.

And so it is here. We are not in any way impervious to the fact that the change we are advocating is profound—that it requires us to literally demolish the foundations upon which our regulatory financial markets are built and replace them with something else entirely. We also know that the financial markets make up a significant portion of the overall economic well-being of both the United States and, by extension, the world. We understand then that the changes we are proposing will have far reaching consequences for most people alive on this planet (whether they invest or not, are a part of the current financial structure or not). We also understand that we cannot predict all of the consequences of our proposed changes (we lost our crystal ball a few months ago).

But here is what we do know: the way that we are currently operating is not working. It just isn't. And the piecemeal, patchwork, two-steps-forward-five-miles-back response by our regulators, our legislators and society as a whole is doing absolutely nothing but making the problem worse. Hopefully, in these pages we have shown you just why we think this is so and how we think we can make it better. But if you're still not convinced, just look up.

Storm's coming.

Notes

1. John C. Coffee, Jr., "The Political Economy of Dodd-Frank: Why Financial Reform Tends to be Frustrated and System Risk Perpetuated," 1082.

2. Olufunmilayo Arewa, "Financial Markets and Networks—Implications for Financial Market Regulation," *78 U. Cin. L. Rev. 613, 624* (2009).

Current Oversight of the Securities Markets

This table illustrates the numerous agencies and organizations with a hand in oversight of securities practices in some way. They range from the traditional regulatory organizations, such as the SEC and CFTC, to SROs, exchanges, state and federal agencies and judicial offices, to those with a less hand's-on orientation, such as the Financial Securities Oversight Board and the Consumer Financial Protection Board.

	Regulatory Organizations		US Treasury/Federal Reserve Board			Self-Regulatory Organizations (SROs)			State Agencies
	SEC	CFTC	OCC/ OTS	FinCEN	CFPB	FINRA	MSRB	NFA	State
Stocks	x			x	x	x			x
Options	x			x	x	x			x
Corporate debt securities	x			x	x	x			x
Municipal bonds	x			x	x	x	x		x
Mutual Funds	x			x	x	x			x
Exchange Traded Funds	x			x	x	x			x
Variable insurance	x			x	x	x			x
Inflation-indexed Securities									
Government Agency Securities									
Treasury Securities	x		x	x	x	x			
Money market funds	x		x	x	x	x			
Commercial paper	x		x	x	x	x			
Currencies	x	x	x	x	x	x			
Currency futures	x	x	x	x	x	x		x	
Commodities		x		x					
Commodity futures		x		x				x	
OTC derivatives**	x	x		x	x			x	
Other derivatives	x	x	x	x	x	x		x	
Hedge funds**	x								
Investment advisors	x								x
Compliance activities									
Rating agencies**									
Securities (as defined by Article 8 of UCC)+									
Broker fiduciary responsibiltiy									

					Exchanges+					
BATS	BYX	BOX+	C2	CBOE	CHX+	EDGA	EDGX	BX	Phlx	NASDAQ
x	x		x		x	x	x		x	x
x		x	x	x				x	x	x
										x
										x
										x
										x
									x	
										x
										x
										x

	Exchanges+						Other Federal Oversight
	NYSE*+	NYSEMKT+	NYSEAcra+	CBOT	CFE	OC	Dept. of Labor
Stocks		x	x			x	
Options	x			x			
Corporate debt securities	x						
Municipal bonds	x						
Mutual Funds	x						
Exchange Traded Funds			x				
Variable insurance							
Inflation-indexed Securities							
Government Agency Securities							
Treasury Securities							
Money market funds							
Commercial paper							
Currencies							
Currency futures							
Commodities							
Commodity futures							
OTC derivatives**							
Other derivatives							
Hedge funds**							
Investment advisors							
Compliance activities							*
Rating agencies**							
Securities (as defined by Article 8 of UCC)+							
Broker fiduciary responsibiltiy							x

| Attorneys General | | General Oversight | | Private-Sector Nonprofit | |
Federal	State	FSOC-US	FSB-Global	PCAOB	SIPC
x	x				
x	x				
x	x				
x	x				
x	x				
x	x				
x	x				
x	x				
x	x				
x	x				
x	x				
x	x				
x	x				
				x	x

NOTES: +Exchanges also act as SROs *Certain regulatory activities allocated to FINRA in 2007 **SEC registration/disclosure may be required but otherwise unregulated + Article 8 of the Uniform Commercial Code can be found at A34+A34+C27http://NASa.gov

Shaded area illustrates changes made by Dodd-Frank.

KEY: Securities & Exchange Commission (SEC); Commodities & Futures Trading Commission (CFTC); Office of the Comptroller of the Currency (OCC); Office of Thrift Supervision (OTS); Financial Crimes Enforcement Network (FinCEN); Consumer Financial Protection Bureau (CFBP); Financial Industry Regulatory Authority (FINRA) (formerly National Association of Securities Dealers (NASD)); Muncipal Securities Rulemaking Board (MSRB); National Futures Association (NFA); BATS Exchange (BATS); BATS Y-Exchange (BYX); BOX Options Exchange LLC (BOX); C2 Options Exchange (C2); National Securities Clearing Corporation (NSCC); The Options Clearing Corporation (OCC); Stock Clearing Corporation of Philadelphia (SCCP); Chicago Board Options Exchange (CBOE); Chicago Stock Exchange (CHX); EDGA Exchange (EDGA); EDGX Exchange (EDGX); NASDAQ OMX BX (BX) (formerly Boston Stock Exchange (BSE)); NASDAQ OMX PHLX (Phlx); NASDAQ Stock Market (NASDAQ); New York Stock Exchange (NYSE); NYSE MKT (NYSEMKT) (formerly NYSE Amex (NYSEAmex), formerly NYSE Alternext US (NYSEALTR), formerly American Stock Exchange (Amex)); NYSE Arca (NYSEArca); Board of Trade of the City of Chicago (CBOT); CBOE Futures Exchange (CFE); Chiacgo Mercantile Exchange (CME); OneChicago (OC); Financial Securities Oversight Commission (FSOC); Financial Stability Board (FSB); Public Accounting Oversight Board (PCAOB); Securities Investor Protection Corporation (SIPC).

Sources: sec.gov, finra.org, msrb.gov, treasury.gov, cftc.gov, cfpb.gov, nasaa.org, cboe.com, nyse.com/regulation, nfa.futures.org, nasaa.org, fdic.gov/regulations, http://www.dtcc.com/, http://www.batstrading.com/, http://www.c2exchange.com/, http://www.chx.com/, http://www.nasdaqtrader.com/, http://business.nasdaq.com/, http://www.cmegroup.com/, http://cfe.cboe.com/, http://www.onechicago.com/

Securities Markets Oversight Legislation, 1933–2015

Year	Significant Legislation, Decisions & Rules
1933	US Banking Act (Glass-Steagall)
	Securities Act
1934	Securities Exchange Act
1938	Maloney Act (creation of NASD)
1940	Investment Advisors Act
	Investment Company Act
1941	*NASD Uniform Practice Code*
1942	*SEC Rule 10b-5*
1946	*NASD registration of brokers*
	SEC v WJ Howey (defines "security")
1956	Uniform Securities Act
1964	Securities Act Amendments
1968	Birth of *NASDAQ*
1970	Securities Investor Protection Corp (SIPC)
1973	*Chicago Board Options Exchange (CBOE)*
1974	Commodities Futures Trading Commission (CFTC)
1975	Municipal Securities Rulemaking Board (MSRB)
	Securities Act Amendments
1982	Futures Trading Act
	Tax Equity and Fiscal Responsibility Act (TEFRA)
1988	Insider Trading and Securities Fraud Enforcement Act
1989	Financial Institutions Reform, Recovery and Enforcement Act
1990	Securities Enforcement and Penny Stock Reform Act
	Market Reform Act
1996	National Securities Market Improvement Act

Year	Significant Legislation, Decisions & Rules
1999	Financial Services Modernization Act (Gramm-Leach-Bliley Act)
2000	Commodity Futures Modernization Act
2002	New Uniform Securities Act
	Sarbanes-Oxley Act
2009	Fraud Enforcement and Recovery Act
2010	Wall Street Reform and Consumer Protection Act (Dodd-Frank)
2012	Stop Trading on Congressional Knowledge (STOCK) Act
	Jumpstart our Business Startups (JOBS) Act

Sources: Securities & Exchange Commission Historical Society, http://www.sechistorical.org/mUseum/timeline/; Commodities & Futures Trading Commission, http://www.cftc.gov/About/HistoryoftheCFTC/index.htm; CBOE, www.cobe.com; Library of Congress, Congress.gov, Legislation https://beta.congress.gov.

FINRA Licensing Registration (Form U4, p. 3–4)

	Rev. Form U4 (05/2009)
	UNIFORM APPLICATION FOR SECURITIES INDUSTRY REGISTRATION OR TRANSFER
INDIVIDUAL NAME:	**INDIVIDUAL CRD #:**
FIRM NAME:	**FIRM CRD #:**

4. SRO REGISTRATIONS

Check appropriate *SRO* Registration requests.
Qualifying examinations will be automatically scheduled if needed. If you are only scheduling or re-scheduling an exam, skip this section and complete Section 7 (EXAMINATION REQUESTS).

REGISTRATION CATEGORY	FINRA	NYSE	NYSE-MKT	BATS-ZX	BATS-YX	BOX	BX	EDGA	EDGX	NSX	ARCA	CBOE	C2	CHX	PHLX	ISE	ISE GEMINI	NOX	MIAX	IEX	ISE MERCURY
OP - Registered Options Principal (S4)																					
IR - Investment Company and Variable Contracts Products Rep. (S6)																					
GS - Full Registration/General Securities Representative (S7)																					
TR - Securities Trader (S7)																					
TS - Trading Supervisor (S7)																					
SU - General Securities Sales Supervisor (S9 and S10)																					
BM - Branch Office Manager (S9 and S10)																					
SM - Securities Manager (S10)																					
AR - Assistant Representative/Order Processing (S11)																					
IE - United Kingdom - Limited General Securities Registered Representative (S17)																					
DR - Direct Participation Program Representative (S22)																					
GP - General Securities Principal (S24)																					
IP - Investment Company and Variable Contracts Products Principal (S26)																					
FA - Foreign Associate																					
FN - Financial and Operations Principal (S27)																					
FI - Introducing Broker-Dealer/Financial and Operations Principal (S28)																					
RS - Research Analyst (S86, S87)																					
RP - Research Principal																					
DP - Direct Participation Program Principal (S39)																					
OR - Options Representative (S42)																					
MR - Municipal Securities Representative (S52)																					
MP - Municipal Securities Principal (S53)																					
CS - Corporate Securities Representative (S62)																					
RG - Government Securities Representative (S72)																					
PG - Government Securities Principal (S73)																					
SA - Supervisory Analyst (S16)																					
PR - Limited Representative - Private Securities Offerings (S82)																					
CD - Canada-Limited General Securities Registered Representative (S37)																					
CN - Canada-Limited General Securities Registered Representative (S38)																					
TD - Securities Trader (S57)																					
AM - Allied Member																					
AP - Approved Person																					
LE - Securities Lending Representative																					
LS - Securities Lending Supervisor																					
ME - Member Exchange																					
FE - Floor Employee																					
OF - Officer																					
CO - Compliance Official (S14)																					
CF - Compliance Official Specialist (S14A)																					
PM - Floor Member Conducting Public Business																					
PC - Floor Clerk Conducting Public Business																					
SC - Specialist Clerk (S21)																					
FL - Floor Clerk - Equities (S19)																					
FP - Municipal Fund (S51)																					
MM - Market Maker Authorized Trader-Options (S57)																					
FB - Floor Broker (S57)																					
MB - Market Maker acting as Floor Broker																					
MT - Market Maker Authorized Trader-Equities																					
IB - Investment Banking Representative (S79)																					
OS - Operations Professional (S99)																					
AF - Floor Broker - Options (S57)																					
AO - Market Maker - Options (S57)																					
AC - Floor Clerk-Options																					
CT - Securities Trader Compliance Officer (S14)																					
TP - Securities Trader Principal (S24)																					
Other _____ (Paper Form Only)																					

Glossary

Algorithmic trading: Computerized trading using models based on proprietary mathematic formulas.

Alpha model: Part of the *black box trading* system, using algorithms to model and predict the behavior of a security.

Angel Investor: A wealthy person who provides funding for start-up businesses in exchange for ownership equity or debt commitments.

BATS: BATS Global Markets, Inc., runs four U.S. equity exchanges and has branched out into forex, options and European equities.

Black Box: The inscrutable, super-secret portion of an algorithmic investment system that contains formulas and calculations used to generate various types of data, including buy and sell signals.

BSE: Boston Stock Exchange

BSECC: Boston Stock Exchange Clearing Corporation

CBOE: Chicago Board Options Exchange

CBOT: Board of Trade of the City of Chicago

CDO: Collateralized Debt Obligation. A structured financial product that pools together cash flow-generating assets and repackages this asset pool into discrete tranches that can be sold to investors. A CDO is so-called because the pooled assets—such as mortgages, bonds and loans—are essentially debt obligations that serve as collateral for the CDO.

CFE: Chicago Board Options Futures Exchange

CFPB: Consumer Financial Protection Bureau

CFTC: Commodities & Futures Trading Commission

CHX: Chicago Stock Exchange

CME: Chicago Mercantile Exchange

CRD: Central Registration Depository

Dark Pool: A private, alternative trading exchange or forum that is not accessible to the public, and where the size and price of orders are not revealed to other participants.

Derivative: A financial contract whose value is based on, or "derived" from, a traditional security (such as a stock or bond), an asset (such as a commodity), or a market index.

DTC: The Depository Trust Company. NOTE: The DTC is a subsidiary of the DTCC.

DTCC: The Depository Trust & Clearing Corporation

Exchange: A brick-and-mortar or electronic marketplace in which securities are bought and sold.

FCIC: Financial Crisis Inquiry Commission

FDIC: Federal Deposit Insurance Corporation

FICC: Fixed Income Clearing Corporation

FinCen: Financial Crimes Enforcement Network

FINOP: Financial operations principal.

FINRA: Financial Industry Regulatory Authority (formerly National Association of Securities Dealers [NASD])

Floor Broker: Member of an exchange who is an employee of a member firm and executes orders, as an agent, on the floor of the exchange for clients.

FSB: Financial Stability Board

FSOC: Financial Securities Oversight Commission

Fundamentals: Information about a corporation's (or firm's) business model, including but not limited to earnings, dividends, interest rates, and risk evaluation.

GAAP: Generally accepted accounting principles. Generally accepted accounting principles are a common set of accounting principles, standards, and procedures that companies must follow when they compile their financial statements. GAAP is a combination of authoritative standards (set by policy boards) and the commonly accepted ways of recording and reporting accounting information. GAAP improves the clarity of the communication of financial information.

HFT: High Frequency Trading. HFT is a program trading platform that uses powerful computers to transact a large number of orders at very fast speeds. It uses complex algorithms to analyze multiple markets and execute orders based on market conditions. Typically, the traders with the fastest execution speeds are more profitable than traders with slower execution speeds.

IEX: Investors Exchange Group

Institutional Investor: Organizations that invest, including insurance companies, depository institutions, pension funds, investment companies, mutual funds, and endowment funds.

Investment Company: A firm that invests the funds of investors in securities appropriate for their stated investment objectives in return for a management fee.

IPO: Initial Public Offering. An IPO is the first sale of stock by a company to the public. A company can raise money by issuing either debt or equity. If the company has never issued equity to the public, it's known as an IPO.

MSRB: Municipal Securities Rulemaking Board

NASAA: North American Securities Administrators Association (NASAA)

NASDAQ: NASDAQ Stock Market

NFA: National Futures Association

NSCC: National Securities Clearing Corporation

NYSE: New York Stock Exchange

OCC: Office of the Comptroller of the Currency

OTC: Over the Counter. OTC is a security traded in some context other than on a formal exchange such as the New York Stock Exchange. The phrase "over-the-counter" can be used to refer to stocks that trade via a dealer network as opposed to on a centralized exchange. It also refers to debt securities and other financial instruments, such as derivatives, which are traded through a dealer network.

OTS: Office of Thrift Supervision

OCC: The Options Clearing Corporation

PCAOB: Public Accounting Oversight Board

Quant: An expert in managing and analyzing quantitative data.

Securities: Paper certificates or electronic records evidencing ownership of equity (stocks) or debt obligations (bonds).

SEC: Securities & Exchange Commission

SIPC: Securities Investor Protection Corporation (SIPC)

SRO: Self Regulatory Organization. An SRO is a non-governmental organization that has the power to create and enforce industry regulations and standards. The priority is to protect investors through the establishment of rules that promote ethics and equality. Some examples of SROs include stock exchanges, the Investment Dealers Association of Canada, and the National Association of Securities Dealers in the United States.

SWIFT: Society for Worldwide Interbank Financial Telecommunications. A member-owned cooperative that provides safe and secure financial transactions for its members. The organization uses a standardized proprietary communications platform to facilitate the transmission of information about financial transactions.

WKSI: A Well Known Seasoned Issuer. A WKSI offering allows a currently listed public company to sell shares directly to the public without having to go through the voluminous paperwork suggested by an Initial Public Offering.

Definitions taken from: NASDAQ, *Financial Glossary*, http://www.NASDAQ .com/investing/glossary/a, and *Investopedia*, Investopedia.com

Bibliography

21st Century Wire, "'White House Attacked, Obama Injured' AP Tweet Hoax Crashes US Stock Market," (2013).

Tracy Alloway & Matt Scully, "Wall Street's Thinking About Creating Derivatives on Peer-to-Peer Loans." *Bloomberg* (Apr 15. 2015).

Gar Alperovitz, "Wall Street Is Too Big to Regulate," *The New York Times* (Jul 22, 2012).

Jena Martin Amerson, "The SEC and Shareholder Empowerment—Examining the New Proxy Regime and its Impact on Corporate Governance," *30 No. 2 Banking & Fin. Ser. Pol'y Report 2* (2011).

James Angel, Lawrence Harris & Chester S. Spatt, "Equity Trading in the 21st Century," Working Paper No. FBE 09–10 (2010).

Olufunmilayo Arewa, "Financial Markets and Networks—Implications for Financial Market Regulation," *78 U. Cin. L. Rev. 613, 624* (2009).

Stephen Bainbridge, "Federal merit review of securities offerings? No thanks!," *Journal of Law, Politics and Culture* (Apr 2012).

———, "Dodd-Frank: Quack Federal Corporate Governance Round II," *95 Minn. L. Rev. 1779* (2011).

Baker Institute Blog, "Hacking the international financial system," *Chron (The Houston Chronicle)* (Jun 13, 2011).

Nick Baker, "NYSE says software upgrade, not a hacking attack, caused outage," *Financial Review* (Jul 10, 2015).

Oren Bar-Gill and Elizabeth Warren's groundbreaking article "Making Credit Work" in the *University of Pennsylvania Law Review, Vol. 158, No.1*.

Joanne Bauer and Elizabeth Umias, "Making Corporations Responsible: The Parallel Tracks of the B Corp Movement and the Business and Human Rights Movement," *Social Science Research Network* (Aug 24, 2015).

Lucian A. Bebchuk & Jesse M. Fried, "Paying for Long Term Performance," *158 U. Pa. L. Rev. 1915* (2010).

Holly A. Bell, "Regulatory, Go Slow on Reining in High-Speed Trading," *The Wall Street Journal*, A13 (Feb 8, 2013).

Barbara Black, "Introduction: the SEC at 75," *78 Univ. Cin. L. Rev. 445, 449* (2009).

Rob Blackwell, "Citi May Soon Regret Its Big Victory on Capitol Hill," *American Banker* (Dec 11, 2014).

Margaret M. Blair, "Corporate Personhood and the Corporate Persona," *2013 Univ. Ill. Law Rev. 785* (2013).

Boston Consulting Group, "Global Asset Management 2014: Steering the Course to Growth," *BCG Perspectives* (2014).

Tony Boyd in "Warren Buffett still says derivatives are 'weapons of mass destruction,'" *Financial Review* (Jul 15 2015).

Allen D. Boyer, "Activist Shareholders, Corporate Directors and Institutional Investment: Some Lessons from the Robber Barons," *50 Wash & Lee L. Rev. 977* (1993).

James A. Brigagliano, "Testimony Concerning Dark Pools, Flash Orders, High Frequency Trading, and Other Market Structure Issues," *US Securities and Exchange Commission: Testimony Before the Senate Banking Subcommittee on Securities, Insurance, and Investment* (Oct 28, 2009).

Yaron Brooks and Don Watkins, "Why the Glass-Steagall Myth Persists," *Forbes* (Nov 12, 2012).

Nathan D. Brown, "The Rise of High Frequency Trading: The Role Algorithms, and the Lack of Regulations, Play in Today's Stock Market," *11 Appalachian J.L. 209* (2011–2012).

Matthais Burghardt, *Retail Investor Sentiment and Behavior: An Empirical Analysis* (Gabler Verlag, 2011).

C.W. Calomiris, "Financial fragility: issues and policy implications," *Journal of Financial Services Research, 9* (1995).

Zach Carter, "Crony Capitalism: Wall Street's Favorite Politicians," *Huff Post Business* (Sept 28, 2010).

Alyssa Chang, "When Lobbyists Literally Write the Bill," *NPR, It's all Politics* (Nov 11, 2013).

Emily Chasan, "Investors: Filings are for Searching, not Reading," *The Wall Street Journal* (Jun 2, 2015).

Kevin Cirilli, "Giuliani rips New York Stock Exchange for messaging," *The Hill* (Jul 8, 2015).

John C. Coffee, Jr., "The Political Economy of Dodd-Frank: Why Financial Reform Tends to be Frustrated and System Risk Perpetuated," *97 Cornell L. Rev. 1019* (2012).

Michael Cohn, "SEC Questions Widespread Use of Non-GAAP Measures," *Accounting Today* (Apr 16, 2016).

Jo Confino, "Will Unilever become the world's largest publicly traded B Corp?" *The Guardian* (Jan 2015).

Jeremy Cooper, "The Regulatory Cycle: From Boom to Bust," from *The Future of Financial Regulation*, Iain G. MacNeil and Justin O'Brien, Eds (Bloomsbury Publishing, 2009).

James Crott, "Structural Causes of the Global Financial Crisis: A Critical Assessment of the 'New Financial Architecture,'" *Working Paper, University of Massachusetts, Department of Economics* No. 2008–14 (2014).

Hon. Richard D. Cudahy & William D. Henderson, "From Insull to Enron: Corporate (Re)Regulation After the Rise and Fall of Two Energy Icons," *26 Energy L.J. 35* (2005).

andre douglas pond cummings, "Still 'Ain't no Glory in Pain': How the Telecommunications Act of 1996 and other 1990s Deregulation Facilitated the Market Crash of 2002," *12 Fordham J. of Corp. & Fin. L. 467* (2007).

Daniel D'Addario, "'The definition of insanity' is the most overused cliché of all time," *Salon* (Aug 6, 2013).

J.E. David, "Ice to Buy NYSE for $8.2 Billion, Ending Era of Independence." *CNBC US News* (2012).

Joe Davidson, "Inadvertent' cyber breach hits 44,000 FDIC customers," *Washington Post* (Apr 11, 2011).

Davis Polk & Wardwell, "Dodd-Frank Progress Report" (2015).

Chris DeRose, "Behind the Ingenious Security Feature that Powers the Blockchain," *American Banker* (May 21, 2015).

Robert W. Dixon, "The Gramm-Leach-Bliley Financial Modernization Act: Why Reform in the Financial Services Industry was Necessary and the Act's Projected Effects on Community Banking," *49 Drake L. Rev. 671, 676* (2001).

Michael Duffy, "By the Sign of the Crooked E," *Time* (Jan 19, 2002).

Jonathan Duong, "Where is the Money? World Market Cap and Sector Breakdown," *Wealthengineers* (Jun 2014).

Matt Egan, "More US families own cats than stocks," *CNN Money* (Sept 9, 2014).

C. Elias, "Regulators globally seek to curb supercomputer trading glitches." *Reuters Financial Regulatory Forum* (2012).

Thomas Eisenbach, Andrew Haughwout, Beverly Hirtle, Anna Kovner, David Lucca, and Matthew Plosser, *Supervising Large, Complex Financial Institutions: What Do Supervisors Do?* (Federal Reserve Bank of New York, 2015).

Maureen Farrell, "Mini Flash Crashes: A Dozen a Day," *CNN Money* (Mar 20, 2013).

Jack Favilukis, "Inequality, stock market participation, and the equity premium." *London School of Economics* (2012).

Manny Fernandez, "Texas Attorney General Faces Federal Securities Fraud Lawsuit," *New York Times* (Apr 11, 2016).

Jill E. Fisch, "Fiduciary Duties and the Analyst Scandals," *58 Al. L. Rev.1083, 1084* (2007).

Deborah Fuhr, "Institutional investors dominate the market," *Financial News* (Oct 21, 2013).

Daniel M. Gallagher, *Emerging Challenges for Regulating Global Capital Markets,* Harvard Law School Forum on Corporate Governance and Financial Reform (US Securities & Exchange Commission, 2013).

Treasury Secretary Tim Geithner, Written Testimony House Financial Services Committee Hearing, March 26, 2009 as cited in Robert J. Shiller's "Democratizing and Humanizing Finance," in *Reforming US Financial Markets, Reflections before and beyond Dodd-Frank* by Randall S. Krozner and Robert J. Schiller (MIT Press, 2011).

Ben Geman, "The Resource Curse, Big Oil, and the Dodd-Frank Battle that Won't Die," *The Atlantic* (Dec 11, 2015).

E. Gerding, "The Next Epidemic: Bubbles and Growth and Decay of Securities Regulation," *38 Conn. Law Review* (2006).

Government Accountability Office, *Management Report: Improvements Needed in SEC's Internal Controls and Accounting Procedures*, Report 15–387R (Apr 30, 2015).

Holly J. Gregory, "SEC Review of Disclosure Effectiveness." *Practical Law: The Journal, Transactions & Business* (Jun. 2014).

Daniel Gross, "Amazon Stock May Be Up, but the Company Still Doesn't Make Any Money," *The Daily Beast* (Oct 25, 2013).

David D. Gruberg, "Decent Exposure: The SEC's Lack of Authority and Restraint in Proposing to Eliminate Flash Trading," *65 U. Miami L. Rev. 263* (2010).

Camilla Hall and Sarah Mishkin, "Wells Fargo Chief Turns to Silicon Valley for Potential Partners," *Financial Times* (Aug 26, 2014).

Shane Hampton, "71% of IPO Companies in 2014 had ZERO earnings." *Hedgeable* (2015).

T. Hendershott, C.M. Jones, and A.J. Menkveld, "Does Algorithmic Trading Improve Liquidity?" *The Journal of Finance, LXVI, 1* (2011).

Peter H. Huang & Michael S. Knoll, "Corporate Finance, Corporate Law and Finance Theory," *74 S. Cal. L. Rev. 175, 187–188* (2000).

Christine Idzelis, "Wirehouses escape the worst of the DOL fiduciary rule," *Investment News* (May 22, 2016).

International Organization of Securities Commissions (IOSCO). "Regulatory Issues Raised by the Impact of Technological Changes on Market Integrity and Efficiency," *Technical Committee, Consultation Report* (2011).

International Swaps and Derivatives Association, "Anatomy of the OTC Market," from *The Value of Derivatives* (2013).

P.K. Jain, "Financial Market Design and the Equity Premium: Electronic versus Floor Trading," *Journal of Finance, 60, 6* (2005).

Jennifer Johnson, "Securities Class Actions in State Court," *Univ. of Cinn. L.Rev., 70, 2* (Aug 2012).

Zura Kakushadze and Dr. Jim Kyung-Soo Liew, "Is It Possible to OD On Alpha," *The Journal of Alternative Investments 18, 2* (2015).

Jonathan G. Katz, "Reviewing the SEC, Reinvigorating the SEC," *71 Univ. Pitt. L. Rev. 489, 501* (2010).

Edward E. Kaufman, Jr. and Carl M. Levin, Senators, "Preventing the Next Flash Crash," *The New York Times, The Opinion Pages* (May 5, 2011).

Mike Konczal, "Sheila Bair: Dodd-Frank really did end taxpayer bailouts," *The Washington Post* (May 18, 2013).

Matt Krantz, "2008 crisis still hangs over credit-rating firms," *USA Today* (Sept 13, 2013).

Randall S. Krozner and Robert J. Schiller, *Democratizing and Humanizing Finance, from Reforming US Financial Markets, Reflections Before and Beyond Dodd-Frank* (MIT Press, 2011).

Jason Lange & Dustin Volz, "Fed records show dozens of cybersecurity breaches," *Reuters* (Jun 1, 2016).

Donald Langevoort, "The SEC, Retail Investors and the Institionalization of the Securities Markets," *95 Va. L. Rev. 1025* (2009).

Jennifer B. Lawrence & Jackson W. Prentice, "The SEC Form 8-K: Full Disclosure or Fully Diluted? The Quest for Improved Market Transparency," *41 Wake Forest L. Rev. 913* (2006).

Robert Lenzer, "Warren Buffett Predicts Major Financial Discontinuity Involving Too Big to Fail Banks, Derivatives," *Forbes* (Apr 30, 2014).

Michael Lewis, *Flash Boys: Cracking the Money Code* (W.W. Norton & Company, 2014).

———, *The Big Short: Inside the Doomsday Machine* (W. W. Norton & Company, 2011).

———, "The Secret Goldman Tapes," *Bloomberg View* (Sept 26, 2014).

Eric Lipton & Ben Protess, "Banks' Lobbyists Help in Drafting Financial Bills," *Dealbook* (May 23, 2013).

Andrew W. Lo & Mark T. Mueller, "WARNING: Physics Envy May Be Hazardous to your Wealth!" *Cornell University Library, v3* (Mar 20, 2010).

Ann C. Logue, *Day trading for Dummies* (For Dummies, 2011).

Heather Long, "Over half of Americans have $0 in stocks," *CNN Money* (Apr 10, 2015).

Megan S. Lynch, "Sequestration as a Budget Enforcement Process: Frequently Asked Questions," *Congressional Research Service* (2013).

Sarah N. Lynch, "Senate, House unveil dueling budget plans for SEC, CFTC," *Reuters* (Jun. 24, 2014).

Timothy Lynch, "Gambling by Another Name: The Challenge of Purely Speculative Derivatives," *17 Stan J.L. Bus. & Fin. 67* (2011).

Jonathan R. Macey and Geoffrey P. Miller, "Origin of the Blue Sky Laws," *Texas Law Review, 70* (1991), 2.

Burton G. Malkeil, *A Random Walk Down Wall Street: The Time-Tested Strategy for Successful Investing, 10th ed.* (W. W. Norton & Company, 2011).

Henry G. Manne, "In Defense of Insider Trading," *44 Harvard Business Review 113* (1966).

L. Marek, "How the sale of the New York Stock Exchange affects CME's future," *Crain's Chicago Business* (2013).

Jerry W. Markham, *A Financial History of the United States* (Routledge, 2001).

Jena Martin, "Changing the Rules of the Game: Beyond a Disclosure Framework," *Securities Regulation 118 W.V. L. Rev. 59* (2015).

Jena Martin and Karen Kunz, "Into the Breach: The Increasing Gap Between Algorithmic Trading and Securities Regulation," *Journal of Financial Services Research* (2013).

Therese H. Maynard, "Commentary: The Future of California's Blue Sky Law, *30 Loyola L. Rev., 1573, 1577* (1977).

John McCrank, "NYSE to take back policing duties from Wall Street watchdog," *Reuters* (Oct 6, 2014).

———, "NASDAQ says software bug caused trading outage," *Reuters* (Aug. 29, 2013).

Brett McDonnell, "Dampening Financial Regulatory Cycles," *65 Fla. L. Rev. 1597* (2013).

Marije Meerman's *Money and Speed: Inside the Black Box*, film (2011).

The Memoirs of President Herbert Hoover (Herbert Hoover Presidential Library and Museum, 1952).

"Microsoft Purchase of LinkedIn is one of the Most Expensive Tech Deals in History: It May not be One of the Smartest," *The Economist* (Jun 18, 2016).

Heidi Moore & Dan Roberts, "AP Twitter hack causes panic on Wall Street and sends Dow plunging," *The Guardian* (Apr 23, 2013).

Stephanie Moore, "The Lemon Law—A Guide to State and Federal Consumer Protection Laws," *Consumer Affairs* (2015).

Gretchen Morganson & Louise Storey, "In Financial Crisis, No Prosecution of Top Figures," *New York Times* (Apr 14, 2011).

Moyers & Company, *Hillary Clinton's Mistake with Glass-Steagall* (Jul 15, 2015).

Edward V. Murphy, "Who Regulates Whom and How? An Overview of U.S Financial Regulatory Policy for Banking and Securities Markets: *Congressional Research Service* (Jan 30, 2015).

Matt Murray, "Fed Approves Citicorp-Travelers Merger," *Wall St. Journal A3* (Sept 24, 1998).

Rishi K. Narang, *Inside the Black Box: A Simple Way to Quantitative and High Frequency Trading* (Wiley, 2010).

Justin O'Brien, George Gillian and Seamus Miller's, "Culture and the future of financial regulation: how to embed restraint in the interests of systemic stability," *Law and Financial Markets Review* (2014).

Mancur Olson, *The Logic of Collective Action: Public Goods and the Theory of Groups, 2nd Ed.* (Harvard University Press, 1971).

Jose Pagilery & Patrick Gillespie, "Federal Reserve under attack by hacker spies," *CNN Money* (Jun 2, 2016).

Theresa A Pardo, Djoko Sigit Sayogo, and Donna S. Canestraro, *Computing and Information Technology Challenges for 21st Century Financial Market Regulators*. M. Janssen et al., Eds. (Electronic Government: 10th International Conference, EGOV 2011, LNCS 6846, 2011), 198–209.

Troy Paredes, "Blinded by the Light: Information Overload and its Consequences for Securities Regulation," *81 Wash. U. L. Q. 417, 422* (2003).

Scott Patterson, "High Speed Traders Turn to Laser Beams," *Wall Street Journal* (Sept 2014).

———, *The Quants: How a New Breed of Math Whizzes Conquered Wall Street and Nearly Destroyed it* (Crown Business, 2010).

Henry Paulson. *Blueprint for a Modernized Financial Regulatory Structure.* (The Department of the Treasury, 2008), from Daniel M. Gallagher, *Emerging Challenges for Regulating Global Capital Markets* (US Securities & Exchange Commission, 2013).

PBS News Hour, *International ATM Cyber Hackers Hid 'in Plain Sight' to Overcome Computer System* (May 10, 2013).

Michael Perion, *Hellhounds of Wall Street: How Ferdinand Pecora's Investigation of the Great Crash Forever Changed American Finance* (Penguin Books, 2011).

Eric A. Posner and E. Glen Weyl, "A Proposal for Limiting Speculation on Derivatives: An FDA for Financial Innovation," *University of Chicago Institute for Law & Economics*, Olin Research Paper No. 594 (2012).

Ilya Pozin, "15 Fintech Startups to Watch in 2015," *Forbes, Entrepreneurs* (2014).

PricewaterhouseCoopers, *PWC Deals Practice, Considering an IPO? The Costs of Going and Being Public May Surprise You* (Sept 2012).

———, *A Roadmap for an IPO: A Guide to Going Public* (2010).

L.O. Rameriz, *High Frequency Trading* (Manuscript, 2011).

Steven Ramirez, *Lawless Capitalism: The Subprime Crisis and the Case for an Economic Rule of Law* (NYU Press, 2014).

Catherine Rampell, "Corporate Profits were the highest on record last quarter," *The New York Times* (Nov 23, 2010).

Victor Reklaitis & William Watts, "Wall Street will always crush the little guy, but the stock market could be fairer," *Market Watch* (Jul 16, 2015).

James Rickards, "Repeal of Glass-Steagall Caused the Financial Crisis," *U.S. News and World Report* (Aug 27, 2012).

Barry Ritholtz, "Where have all the public companies gone?" *Bloomberg View* (Jun 24, 2015).

Sally St. Lawrence (ed.), *Organizing Corporations in California* (Continuing Education of the Bar, Feb 2016 Update), §4.116(b).

Larry A. Schwartz, "Suggestions for Procedural Reform In Securities Market Regulation," *Brooklyn Journal of Corporate, Financial & Commercial Law, v1, 2* (Nov 10, 2006).

Steven L. Schwarz, "Enron and the Use and Abuse of Special Purpose Entities in Corporate Structures," *70 Univ. Cinn. L. Rev. 1309* (2002).

Kenneth B. Scott and John B. Taylor, "Why Toxic Assets Are So Hard to Clean Up: Securitization was maddeningly complex. Mandated transparency is the only solution." *The Wall Street Journal* (Jul 21, 2009).

"SEC is Unequal to the Job," *Time Business* (Jul 16, 1956).

Joel Seligman, "The SEC in a Time of Discontinuity," *95 Va. L. Rev., 679* (2009).

———, *The Transformation of Wall Street: A History of the Securities and Exchange Commission and Modern Corporate Finance, 3rd Edition* (Aspen Publishers, 2003).

David M. Serritella, "High Speed Trading Begets High Speed Regulation: SEC Response to Flash Crash, Rash," *2010 Univ. Ill. J.L. Tech & Pol'y 433* (2010).

Adam Shell, "NASDAQ: Tech glitch caused 'brief outage,'" *USA Today* (Sept 4, 2013).

Jonathan Spicer and Emily Stephenson, "Secret tapes of Fed meetings on Goldman prompt call for US hearings," *Reuters' Business News* (Sept 26, 2014).

Cole Stangler, "As Market Mayhem Grips Investors, Fewer Americans Have a Stake in What Happens On Wall Street," *International Business Times* (Aug 25, 2015).

Lynn A. Stout, "Regulate OTC Derivatives by Deregulating Them," *Cornell Law Faculty Publications*, Paper 754, *Cornell University Law Library* (2009).

———, "Why the Law Hates Speculators: Regulation and Private Ordering in the Market for OTC Derivatives," *48 Duke L.J. 701* (1999).

Paul Sullivan, "Assessing the Value of Owning Dividend-Paying Stocks," *NY Times* (Jun 3, 2011).

Ken Sweet, "Flash Crash Worries Go Global," *CNN Money* (May 6, 2011).

Steven L. Taylor, "The Recent History of Congressional Resolutions," *Outside The Beltway* (2013).

Trefis Team, "Why LinkedIn's Fundamentals Don't Support Its Share Price," *Forbes* (Jul 15, 2011).

Jessica Tollestrup, "Continuing Resolutions: Overview of Components and Practices," *Congressional Research Service* (2012).

US Securities & Exchange Commission, "Investor Bulletin: Crowdfunding for Investors," *Investor Bulletins and Alerts* (Feb 16, 2016).

Philip van Doorn, "Time to sell your dividend stocks? Not so fast," *Market Watch* (Apr 10, 2014).

Dustin Voltz and Jeremy Wagstaff, "Cyber firms say Bangladesh hackers have attacked other Asian banks," *Reuters* (May 27, 2016).

Daniel Wagner & Allison Fitzgerald, "Meet the Banking Caucus: Meet Wall Street's Secret Weapon in Washington," *Citizens for Public Integrity* (Apr 24, 2014).

Elaine Wah and Michael P. Wellman, "Latency Arbitrage, Market Fragmentation, and Efficiency: A Two-Market Model," *Univ. Mich., Strategic Reasoning Group* (Conference Proceedings) (2013).

Elizabeth Warren, "Where is Wall Street Accountability," *Politico* (2011).

Elizabeth Warren & Oren Bar-Gill, "Making Credit Safer," *157 U. Pa. L. Rev. 1, 4* (2008).

John W. White, *The Promise of Transparency—Corporation Finance in 2007* (The Securities & Exchange Commission, 2007).

Mary Jo White, *Statement at an Open Meeting on Regulation S-K Concept Release* (Securities & Exchange Commission, Apr 13, 2016).

————, *Testimony on "Oversight of the Financial Stability Oversight Council."* Testimony before the Committee on Financial Services, United States House of Representatives (Securities & Exchange Commission, Dec 8, 2015).

The White House, *Historical Tables* (Office of Management and Budget, 2015).

Jane Wild, Martin Arnold and Philip Stafford, "Technology: banks see the key to blockchain," *Financial Times* (Nov 1, 2015).

Lauren C. Williams, "The NYSE Shutdown Isn't Just a Glitch, It's a Glimpse into Our Chaotic Future," *Think Progress* (Jul 9, 2015).

Wallace Witkowski and Sital S. Patel, "Twitter trading influence laid bare by fake tweet," *Market Watch* (Apr 24, 2013).

Wonkblog, "Twitter could end up being really profitable. But it's a super risky stock," *Washington Post* (Nov 4, 2013).

Stu Woo and Lynn Cowan, "LinkedIn 4.2 Billion Valuation Raises Eyebrows," *The Wall Street Journal* (May 19, 2011).

Yesha Yadav, "Beyond Efficiency in Securities Regulation," *Vanderbilt Law and Economics Research Paper No. 14–8* (2014).

Matthew Yglesias, "The Prophet of No Profit: How Jeff Bezos won the faith of Wall Street," *Slate* (Jan 30, 2014).

Todd Zenger, *"What is the Theory of Your Firm?,"* *Harvard Business Review* (2013).

Zachary J. Ziliak, "Regulation Ahead: Advice and Options for Automated and High-Frequency Traders," *Bloomberg* (Apr 22, 2013).

Index

About the Authors

Karen Kunz is an associate professor in the Department of Public Administration, in the John D. Rockefeller IV School of Policy & Politics at West Virginia University. She teaches courses on public financial management, public budgeting, economic fiscal policy and advocacy, and civil disobedience and was named an outstanding teacher by the WVU Foundation in 2016. Her research interests include public finance and fiscal policy, political economy, and financial markets regulation. She received her doctorate in public administration from the University of Illinois at Springfield in 2008.

Karen brings over 25 years of professional experience in the financial markets industry to her academic endeavors. She began her career in the municipal bond markets before starting one of the first female-owned consulting firms in the industry, specializing in regulatory compliance and development of new broker-dealers.

Karen serves on the board of directors for the American Association of Budget and Program Analysts (AABPA) and Public Financial Publications (PFP). She is a former board member of the West Virginia Center on Budget and Policy. In addition, she is a veteran, having served in the US Army.

More information about Karen can be found at her WVU webpage: http://publicadmin.wvu.edu/faculty-staff/mpa-faculty/karen-kunz

Jena Martin is a professor of law and the associate dean for innovation & global development at West Virginia University. She teaches in the areas of business and securities regulation, both at the College of Law and for the College of Business and Economics. After practicing for a number of years as a litigator for a boutique law firm in Washington, D.C., she joined the United States Securities & Exchange Commission's Division of Enforcement where she was involved in a number of investigations and enforcement actions.

Jena's current scholarship is in the burgeoning academic field of business and human rights issues. Her research and scholarship in this area has resulted in a Faculty Scholarship Award. She has also presented her work at the UN Forum for Business and Human Rights in Geneva, Switzerland.

You can find more information about her at: http://www.law.wvu.edu/faculty-staff/full-time-faculty/jena-martin.

Lightning Source UK Ltd.
Milton Keynes UK
UKHW011532160819
348010UK00013B/191/P